LLOYDS BANK
1918-1969

LLOYDS BANK

1918–1969

J. R. Winton

OXFORD   NEW YORK

OXFORD UNIVERSITY PRESS

1982

Oxford University Press, Walton Street, Oxford OX2 6DP

London Glasgow New York Toronto
Delhi Bombay Calcutta Madras Karachi
Kuala Lumpur Singapore Hong Kong Tokyo
Nairobi Dar es Salaam Cape Town
Melbourne Auckland
and associates in
Beirut Berlin Ibadan Mexico City Nicosia

British Library Cataloguing in Publication Data

Winton, J. R.
Lloyds Bank 1918–1969.
1. Lloyds Bank—History
I. Title
332. 1'2'0941   HG3000.L84L7
ISBN 0-19-920125-0

Printed in Great Britain
at the University Press, Oxford
by Eric Buckley
Printer to the University

Preface

In 1957 the Oxford University Press published *Lloyds Bank in the History of English Banking* by Professor R. S. Sayers (now out of print), which traced the history of the bank from the establishment of the partnership of Taylors and Lloyds in Birmingham in 1765 to just after the end of the first world war. This book carries the story forward another fifty years to 1969, when Sir Eric Faulkner succeeded Sir Harald Peake as chairman. Professor Sayers's study virtually ended with the amalgamation in 1918 of Lloyds Bank with Capital and Counties Bank, which I have thus covered only summarily. The record occasionally extends beyond 1969, but events in these years are not treated in any great detail.

This book is based, in the main, on material in the archives and records of Lloyds Bank and I gratefully acknowledge the considerable assistance given me by Mr. M. D. Roberts, one of the bank's archivists, and by many busy officials in head office. A number of other people have also helped me and for their comments and recollections I am indebted to Lord Barnby, the late Mr. S. A. C. Bartlett, Mr. John Brough, Miss M. A. E. Cotterell, the late Mr. A. H. Ensor, Lord Franks, Mr. H. C. Gotts, Mr. F. E. Goudge, Mr. C. A. Haines, Mr. C. B. Howland, Mr. J. I. Kennan, Mr. A. C. King, the late Sir Henry Lawson, the late Sir Harald Peake, the late Mr. F. Pritchard, the late Sir Jeremy Raisman, Lord Robbins, Lord Runciman, Mr. H. B. Savill, the late Mr. F. H. Shann, Mr. H. A. Steerwood, Mr. F. J. Thomas, Mr. E. S. Tibbetts, Sir Reginald Verdon-Smith, Mr. E. J. N. Warburton, Lord Wardington, Sir Michael Wilson, and the late Mr. E. G. Woolgar. I am additionally grateful to Mr. Tibbetts for reading in draft the chapter on the bank's Eastern business and to Mr. Gotts for allowing me to quote from his diary in this chapter, and to Mr. R. H. Ball for reading in draft the section on the computer revolution.

I have other debts to acknowledge. The Governor and Company of the Bank of England and the Committee of London Clearing Bankers permitted me to consult their archives; Mr. Lloyd Howard Fox gave me details of the history of Fox, Fowler & Co.; Mrs. Gwen Watkins provided information on the life of her husband, Mr. Vernon Watkins; Mr. Michael Harris, of Commercial Union Assurance Co. Ltd., Mr. H. H. Reeves, of Trollope & Colls Ltd., and Mr. Gordon Tait, of Sir John Burnet, Tait & Partners, supplied particulars about the building in the 1920s of the bank's new head office; Mr. Jon Robinson gave me information on the history of the National Union of Bank Employees (now the Banking, Insurance, and Finance Union) and details of the membership of Lloyds' staff. I am grateful to Mrs. Valerie Eliot for permission to use extracts from her introduction to *The Waste Land, a facsimile and transcript of the original drafts*, published by Faber & Faber Ltd., to the Hon. Ewen Montagu, for allowing me to reproduce a letter from his book *The Man Who Never Was*, published by Evans Brothers Ltd., and to the Guildhall Library for permission to reproduce the photograph of Cornhill in 1922. I have made much use of the library of the Institute of Bankers, the unfailing help of whose staff I acknowledge with thanks. Most of the economic statistics have been taken from *The British Economy Key Statistics 1900–1970*, published by Times Newspapers Ltd., for the London and Cambridge Economic Service, and from *Statistical Tables of National Income, Expenditure and Output of the U.K. 1855–1965* by C. H. Feinstein, published by the Cambridge University Press.

Throughout my work on this book I was assisted by Mr. Norman Dommett, who searched for material, gathered statistical data, and also drew the charts and diagrams. I am very much in his debt. My warm thanks are also due to Mrs. Jean Durrant who, starting from a barely legible manuscript, efficiently and uncomplainingly typed successive drafts.

J. R. Winton
London, 1980

Contents

List of Illustrations

List of Figures

———————— ∽ ————————

A General Review

1918 and 1969

The story of a large commercial enterprise like Lloyds Bank over the years 1918 to 1969, as might be expected, is in some ways a microcosm of the economic and social history of Britain during this half century. Its business and fortunes largely parallel the general movements of the economy; the men and women who carry out its operations reflect the extensive shifts in social conventions and education; the offices and branches in which they work typify the changes in interior styling and architectural taste.

By 1918 the structure of the bank on which the development of the next fifty years was built had nearly been completed. Hitherto, particularly from the 1890s onwards, growth had gone hand-in-hand with amalgamation, as one bank after another had joined forces with Lloyds. The merger with Capital and Counties Bank in 1918, itself a large institution, was almost the end of this process. There were to be three more amalgamations in the next five years, one of which extended Lloyds' branch network overseas, but these altered the figures relatively little.

Expansion, as we shall see, was not by any means uniform during the years between 1918 and 1969. The half century divides itself into two periods of twenty or so years of peace, separated by six years of war. These six years were a significant dividing line for Lloyds, as for the other banks. The environment in which the bank conducted its business after 1945 was radically different from that before 1939. As the years went on, moreover, the pace of change quickened, with an ever-widening range of services and facilities provided for customers and followed, in the 1960s, by a complete revolution, with the advent of the computer, in the way the bank came to handle its multifarious kinds of business. Although the principles on which Lloyds conducted its affairs were basically the same, the bank had changed very considerably from the institution of 1918.

For almost half this entire period, from a few years after the end of the first world war until just after the end of the second, there was no change of chairman. In 1922 J. W. Beaumont Pease became chairman and continued in office until December 1945, a length of term that must be unique in English commercial banking, and equalling those of his three successors put together. Pease, through his mother, Helen Maria Fox, was directly descended from Sampson Lloyd II, one of the four founding partners in 1765 of Taylors and Lloyds to whom Lloyds Bank owes its origin. The connection with the Lloyd family went on. In 1957, Lord Lloyd, another direct descendant, was elected to the board; his father had also been a director from 1912 to 1918 and again in 1924-5.

Let us look briefly at the bank at the beginning and end of the half century. A few figures will sum up the enormous change in size. In December 1918 the bank's deposits stood at £267m.; by December 1969 they had increased over seven-fold, to £1,935m. If allowance is made for the increase in prices between these two years the growth in deposits is, of course, very much less: in 'real terms' their level in 1969 was just over twice that in 1918. In 1918 total accounts numbered less than a million; by 1969 they had increased to over 4½m. In 1918, there were 1,273 offices in England and Wales; by 1969 these had nearly doubled, to 2,307. In 1918 the bank's staff was just on 11,400,[1] of whom under a third were women; by 1969 the number had risen nearly three-fold to 32,500, of whom more than half were women.

In 1918 the regional structure was rudimentary. Apart from the main board in London, there were three local committees of directors, all the result of previous mergers. The committee in Liverpool was the product of the merger with Liverpool Union Bank in 1900, that in Salisbury followed the amalgamation with Wilts and Dorset Bank in 1914, while the third, in London, resulted from the recent merger with Capital and Counties Bank. A district office had been set up in Birmingham under an assistant general manager when head office had been finally moved to Lombard Street in 1910,[2] while district managers were established also at Salisbury and Newcastle, the latter following the merger with Hodgkin, Barnett, Pease, Spence & Co. in 1903. By 1969 the whole branch network in England and Wales, apart from a number of branches in Central London, was organised into sixteen regions, each with its own regional manager, under fifteen regional boards.[3]

[1] This *includes* the approximately 4,000 men on the permanent staff serving with the Forces.

[2] But not until 1925 was the annual general meeting transferred to London, held at the Cannon Street Hotel in the City.

[3] In 1969 the regional office at Birmingham was divided into two: one office for Birmingham and the other for the West Midlands, both under the same board. Similarly, in 1970 the Greater London region was split into Greater London (North) and Greater London (South), under one regional board. In 1975 a new region was formed of Central London branches, excluding those in the City and, finally, in 1979 these too (excluding City Office) were brought together into a separate region. There were now eighteen regions and fifteen regional boards.

In 1918 Lloyds had a controlling interest in only two affiliates,[4] together with an equal voice in the so-called auxiliary, Lloyds and National Provincial (Foreign) Bank. In 1969 the bank could claim seven wholly-owned subsidiaries.

This widening spread of interest was matched by the proliferation of the services and facilities provided for the public. Specific services available to customers totalled only seven in 1918.[5] By 1969 the number had increased to over twenty. Traditional commercial banking remained the backbone, current and deposit accounts on one side and loans and advances on the other. But, in addition, there were now unit trusts, cheque cards, special lending schemes for exporters, a pay service for companies, and so on.

The methods by which the bank carried on its business had been transformed. In 1918, although most branches had a typewriter, all the book-keeping was done by hand and accounts kept in ledgers, with the copies for customers written, preferably in copper-plate, in pass books. By 1969 this was a memory for a few but ancient history for the great majority, together with high stools, long ebony rulers, and cashiers' scales. By the end of the 1960s in most of Lloyds' branches the computer had taken over all the drudgery, keeping the accounts, providing statements, working out interest, balancing the books. The ledger clerks tediously toiling away had been replaced by a kind of teleprinter, a terminal linking the branch to a piece of electronic machinery miles away.

The personal element remained, however, at the counter, although here, too, things were not quite the same. No longer could a customer cash a cheque across an open mahogany counter; now he, or as often as not she, was confronted by a roof-high glass grille. Seldom was the cashier a man in stiff white collar and black jacket; as often as not, it was an attractive young lady in a mini-skirt. And if a customer had to wait a few minutes to see the manager, there was now a rack of the bank's colourful publications to thumb through or possibly indoor plants to admire, as well as the framed copy of the bank's balance sheet to inspect.

Growth of the bank

As a broad indication of the growth of Lloyds' business over the period one can take the movements in total deposits, and these are shown in the top part of Figure 1.[6] From 1921 until the outbreak of war in 1939, it will

---

[4] National Bank of Scotland and London and River Plate Bank.

[5] Conducting current, deposit and savings accounts, undertaking security transactions, overseas business and executor and trustee work, and providing safe deposit facilities.

[6] The figures on which this chart is based are those published by the Committee of London Clearing Bankers, which start in 1921. On 31 December 1918 Lloyds' total deposits were £267m., rising to £345m. in December 1920.

FIGURE I. *Lloyds Bank: Total deposits, 1921-70*

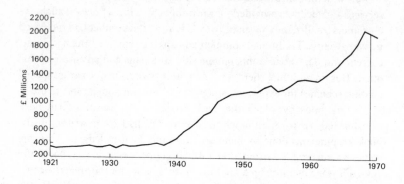

Lloyds Bank: Total deposits as per cent of big five banks and London clearing banks

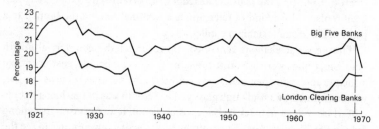

Notes: (1) Figures are for current, deposit, and other accounts: 1921-38 for average weekly balance in December; 1939-58 for 31 December; 1959-70 for second Wednesday in December. (2) 'Big Five' banks: 1921-69 Lloyds, Barclays, Midland, National Provincial, and Westminster Banks; 1970 Lloyds, Barclays, Midland, and National Westminster Banks. (3) London clearing banks: 1921-35 10 banks, 1936-69 11 banks, 1970 6 banks. (4) Following changes in accounting procedures, figures for 1970 are not strictly comparable with those for previous years.

Source: Committee of London Clearing Bankers.

be seen, there was little significant change in deposits. In 1930 the total was only £12m. higher than in 1921. The depression years of the thirties made little impact, except for a dip in 1931. Thereafter, there was a modest increase, of £17m. net, between 1932 and 1938. The war years saw a sharp jump, deposits doubling between 1939 and 1945. From about 1948 to the end of the 1950s came another period of relatively slow growth. This was then followed by a further upsurge in the 1960s, the fastest rate of expansion—excluding the war years—in the whole period covered.

The bottom part of Figure 1 shows Lloyds' deposits in relation to those of the big five clearing banks and of those of all the clearing banks.[7] As the big five held around 90% of all clearing bank deposits, it is not surprising that the two lines of ratios run parallel. After rising to a peak in 1925 there was a decline until 1937. (The fall between 1935 and 1936 in the all-bank ratio was partly due to the inclusion of District Bank in the figures—see footnote 7.) In other words, from the mid-1920s until just before the war there was some erosion of Lloyds' competitive position. If Lloyds' share of clearing bank deposits in 1937 had been the same as in 1925 the total would have been some £70m. (18%) higher than it was. From 1937 until 1951 there was a gradual recovery, followed by a downward trend to 1965. The last half of the 1960s, a time of innovation and increasing change—in spite of severe credit restrictions—saw a rapid improvement in the bank's competitive stance, Lloyds' share of clearing bank deposits rising from 17.5% in 1964 to 18.9% in 1968, a gain of about £160m. The bank's relative position was back to where it had been forty years previously, at the end of the 1920s.

These changes are for Lloyds *vis-à-vis* the clearing banks. Until the end of the 1950s there was not much more to be said. These banks dominated the banking market in Britain. In the 1960s, however, American and other overseas banks greatly expanded their business in Britain, with a corresponding decline in the relative share of the clearing banks. In 1918 Lloyds had just over 13% of all bank deposits in Britain, and in 1959 the share was approximately the same. By 1969 the figure had dropped to 6%. However, in the 1960s there was a great expansion of London's Euro-currency market: in 1969 over eight-tenths of the deposits of the overseas

---

[7] Ten banks until 1935 and, with the addition of District Bank in 1936, eleven banks 1936-69. The inclusion of District Bank in 1936 was responsible for a fall of about ½% in Lloyds' share of all clearing bank deposits between 1935 and 1936. Most of the other clearing banks carried out a number of mergers and amalgamations during the period 1921-67. However, these were all with relatively small banks and made little difference to Lloyds' share of either big five or all clearing bank deposits and advances. Then in 1968 came the National Provincial-Westminster and Barclays-Martins mergers, which, for CLCB statistical purposes, were treated as four separate banks until 1970.

banks were denominated in currencies other than sterling. In the domestic sterling market Lloyds and the other clearing banks still predominated.

So far we have considered only deposits in total, but some marked changes in their composition were experienced during these years, as Table 1 brings out.

TABLE 1. *Percentage of total deposits*

	Current accounts	Deposit accounts	Savings bank accounts
1919	62	37	1
1929	45	54	1
1939	55	41	4
1949	69	29	2
1959	63	35	2
1969	56	42	2

Note: Figures are annual averages and for 1929–59 exclude Eastern branches. 'Other accounts' also excluded.

For most of the period, current account balances predominated but to different extents at different times. Their share increased particularly between 1929 and 1949, from less than half to over two-thirds of the total. These were the years when, from 1932 to 1951, excepting a brief flurry on the outbreak of war, Bank Rate was stuck at 2% and London deposit rate at ½%. It is understandable that there was a relative decline in deposit balances—and an absolute decline from 1929 to 1939 (£172m. to £149m.). After 1951, the general upward movement in deposit rate was accompanied by a relative increase in deposit balances, which rose from 29% of total deposits in 1949 to 35% in 1959, and 42% in 1969.

All the changes in deposits discussed above relate to the figures as they appeared in the bank's accounts at the time; they are all in terms of the current value of money. However, if allowance is made for the movements of prices, then a rather different picture emerges, particularly for the years since the war. Table 2 shows that, once the 1918–20 boom subsided, there was not much difference between the courses of the two indices in the period up to 1939. But from then on they diverged, increasingly so in the years after the war with the virtually uninterrupted rise in prices. The adjusted index reached a peak in 1946 (270) then, as prices rose faster than deposits, fell gradually during the 1950s until 1961 (185). Thereafter, with the growth of deposits outpacing that of prices, there was some recovery in the adjusted index, to touch a peak in 1968 (222).

TABLE 2. *Indices of total deposits 1918 = 100*

	Actual	Adjusted for changes in prices
1919	122	103
1929	131	143
1939	163	171
1949	425	251
1959	501	195
1969	752	212

Note: The index of actual deposits 1929–69 is based on the figures as published by the CLCB (see Figure 1); the values for 1918 and 1919 are for 31 December. This index is adjusted for changes in prices by using a 'GDP deflator' (the estimate of gross domestic product at factor cost at current prices divided by that at constant prices). As this deflator is annual 1918–49 and for the last quarters of 1959 and 1969, while the figures for actual deposits are for December, the values of the adjusted index in the above table (and elsewhere in this study) are only approximate.

The movement of Lloyds' advances, traditionally the largest single and most profitable of the bank's assets, is shown on Figure 2. In general, it follows that of deposits, but the fluctuations are wider. In the boom following the first world war advances nearly doubled, from £81m. in 1918 to £151m. in 1920. After a short relapse in the post-war recession there was a further rise in the late twenties to a peak of £204m. in 1929, when advances equalled 58% of deposits, against less than 40% at the beginning of the decade, and a ratio not reached again until the 1970s. The great depression had a much greater influence on advances than on deposits: lending dropped by £64m., or by nearly a third, between December 1929 and the end of 1933. With the economy's recovery of the late 1930s advances picked up, to slump again during the war to equal only 16% of deposits in 1945. The years after 1945 saw a general upward movement, punctuated by the consequences of crises and with sharp increases in the only two brief periods of freedom from official lending restraints in 1958–61 and 1962–4. By the end of the 1960s advances had climbed back to represent 50% of deposits.

The swings in Lloyds' share of advances, as shown in the lower part of the chart, follow broadly those of deposits but are more pronounced. During the depression years of the 1930s, Lloyds' share of 'big five' advances slid from 22.9% in 1929 to 20.9% in 1933. Economic recovery later in the decade saw no improvement. Although there was some increase in total lending, in relation to the other banks Lloyds fell behind

FIGURE 2. *Lloyds Bank: Advances, 1921–70*

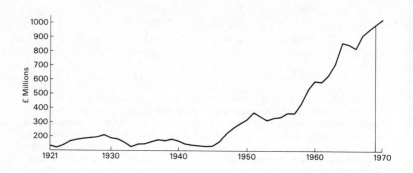

Lloyds Bank advances as per cent of big five banks and London clearing banks

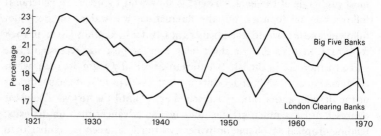

Notes: (1) Advances include *items in transit* for Lloyds Bank 1928–57 and for Martins Bank 1930–42 (included in total for London clearing banks). (2) See Figure 1 for dates of plots and banks covered.

Source: Committee of London Clearing Bankers.

and the ratio dropped to just under 20% in 1938. This weakening of com-
petitiveness must have owed much to the cautious attitudes engendered by
the sharp decline in profits earlier in the decade: between 1932 and 1933
gross profits slumped by nearly two-thirds. In the early war years, lost
ground was partly recovered but in 1944, particularly, there was another
set-back. Lloyds' share rose again with the peace but fell away once more
in 1953-4, partly, it seems, because of the strict respect given to official
wishes to restrict lending to 'essential' purposes. After this set-back
had been made good Lloyds' share dropped again until the early 1960s,
following which, as with deposits, there was a rise in the ratio.

Figure 3 shows the growth of Lloyds' business as shown by the increase in
the number of accounts. The greatest expansion was in the 1960s: between
1959 and 1969 the total increased by 1.82m., rather more than the growth
in the whole forty years from 1919 to 1959. The distribution of the total
among the three kinds of account during these years is shown in Table 3.

TABLE 3. *Percentage of total numbers of accounts*

	current	deposit	savings bank
1919	57	39	4
1929	51	35	14
1939	52	25	23
1949	65	19	16
1959	66	23	11
1969	61	30	9

Note: Figures are for end-years and for 1929-59 exclude Eastern branches.

The changes in the distribution of the three kinds of account are broadly
the same as those for their corresponding balances, as given in Table 1,
except for deposit accounts in the 1920s. In total, current accounts
increased by over half in the ten years 1959-69, from 1.86m. to 2.84m., but
the number of deposit accounts more than doubled, from 630,000 to
1,384,000. Apart from a small increase in 1944-5, deposit accounts fell in
number in every year from 1933 to 1951. The sharp rise in savings bank
accounts in 1929 (and 1930) was the result of a successful special campaign
in those years.

The increase in the staff of the bank over the half century reflects the
growth of business and, in its distribution between men and women, is a
measure of the considerable social and economic changes in society in

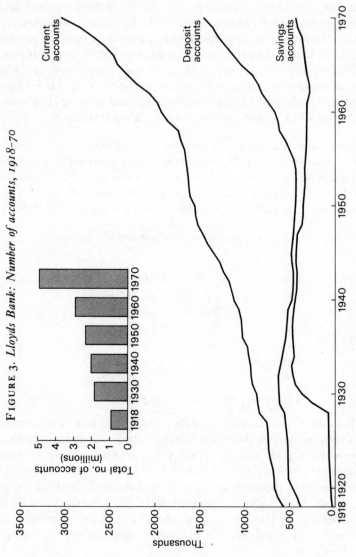

FIGURE 3. *Lloyds Bank: Number of accounts, 1918–70*

Notes: (1) Figures are for end-year. (2) Cox & Co. 1923–7 and Eastern branches 1923–60 excluded.

general. Total staff grew by some 6,200 between 1918 and 1938 but nearly half this increase was in the immediate post-war period.[8] There was little difficulty in recruiting enough young men in the inter-war years, indeed there were often waiting lists. Many women came into the bank in the first world war but after 1918 their numbers declined: from 3,300 in 1918 to 1,380 in 1927. Except for such jobs as typists and filing clerks general recruitment of women ceased during these years and was not resumed until the start of mechanisation at the end of the 1920s. All these were single, for until 1949 any women on the permanent staff who married had to resign. Though increasing in numbers through the 1930s women in 1938 still accounted for less than a fifth of all employees.

The war was a watershed, in this as in so much else. With men leaving for the Forces, the number of women again increased quickly (see Figure 4) to total nearly half the staff in 1944. Peace brought back the men to the bank but until the end of the 1950s there was a gradual slight decline in the total of male staff. There had been fundamental changes in the labour market that, in pre-war days, the bank had been able to tap so easily, although it was many years before its policies were correspondingly adapted. For one thing, in the immediate post-war years, there were fewer young men in total, as a result of the decline in the birthrate in the early 1930s and, until 1962, there was also national service. Many more young men now went to university and, for those who did not, opportunities for employment, often better paid than in banking, were much wider than before the war. Recruitment was rarely easy and there were moments of anxiety.

The number of women, in contrast, rose sharply in these years, doubling between 1946 and 1960. Most of these were girls and young women: in 1960 nearly half the female staff in the bank were twenty years old or younger, against just over a quarter in 1938. Here, too, things had changed radically since before the war; other jobs were easy to come by, particularly in London, and often paid better and offered regular hours. Turnover increased, and by the late 1950s nearly a fifth of the total female staff were leaving each year, against well under a tenth in the 1930s.

More men were attracted during the 1960s to handle the bank's rapidly expanding business, partly the result of improvements in pay scales and, in the early years of the decade, partly the result of some easing in the labour market. By now, the change in the scale of the bank's operations and the growing diversity of its services, together with the revolutionary impact of

[8] This relates to the staff at work in the bank and excludes in 1918 the 4,000 or so men on the permanent staff serving with the Forces. All figures for staff in this study exclude those in the Eastern branches (1923-60).

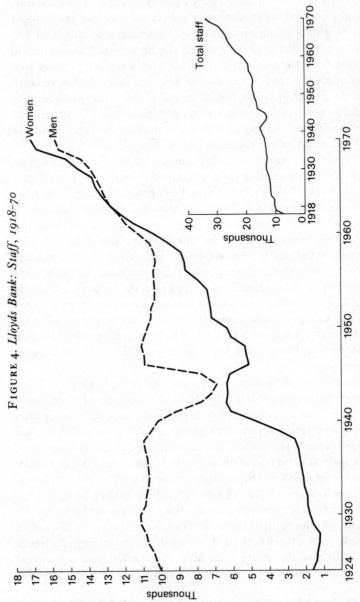

FIGURE 4. Lloyds Bank: Staff, 1918–70

Notes: (1) Figures are for end-year. (2) Staff at Eastern branches 1923–60 and on service with H.M. Forces 1918 and 1939–62 excluded. (3) Messengers included.

the computer, had brought the realisation that the old ways of recruitment were no longer feasible. In 1966 'two-tier' recruitment was at last introduced but not really properly implemented until 1969.

The increase in the men—by nearly half between 1959 and 1969—was far exceeded by that in the number of women—by just on four-fifths over the same years. In 1963, for the first time, there were slightly more women than men in the bank. Recruitment had to be increased, however, to offset the higher rate of turnover: in 1969 the 'wastage rate' for women was 28%, against 18% ten years earlier.[9] Women were employed as typists, clerks, and in the arcane processes of the computer but also, increasingly, in more responsible and senior jobs. By 1968 nearly half the 6,000 or so cashiers were women, there were sixty-four women with 'chief general manager's' appointments and eight with board appointments.

There were significant changes during the fifty years in policy on the extension of the bank's branch network. In 1919 over 200 offices were opened (see Figure 5) but nearly half were offices that had been closed during the war and there was also the amalgamation with West Yorkshire Bank. The last merger which extended Lloyds' existing branch network in England and Wales was in 1921 with Fox, Fowler and Co., so that extension in future had to come from the opening of new offices. In the second half of the 1920s a considerable number of new branches were opened, a development that came to an abrupt halt with the depression. Branches were now closed, sometimes in collaboration with other banks. More offices were closed during the war, so that by 1945 the total of branches open, 1673, was the lowest since 1925. Numbers built up gradually during the 1950s until, once again, during the first half of the 1960s an extensive branch programme was put in hand, partly to meet the expected consequences of the Payment of Wages Act 1960. In the six years 1960-5 a total of 330 branches was opened, and half this number in the next five years.

The look of these branches, both inside and outside, was distinctly different from that of offices put up in the 1920s. Then bank branches were usually built in either classical or neo-Georgian style, although occasionally a branch would be designed in the so-called Art Deco style. Interiors were not much more welcoming than the usually staid exteriors, with an emphasis on marble, mahogany, and Corinthian columns. For Lloyds, the most notable structure of these years was the new head office in Lombard Street, built in the classical manner and completed, not without drama, in July 1930.

---

[9] The number who left the bank during the year, for whatever reason, as a percentage of the staff at the beginning of the year.

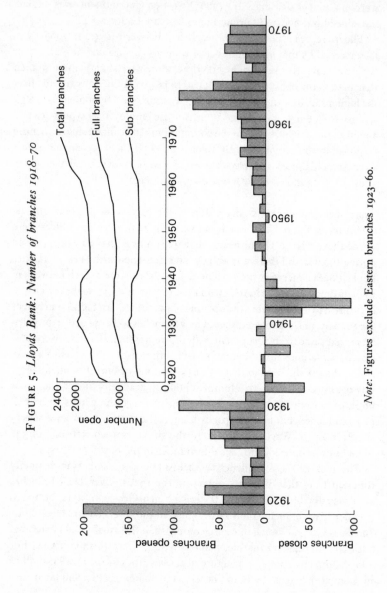

FIGURE 5. *Lloyds Bank: Number of branches 1918–70*

Note: Figures exclude Eastern branches 1923–60.

After the war, when building again became possible, Lloyds rather lagged in adopting so-called 'modern' architectural styles. From about the mid-1960s to the end of the decade, however, lost ground was more than made up. Branches were built or rebuilt in an elegant modern style. Gone was the forbidding fortress-like aspect.[10] Interiors, too, were transformed, with an accent on informality and a friendly atmosphere, somewhat blunted by the anti-bandit screens that unfortunately became necessary.

The bank occupies properties of one kind or another throughout England and Wales—and the Channel Islands and Isle of Man, and Edinburgh—running into thousands, of varying age, design, and style. Of these, 208 are listed[11] under the Town and Country Planning Act, 1947, as being of historic or architectural interest. Usually, branches have a sign swinging outside of a black horse on a green background and also have a green fascia. Lloyds started to use green as its house colour in the early 1920s. Major R. C. Garton, a director 1918–23 and a keen yachtsman, had a boat kept in Poole harbour covered with tarpaulins dyed 'Willesden green', a colour which, Garton claimed, stood out well and enabled him to pick out his boat easily. He convinced the premises committee, of which he was a member, that Lloyds' signs in this colour would also be visible at a distance and so it was adopted.[12] The bank had used the sign of the black horse since 1884, when it merged with the Lombard Street house of Barnetts, Hoares, Hanbury and Lloyds, but not until 1956 did it have a coat of arms. In the early 1950s the clearing house in Lombard Street was rebuilt, and the clearing banks' arms and devices were to be carved near the main entrance. Lloyds found that, apart from Coutts, it was the only bank without arms, which, on application to the College of Arms, it was granted in February 1956.[13]

---

[10] The tradition that bank counters had to be on the ground floor was also broken: New Street, Birmingham, branch was rehoused in 1964 on the first floor, reached by escalator. Other branches were similarly designed.

[11] In April 1977.

[12] A somewhat darker shade than Willesden green is now used.

[13] The shield of the arms derives from the arms of the Lloyd family, to which have been added five bezants—formal representation of ancient gold coins—to indicate the nature of the bank's business. The black horse forms one of the supporters and a goat from the Lloyd family arms the other. The sword and mural crown in the crest refer to the bank's connection with the City of London. The griffin is the traditional guardian of treasure; the unicorn is one of the old Lombard Street signs which hung in the seventeenth century on the site of the bank's head office.

Esto Vigilans (Be Watchful) is the motto of the Lloyd family. Lloyds' black horse, and the arms of the other clearing banks, were incorporated not near the main entrance but on the King William Street frontage of the clearing house building (10 Lombard Street) at the first-floor level.

Finally, to round off this fifty-year survey, let us look at the changes in
the bank's capital structure. Most of these were after the war. In December 1918 authorised capital was £60m., in £50 shares, paid-up capital
standing at £8.95m. Following a re-organisation in 1920, and in line with
the trend towards a smaller par value for shares, Lloyds' authorised capital
became £72.5m. (14.5m. shares of £5), with paid-up value of £14.14m. In
1926 there was another re-organisation, which raised the authorised
capital to £74m. and paid-up capital to £15.81m. Authorised capital
remained unchanged from then on, until 1973, and so did paid-up capital
until the 1950s.

During the war there was a sharp deterioration in the relationship
between the bank's capital funds and the increasing volume of its business.
In December 1937 paid-up capital and total reserves (published and
inner) were equal to just over 8% of total resources,[14] only a shade below
the figure for the early 1920s. By 1947, however, the ratio had been almost
halved, to under $4\frac{1}{2}$%, and the next few years saw only a gradual increase.
One of Lord Franks' prime aims during his term as chairman (1954–62)
was to restore the ratio to a level more in keeping with the bank's scale of
business and this he succeeded in doing. Four capital re-organisations in
the 1950s raised paid-up capital by December 1959 to £34.8m. which,
together with the building up of reserves, meant that capital funds now
equalled 7.5% of total resources. In the 1960s the capital structure was
strengthened further. Paid-up capital by 1969 had nearly doubled in the
ten years, to £64.9m.,[15] while total reserves had considerably more than

---

[14] The total of paid-up capital, published reserves and current, deposit, savings, and other
accounts.

[15] In detail, the changes in paid-up capital over the period 1918–69 were as follows:

December		£m.
1919	amalgamation with West Yorkshire Bank and additional shares in National Bank of Scotland and London & River Plate Bank.	9.421
1920	£2 per share paid up from reserves, £50 shares now £10 paid up, sub-divided into £5 shares, £1 paid up.	14.138
1921	amalgamation with Fox, Fowler & Co.	14.373
1926	£1 fully-paid 'B' shares issued, as bonus of 1 share for every 10 £5 'A' shares	15.810
1942	'B' shares converted to stock (in £1 units)	15.810
1955	5/- per share paid up from reserves, making £5 shares £1. 5s. paid up.	19.403
1956	5 £1 fully-paid shares for each 4 £5 shares and 5 for each £12 'B' stock. Capital now all £1 fully-paid shares	18.565
1958	scrip issue, 1 for 2 shares held	27.848
1959	rights issue, 1 for 4 shares held at 37/6 per share.	34.810
1961	scrip issue, 1 for 5 shares held	41.771
1962	scrip issue, 1 for 6 shares held and rights issue, 1 for 10 shares held at 50/- per share	53.607
1964	scrip issue, 1 for 7 shares held	61.265

doubled from £73m. to £189m. In relation to total resources, Lloyds' capital funds in December 1969 stood at 11.3%, the highest figure in the half century covered by this study.

1966　acquisition of National Bank of New Zealand, 11 Lloyds' shares for every
　　　10 NBNZ shares.　　　　　　　　　　　　　　　　　　　　64.883

2

The Structure Established

The last amalgamations

The early years after the first world war marked the end of the great movement of amalgamation among banks in England and Wales that had started in the middle of the nineteenth century and gathered pace in the 1890s and the first decade of this century. Lloyds Bank absorbed four other banks during the period 1918-23, three by mutual agreement— Capital and Counties in 1918, West Yorkshire in 1919, Fox, Fowler & Co. in 1921, and one requested by the Bank of England, with Treasury approval, Cox & Co. in 1923. With this last takeover, the basic structure of the bank was completed. There were, it is true, various changes in later years affecting its subsidiary and associated banks and the sale in 1960 to National & Grindlays Bank of the Eastern business that had been acquired with Cox & Co. in 1923. But no longer was the growth in business partly a reflection of absorption and merger. It was on the foundations completed in 1923 that the development of the bank in England and Wales was built in the years that followed.

The amalgamation drive of the banks up to the early years of the century had been characterised by small, local, and private banks taken over by larger and more widely spread joint stock banks, and had been carried through without much serious opposition or public resentment. In the period just before 1914, however, there was some change of direction and now large banks began to merge with other banks of equal size. This development accelerated during the war. Reacting to the public concern and criticism such mergers provoked, a Treasury Committee under Lord Colwyn was set up in March 1918, with Sir Richard Vassar-Smith, chairman of Lloyds, as one of its twelve members. With exemplary speed the Committee reported on 1 May, and concluded that the possible dangers of further large amalgamations, particularly of reduced competition or possible monopoly, were material enough to outweigh the arguments against government interference. It recommended legislation to require prior approval of the government for proposed mergers and other agreements, for example, the purchase by one bank of the shares of another, with a committee to advise the Treasury and Board of Trade.

No legislation was ever passed but an Advisory Committee was soon established, to which proposals for amalgamation or purchase of bank shares were subsequently referred.

The conclusions of the Colwyn Report were to inform official policy towards bank mergers for the next half century. It was not until 1967, with the report of the National Board for Prices and Incomes on *Bank Charges*, that it appeared that the authorities' attitude to mergers might have changed. We shall come to this and the misunderstandings of the time later in the story. Now we must turn back to 1918.

One of the first merger proposals submitted to the Advisory Committee was that between Lloyds and Capital and Counties Banks. Lloyds then had deposits of £193m. and 888 branches, while Capital and Counties had deposits of £60m. and 473 branches, so that the proposed amalgamation was very much one between two large banks, which might have been difficult to reconcile with the Colwyn Committee's views. However, in July the merger was approved, but Lloyds was asked for an undertaking that no further proposals for amalgamation with another bank would be put forward for the next three years. In the event, this ban was lifted in the following June, although it was not intended that any large-scale amalgamations would be sanctioned.

Capital and Counties had been formed in 1877 by the merger of Hampshire Banking Co. and North Wilts Banking Co. to form Hampshire and North Wilts Banking Co., which changed its name the following year. Both partners had taken over a number of banks, mainly in the west and south of England, and after 1878 the new institution continued the policy of absorption. Discussions for a merger with Lloyds were started early in 1918, prompted mainly by the needs to secure a wider branch coverage and to obtain the benefits of size in financing overseas trade. As regards the former, the merger brought Capital and Counties' customers facilities in nearly 670 new places, while Lloyds obtained branches in some 260 places where it had no existing office. There was thus a considerable overlap, resulting in subsequent years in a number of closures. The merger terms were one Lloyds share and £2 cash bonus for each of the 175,000 Capital and Counties' shares, which, in view of the relative market prices, meant the holders of the latter were in pocket on the transaction.

For some time after 1918 Capital and Counties continued to operate very much as a separate business under a Capital and Counties committee of directors, originally of fifteen members. As time went on, the numbers —and business transacted—dwindled, but the committee continued. By

1949 the sole surviving member was Lord Bledisloe, and with his death in 1958 the committee at last came to an end.

The next amalgamation came in September 1919 when, with official approval, Lloyds absorbed the West Yorkshire Bank. This relatively small bank, with deposits of £10m., 215 staff and 29,000 accounts, over a third savings bank accounts, dated back to 1829, and as Halifax Joint Stock Banking Co. had merged with Halifax and Huddersfield Union Banking Co. in 1910, changing its name the following year. At that time, it did not wish amalgamation to go any further. However, 'the war has changed the position of everything', explained J. H. L. Baldwin, West Yorkshire's chairman in 1919. Increased demands for capital by industry required a merger with a strong bank to secure the advantages of larger resources. From Lloyds' point of view, the merger brought a welcome thirty-four offices in an area where it had relatively few branches. Lloyds gave 50,000 shares for West Yorkshire's 40,000 shares, together with £5 cash for each share, the latter's shareholders about breaking even on the transaction. Two directors of West Yorkshire joined Lloyds' board, and a local board and district office were established in Halifax.

In February 1921 the amalgamation was announced of Lloyds Bank with Fox, Fowler & Co. This was a merger of particular significance in banking history, since it marked the end of the last private bank note issue in England and Wales.

This family bank dated back to 1787, when Thomas Fox founded it as an adjunct to his woollen business carried on at Wellington, Somerset. A century later the partnership was widened to include two Fowler brothers, members of a wealthy London family with which one of the Fox partners was associated by marriage, and banking was henceforward separated from woollen manufacturing. Encouraged by the Fowler family, a number of branches were opened in Somerset and Devon. However, unwise lending, largely by the Fowler brothers, resulted in some considerable bad debts and for a time the bank was in the red. In the new century the Fowlers were gradually eased out and effective command came into the hands of John Howard Fox, a nephew by marriage of Howard Lloyd (general manager of Lloyds until 1902 and a director until his death in 1920), and a cousin of Beaumont Pease, then deputy chairman. The position improved and profits were restored, but the firm's finances were still not wholly secure. The bank was solvent but reserves were inadequate. The partners feared that legislation might require publication of their balance sheet and also felt that the risks ahead after the 1920 boom were

too great for them to shoulder. Negotiations were opened for a merger
with Lloyds. Fox, Fowler & Co. then had £3.5m. in deposits at twenty-
one branches and forty-four sub-branches. Under the amalgamation
agreement Fox, Fowler received 235,000 Lloyds' shares as consideration,
and J. Howard Fox joined Lloyds' board, continuing in charge of a
committee at Wellington supervising the former Fox, Fowler branches.
His interest never flagged and until the end of the second world war on
most days he visited Wellington. On his death in 1951 the committee was
wound up but his son, Lloyd Howard Fox, continued the association with
Lloyds as a member of the Devon and Cornwall committee until 1967.

The number of note-issuing banks in England and Wales had been
shrinking over the years, as the provisions of the Bank Charter Act of 1844
combined with amalgamations to extinguish one note issue after another.
In December 1919 the last country joint stock bank issue disappeared,
with the merger of Halifax Commercial Bank with the Bank of Liverpool
and Martins. The amalgamation of Fox, Fowler with Lloyds in 1921
marked the end of the issue of bank notes by private banks in England and
Wales. Fox, Fowler's issue of £5 notes had stood at £4,300 since the
beginning of 1918, with about £2,850 in circulation and the rest in its tills.
In the six months after the merger a large number of notes were paid in
and by 1923 only some £150 was still outstanding. Over the next twenty
years this was reduced to £105, a figure that remained until 1962, when the
ledger was finally ruled off. As notable collectors' items, each of these
twenty-one notes is, of course, now worth vastly more than its £5 face
value.

Note issues of banks in Scotland continued, of course, and in the Isle of
Man, too, Lloyds Bank still issued notes over the signatures of the
manager and accountant of Douglas branch. In 1918 the bank obtained a
licence for the issue of one pound notes to a limit of £15,000, against the
deposit of War Stock, and, later, other gilt-edged securities. In December
1919 the issue stood at £5,000, increasing to the authorised limit by 1922
and there was then little change until 1928. In 1929 the issue was £6,000, a
level generally maintained until the war. From 1940 to the end of the 1950s
the total fluctuated around £10,000, then in December 1961, with the
issue at £4,000, the Isle of Man authorities assumed sole responsibility for
the local note issue and Lloyds' issue came to an end.

The last Lloyds absorption of another bank in this period came literally
out of the blue in February 1923, with the takeover of Cox & Co., the West
End Army bankers with branches in India, Burma, and Egypt. 'We have

not sought or initiated these arrangements', wrote Henry Bell, Lloyds' general manager, but 'any other avenue of escape from the present impasse is for all practical purposes closed.' There is no doubt that Lloyds' agreement to the merger, made with little enthusiasm, averted a serious crisis.

It is not possible here to retrace Cox's romantic history since Mr. Richard Cox was appointed in 1758 to keep the accounts of the 1st Foot Guards.[1] Army business had expanded enormously during the war but fell away after 1918. However, it was as regards ordinary commercial banking that Cox's had become vulnerable. In 1918 there were already rumours, which came to the ears of Sir Brien Cockayne, Governor of the Bank, about their industrial and financial business. The reaction from the short-lived post-war boom revealed over-trading by certain customers, while some injudicious loans had also been made. In India, where Cox's had opened its first branch in 1905 at Bombay, docks and warehouses were full of unsold goods. In the six months to March 1921 net profit was less than a fifth of that for the previous half year. A year later a substantial loss was recorded, and it was only after a special reserve of £210,000 had been set aside for contingencies that the auditors were satisfied.

It was in this rickety position that, six months on, in October 1922, Cox's took over the firm of Henry S. King & Co.[2] King & Co., founded in 1816, carried on a banking and agency business from its office in Cornhill and branches in India. The sole partner for the past forty-four years had been Sir Seymour King, also a director of Lloyds from 1909 to 1933. Then aged seventy, recently recovered from a serious illness and with no successor in sight, King understandably decided to sell. In the same month, confidence was shaken with the failure of Sir Charles R. McGrigor & Co., one of the three banks then acting as Army Agents. This did nothing to allay existing qualms about Cox's position, one of the other two agents (the third was Holt & Co.). One customer wrote from Egypt offering the balance of his account if it would help, but unfortunately the balance was an overdraft. Cox's employees had also heard the rumours and realised the firm was in trouble when men on the permanent staff were given three months notice to quit.

Things rapidly came to a head. On Monday, 29 January 1923, Sir William Plender called on the Governor, now Montagu Norman, and told him that, as auditor, he had examined Cox's accounts, which showed a loss of about £1m., against capital and reserve of little more. The position was

---

[1] See R. S. Sayers, *Lloyds Bank in the History of English Banking*, Oxford University Press, 1957, pp. 190–3.

[2] In May 1922, Barclays Bank had bought Cox's interest in Cox & Co. (France), which had been established in 1915 to handle the firm's Continental business.

extremely serious—'a state of jeopardy existed'—and a run was daily expected. At Sir William's suggestion, Norman then saw Beaumont Pease and Paine, Lloyds' legal adviser and a joint general manager, who told him that in fact six weeks previously Cox's had asked to be taken over. This was refused. Cox's were told to try Barclays, the clearing bank with which they had a special relationship. However, Cox's were adamant,[3] so, in view of the grave position, Lloyds agreed to ask their own auditors to go over Cox's accounts. This had taken five weeks and abundantly confirmed Sir William Plender's dire audit.

Norman now pressed Pease to take over Cox's—'in the interests of the community it appeared essential that the proposed amalgamation be carried through with the least possible delay'—and Pease agreed, subject to guarantees from the Bank, without which Lloyds would not have moved. On 6 February the announcement was made that, with the consent of the Treasury and the Army Council, Lloyds were taking over Cox & Co. and that Henry S. King & Co. would also become part of Lloyds Bank. At the suggestion of Henry Bell, Norman sent a cable to the Government of India giving the news and hoping that the 'intrusion into India of an English joint stock bank might prove to be only temporary'. This was prudent, since in 1918 Indian government objections had led the Colwyn Advisory Committee to refuse Lloyds permission to buy an interest in the National Bank of India. As it turned out, the temporary intrusion lasted nearly forty years. Lloyds received two guarantees from the Bank of England totalling £900,000, one covering general assets and the other premises—the latter was covered by the Treasury but taken over by the Bank in 1927—and it was provided that Lloyds would run Cox & Co., including the branches in India and Egypt, as a separate business over a 'management period' ending in December 1927, when the assets would be valued and any liability of the Bank of England under its guarantees assessed.

In February 1923 Cox's deposits in London stood at £11m., with £2.8m. at the eight Indian and Rangoon offices and just over £1m. in Egypt, and a staff of some 900 in London and about eighty Europeans overseas. Head Office was at 16 Charing Cross and city office in Grace-church Street. New premises were being built at 6 Pall Mall, which Lloyds took over—'probably the finest bank premises in England', thought Sir Austin Harris, Lloyds' deputy chairman. The Charing Cross premises were sold to the National Bank and the Gracechurch Street office closed

---

[3] The records do not reveal why Cox's insisted on Lloyds but it may well have been Sir Seymour King, a director of Lloyds who had become associated with Cox's, who pressed the issue.

and its business transferred to other Lloyds' branches. In London, King's had deposits of only £1m. and a staff of about 120, with twenty-seven Europeans in India, where its deposits totalled £590,000.

For the whole management period to the end of 1927, the 'Cox's Section' of Lloyds showed a net loss of over £180,000, but this was heavily concentrated in the early years. By 1927 a substantial profit was recorded, reflecting in the main a sharp improvement in the fortunes of Pall Mall. The position now had to be assessed *vis-à-vis* the Bank of England, under its guarantees, but it took until the beginning of 1930 to draw up the accounts. These put the deficiency on general assets account at £347,000, but allowance had now to be made for the considerable income tax relief Lloyds had received in respect of losses incurred by Cox & Co. before 1923 and by the Cox & Co. section since. After allowing for this windfall tax relief and making no allowance for any liability on unclaimed balances, there was a surplus of £267,000 on general assets account. Premises account showed a deficiency, after crediting the £267,000, of £160,000. This sum, together with interest (£12,000) from December 1927, Lloyds received from the Bank. Unclaimed balances totalled £178,000, largely at Pall Mall, and to cover Lloyds' liability the Bank transferred government securities to this value, to be realised as and when needed to meet any claims, but the income on which was to be paid by Lloyds to the Bank. The total of such balances fell gradually in succeeding years, to stand at £140,000 in the early 1940s, but going down by only £2,000 in the next ten years. In 1955 Lloyds agreed on a final settlement with the Bank of £5,000. The total cost to the Bank under its guarantees given in 1923 thus came to £217,000. However, the Bank also contributed £50,000 in 1926 towards the National Bank of Egypt's purchase of Lloyds' Egyptian business (see chapter 6) and, as Lloyds was in Egypt only because it had been forced to take over Cox & Co., this, too, should properly be included in the cost to the Bank of the whole rescue operation, raising it to £267,000.

After 1927 the Cox & Co. section was absorbed into the ordinary administrative and operational structure of Lloyds Bank, and a number of former Cox's and King's staff subsequently rose to positions of authority in the domestic bank and in the Indian branches. This side of the business was built up into a profitable enterprise until, for reasons we will come to later, it was sold to National & Grindlays Bank in 1960. At home, 6 Pall Mall remained one of the largest bank branches in the country, with its connections continuing with the Army and R.A.F.[4] The second world

---

[4] The name of Cox & Kings did not disappear. After Lloyds acquired Cox & Co. in 1923, Cox's Shipping Agency and King's agency business was sold, to become the present-day firm of tour operators and travel, insurance, and shipping agents.

war, like the first, meant a great increase in its business, to cope with which special machinery was installed, and later the branch became the testing ground for the application of computer techniques to bank accounting.

The enforced take-over of Cox & Co. did not entirely blunt Lloyds' appetite for further amalgamation. Indeed, in the same month that the Cox merger was announced a request by Lloyds to absorb the small West End bank, Childs, was referred to the Colwyn Advisory Committee. Although the Treasury had been inclined to agree, the merger was turned down, and in 1924 Childs joined forces with Glyn, Mills & Co. More disappointing was the fruitless attempt by Lloyds in 1925 to amalgamate with Manchester & County Bank, for this would have added to Lloyds' network over 160 branches in a part of the country where, as on the other side of the Pennines in 1919, its branch coverage was somewhat sparse.

Discussion about policy on amalgamations between Norman, the Treasury, and the Colwyn Advisory Committee since early in 1923 had produced two principles: that no amalgamations among the big five London clearing banks would be permitted and that there should be no extension of their interests in banks abroad. By March 1924 Norman and the Chancellor (Snowden) had agreed on a division of domestic banks into five groups, the first of which, the big five London clearing banks, were not to amalgamate either among themselves or with any other bank.[5]

When, therefore, Pease informed Norman in June 1925 that Lloyds was about to open negotiations to amalgamate with Manchester & County Bank he was left in no doubt about how the proposal would be received. Norman was 'entirely opposed to any amalgamation or ownership, whether at home or abroad, which would increase the five large Clearing Banks'. There were further talks between Pease and Norman, who also saw Sir Austin Harris and Sir Robert Horne, a director of Lloyds and former Chancellor. Pease soon realised defeat was inevitable and he told the Chancellor (now Churchill) that Lloyds did not intend to go ahead. Ten years later Manchester & County Bank merged with the District Bank.

By the outbreak of the first world war Lloyds had been faced on a great number of occasions with the problems of absorbing yet another bank into its system. Methods of working had to be brought into line, staff assimilated and a whole range of details of greater or lesser importance reviewed—stationery, salary scales, holiday arrangements, how cheques

---

[5] R. S. Sayers, *The Bank of England 1891–1944*. Cambridge University Press 1976, Volume 1, pp. 242–3. Not until 1940 did one of the five merge with another bank in England (Barclays with Union Bank of Manchester).

were filed, and so on.[6] The larger the bank, the greater the job. Much experience had been built up and a routine established. Inspectors were issued with a list of twenty-four instructions to be followed when arriving at a bank that had thrown in its lot with Lloyds: the first, to count the cash on arrival, the last, the underlined admonition that 'members of our staff are particularly requested to treat their new friends with every courtesy and to refrain from making any comparisons whatever'.

The amalgamation with Capital & Counties in 1918 presented all these problems once again on a large scale. One that took some months to overcome was the difference in book-keeping systems: Lloyds worked on double entry, and Capital & Counties on single entry. Both banks had extensive branch networks and in a number of places both had offices, mainly in the South West Midlands and the South East. To eliminate duplication meant the closure and sale of a number of branches in the early 1920s, sometimes those of Lloyds, sometimes of Capital & Counties. The process of merging the two businesses into one office often presented difficulties: premises had to be altered or enlarged, desks or furniture changed; staff arrangements were also affected: for a time Plymouth branch had three managers—of Lloyds, Wilts & Dorset, and Capital & Counties Banks respectively. By 1925 there had been just on ninety branch mergers but in 1933 only five places remained where there were still two branches. Today, only in Bath do two remain: Lloyds at one end of Milsom Street and Lloyds (C & C) at the other. Such changes inevitably caused disturbance and upset of expectations to the men and women affected, and the 'new friends' were not always treated with every courtesy. At least at the outset, there was some antagonism and ill-will between the staffs of the two banks, and, perhaps naturally enough, Capital & Counties' staff did not always find it easy to regard themselves as Lloyds' employees.

The amalgamation with West Yorkshire Bank and Fox, Fowler, much smaller enterprises, presented far fewer difficulties. But working methods had to conform to Lloyds' routines, former ways of doing things abandoned, old privileges given up. Fox, Fowler's managers, for example, had to forgo a bonus scheme they had enjoyed, of $2\frac{1}{2}\%$ of the net branch profit. The take-over of Cox & Co. in 1923, however, was another question. Admittedly, the business was run as a separate operation until 1927 and the problem of assimilating branches did not arise; the offices in Egypt and India were a special case. Yet, partly because of the peculiarities

[6] The result of former practices still sometimes lingered on. In 1911 Lloyds amalgamated with the small Smithfield bank of Hill and Sons, which used to recruit some of its staff from an orphanage. In the 1920s there were still a number of elderly ledger-keepers in the office who had joined the bank in this way.

of its work as an Army Agent, Cox's had developed certain practices which Lloyds sought to change on the amalgamation. The business at Charing Cross had been divided into ten sections. These were formed into ten individual branches. Cox's stock department had bought and sold securities in its own right and operated on a considerable scale; a memorandum on the take-over notes that 'jobbing in War Loan, Conversion Funding and Victory Bills ceased, upon instructions from the Manager, on the evening of 5th February 1923'. Managers had to stop signing letters 'your obedient servant' and change to 'yours faithfully'. On Lloyds' side, there was some fear of competition from Cox's men and the years afterwards showed this was not entirely groundless. A number of Cox's men were able to take advantage of the greater scope open to them, and did well. In the colonial and foreign department in 1928, for example, of the four managers, two were former Cox's staff, while the chief manager (W. H. Taylor) had come from Brown, Shipley.

Investments in other banks

By the early 1920s the foundations had been laid not only for the development of Lloyds Bank during the next half century, but for that of the international Lloyds Bank Group which became a conscious aim of policy in the years after 1969. Lloyds made the investments in those other institutions which were ultimately to come together as members of the Group.

The first step had been taken in 1911, when Lloyds Bank (France) was established by the purchase for approximately £40,000 of Armstrong & Co., with branches in Paris and Havre. In 1917, as National Provincial Bank needed offices in France, a fifty-fifty partnership was formed and the name of the 'auxiliary', as it was called, changed to Lloyds and National Provincial (Foreign) Bank. Describing itself as 'a British bank, conducted on British lines', and modelling its services on those of its English owners, its business was mainly with British companies operating on the Continent and British nationals living abroad. By 1938 nine branches had been opened in France, two in Belgium, one in Switzerland, and two in London. But its deposits were still only £12m., against £10m. in 1930. In the post-war years retail deposit banking continued to be the mainstay of the business until the development of the Euro-currency market and 'wholesale banking' in the 1960s. In the meantime, in 1955 National Provincial's holding had been purchased and the bank, as Lloyds Bank (Foreign), became a wholly-owned subsidiary, in 1964 the name being changed again, to Lloyds Bank Europe. The following years were a period of rapid growth, with a substantial increase in capitalisation and a total of nineteen branches in Europe by 1970. Between 1960 and 1970 deposits grew from £41m. to £561m. In May 1971 the bank was merged with Bank of London and South America to form Lloyds and Bolsa International Bank, in which Lloyds had a 51% shareholding. Two years later this became a wholly-owned subsidiary and in 1974 its name was changed to Lloyds Bank International.

Lloyds' interest in the other, and larger, constituent of L.B.I. originated in 1918 when, with official approval, control was acquired of the London and River Plate Bank, the oldest British bank in South America. In 1923 Lloyds merged the London and Brazilian Bank with the London and River Plate to form the Bank of London and South America. Lloyds was now joined by some 3,000 other shareholders but it retained a controlling interest of 56.9%. Norman had doubts about this extension[7] but decided nothing could be done to stop it. Over the years that followed, Lloyds' stake was reduced, to stand at 31.4% by the beginning of the 1960s, and there was a further decline during the rest of the decade. The story after that is beyond the scope of this book: capital transactions that, in partnership with Lloyds Bank Europe, produced Lloyds Bank International.[8]

Another banking investment was made in 1918 when, again after submission to the Colwyn Advisory Committee, Lloyds acquired 96.4% of the issued stock of the National Bank of Scotland. This remained a subsidiary until it merged with Commercial Bank of Scotland in 1959, when Lloyds' holding was exchanged for shares representing approximately 37% of the capital of National Commercial Bank of Scotland. In 1968, this bank in turn amalgamated with the Royal Bank of Scotland and Lloyds' holding became 16.4% of the share capital of the holding company set up.

The following year Lloyds again looked overseas and, after official sanction, acquired interests in The National Bank of New Zealand and in the Bank of British West Africa. In 1919, Lloyds bought 50,000 shares in N.B.N.Z. The 1920s saw a few sales and purchases, thereafter the bank's holding remaining unchanged until a capital reorganisation in 1957 and a scrip issue in 1959. By 1965 Lloyds' stake was still only 6% of N.B.N.Z.'s issued capital of 3,500,000 shares. The idea was now floated of an offer to buy the approximately 3,290,000 shares held by the public, to make N.B.N.Z. a wholly-owned subsidiary. This was not only because of the bank's importance in New Zealand (it had about a fifth of the country's

---

[7] Sayers, *op. cit.*, p. 244.
[8] For the history of the Bank of London and South America see David Joslin, *A Century of Banking in Latin America*, Oxford University Press, 1963.

bank deposits) but also because it might provide an entry into the Australian banking market. For some time, Harald Peake, chairman since 1962, had wished to extend Lloyds' interest in Australia. N.B.N.Z. had no branches in Australia and it was believed the New Zealand government would not approve its absorption by an Australian bank. However, if Lloyds acquired N.B.N.Z. it might encourage an Australian bank to invite a participation from Lloyds. These arguments won over the board, and, with the assent of the Governor, Lord Cromer, an offer to N.B.N.Z.'s shareholders was made in November 1965, of ten new Lloyds' shares in exchange for eleven of theirs. The vast majority accepted and in February 1966 The National Bank of New Zealand became a wholly-owned subsidiary. In the event, Lloyds' interest in Australia has come not from any sizeable stake in an Australian bank, but from an extension of the business of L.B.I.

In 1919, in three operations, Lloyds acquired 37,500 shares in the British Bank of West Africa, beginning a connection that was to last until 1965. Friendly relations had already been established between the two banks, in particular between Lloyds' managers and Roy Wilson, then assistant general manager of British Bank of West Africa (and father of Michael Wilson, chief general manager of Lloyds in the 1960s). Apart from the capital investment, the two chairmen, Lord Selborne and Sir Richard Vassar-Smith drew up 'A Treaty of Alliance': each bank was to appoint the other as correspondent, the British Bank of West Africa was to transfer accounts to Lloyds, Lloyds was to finance B.B.W.A.'s seasonal and other requirements.[9] One particular consequence came in 1925, when Lloyds took over the Egyptian branches of B.B.W.A. There were few changes in Lloyds' holding until the end of the 1950s, when its stake represented about 14% of B.B.W.A.'s issue of stock units. In 1965, the Bank of West Africa, as it was now named, merged with the Standard Bank to form the Standard Bank of West Africa. In the meantime, Lloyds had become a large shareholder in National and Grindlays Bank, to which it had sold its Eastern business in 1960, and which was a competitor of Standard in East Africa. To resolve the conflict of interest, Lloyds sold its shares in the Bank of West Africa.

Lloyds had investments in a few other overseas banks at this time, many of which were sold by the mid-1930s. There was, in particular, the stake in the Banca Italo-Britannica, which we will come to in the next chapter.

[9] For the details, and history of British Bank of West Africa, see Richard Fry, *Bankers in West Africa*, Hutchinson Benham, 1976.

There seems to have been little consistent policy as regards these various investments, and no conscious strategy for the development of Lloyds' interests overseas or, for that matter, its investment interests at home. In 1919, admittedly, Pease proposed the formation of a high-sounding general intelligence council, to be made up of Lloyds' directors and representatives of the other banks, to consider financial, commercial and political matters in the various countries. But nothing seems to have come of the idea. Nor was there any official encouragement. In 1923, as we have seen, the principle was accepted that there should be no extension by the big five banks of their interests in banks abroad, and, as occasion arose, Norman tried, but with little success, to enforce this rule.[10] In 1925, when Norman was pressing Pease to sell the Indian branches Lloyds had acquired with Cox's in 1923, Norman wrote, about Lloyds' overseas affiliations with The National Bank of New Zealand, the 'auxiliary' and the rest: 'there is nothing to be said for these; they are apt at any time to be a danger to Lloyds who are a Bank and not a Trust Company'.

Several years later another attempt was made to promote closer co-operation. In 1943, the chief general managers, R. A. Wilson and Sydney Parkes, set down their thoughts about Lloyds' investments in other banks in the context of possible post-war expansion. They noted that under existing arrangements the bank's three affiliates, National Bank of Scotland, BOLSA, and Lloyds and National Provincial (Foreign) Bank, kept very much aloof from Lloyds: 'there is an entire lack of cohesion between these institutions and the parent'; and they suggested ways be sought through which closer relationships might develop, such as regular meetings of the various general managers or exchanges of staff. But, once again, little happened. It was to be another thirty years before any real practical expression was to be given to the belief of Wilson and Parkes that 'our united thoughts should be applied continuously to the development of the "Lloyds Bank Group"'.

The post-war boom and after

The eighteen months after the end of the war in November 1918 saw a very sharp upturn in economic activity, followed by a drawn-out recession. Manufacturing production in 1920 was nearly a quarter higher than in 1918 but in 1921 fell by about the same proportion, then recovered the following year; merchandise exports rose 60% in value between 1919 and 1920 to £1,585m.—a level not reached again until 1948—and in 1921 dropped by about half; company trading profits in 1920 rose to £621m., and the next year were down to £343m. Prices also were subject to a

[10] See Sayers, *op. cit.*, pp. 243–8.

violent fluctuation. Wholesale prices rose 12% in 1919, followed by a 20% jump in 1920, but slumped by 37% in 1921, with comparable movements in retail prices: up 23% in the two years 1918 to 1920, down 27% in the two years 1920 to 1922.

These wide swings were reflected in the banks' business. Lloyds' advances rose from £81m. at end-1918 to £136m. twelve months later, an increase of nearly 70% (only very little of which was due to the merger with West Yorkshire Bank). Some years after, R. H. (later Lord) Brand, who had joined the Board in 1916, recollected:

My impression of Board meetings . . . at that time was that we ladled out money; we did it because everybody said they were making and were going to make large profits, and while you had an uneasy feeling yet you thought that while they were making large profits there could be nothing said about ladling out the money.[11]

In 1920 the pace slowed down, advances standing at £151m. in December, to represent 44% of total deposits, against 30% in 1918. In the meantime, official reaction had come in a rise in Bank Rate, to 6% in November 1919 and 7% in April 1920. This was accompanied, moreover, by the kind of official 'request' with which the banks became so familiar in the years after 1945 and couched in much the same kind of language. In March 1920 the bank chairmen had talked with the Chancellor (Austen Chamberlain) who, later in the month, wrote that he was

relying on their co-operation in putting into effect a policy of gradual deflation of credit which in my opinion will require a gradual but progressive reduction in the amount of accommodations granted by the banks of this country to their customers.[12]

In the spring, however, the boom broke, before the banks' restrictions could have much effect. It had been a short-lived spree. At the annual general meeting in February 1921 Vassar-Smith commented on how fast things had changed during 1920: at the end of the year industry suffered 'extreme depression', while at the beginning there had been 'extremely active and prosperous conditions'. By the end of 1922 Lloyds' advances had fallen to £122m., 37% of deposits.

The changes in deposits mirrored those in advances, but somewhat less violently. Between December 1918 and December 1920 Lloyds' total deposits rose by about 30%, from £267m. to £345m., and in the succeeding two years fell by only £14m. In the rates offered for deposit (term)

[11] Susan Howson, *Domestic Monetary Management in Britain 1919–1938*, Cambridge University Press, 1975, p. 10.
[12] Committee of London Clearing Bankers' Minutes, 18 March 1920.

money, Lloyds adhered to those agreed by the Committee of London Clearing Bankers. This cartel was not, however, quite so wide in scope as has sometimes been supposed. Agreement between the clearers in the 1920s was restricted to the maximum rates to be offered for deposits, domestic and foreign, plus, from 1925, call money lent to the discount market. In early 1918, with Bank Rate at 5%, London deposit rate stood at $3\frac{1}{2}$%, the margin of $1\frac{1}{2}$% that had been established in the 1880s. In February, however, the banks agreed, to stimulate the sale of government bonds, to reduce the maximum rate to 3%, thus widening the margin to 2%. The rate undertaking given by the banks in 1918 ended in August the next year but deposit rate stayed at 3%, still two points under Bank Rate. Except during the war, a 2% margin was thereafter generally maintained over the whole period covered by this study.

Interest was widely given on current accounts in this period and the 3% maximum of 1918 applied also to these. After the rate undertaking ended in 1919, however, some current accounts attracted rates that were fixed independently of Bank Rate. Deposit rate at country branches was not geared to Bank Rate and moved much less frequently. In 1920, for example, London deposit rate became 5% when Bank Rate was raised to 7%, but country deposit rate stayed at $3\frac{1}{2}$%. There was some resentment among Lloyds' country customers at this difference in treatment and some demanded, and got, London rate; but then later, when London rate went down in 1922 and country deposit rate became relatively more favourable, wished to change back. But this was not permitted.

Savings bank accounts, which Lloyds introduced in 1915 'to meet the requirements of the small depositor', generally earned the going rate for country deposits at this time; with the result that managers in London had to try to stop transfers from deposit to savings accounts when the rate on the latter became more favourable.

The increase in London deposit rate in 1919–21 was reflected in a significant rise in the number of Lloyds' deposit accounts—by 32% over the three years—but with the run-down in the rate after the collapse of the boom the rate of increase tailed off, and in 1922 and 1923 there was practically no growth at all. In 1918 deposit balances accounted for only a third of all deposits,[13] but rose to over two-fifths in 1920 and to about a half in 1922–3. Over the whole five years from December 1918 to December 1923 the total number of accounts grew by some 290,000, of which current accounts accounted for 135,000, deposit accounts for 129,000, and savings accounts for 26,000. This increase included about

---

[13] Excludes 'other accounts', as do all other references in this study to the shares of current, deposit, and savings bank accounts.

50,000 accounts as a result of the West Yorkshire and Fox, Fowler amalgamations but did not include Cox's business which, it will be remembered, was run as a separate section until 1927.

In spite of the mergers of branches necessitated by amalgamation, each year during this period recorded a net increase in the number open, to total 1,626 in December 1923. In November 1918 war-time official restrictions on the opening of new branches were lifted and requests to close branches withdrawn, in anticipation of which a branch extensions committee had been formed. In a month a list of sixty new branches was drawn up and approved, to be added to as time went on. In 1919, no less than 203 offices were opened for business. However, nearly half of these were branches that had been closed during the war and now re-opened and there were also the additional offices from the merger with West Yorkshire Bank. Most of the rest were sub-branches opened as part of the post-war expansion programme.

The premises department of the bank during these early post-war years was kept busy not only in merging branches, in acquiring premises for new offices and seeing to their design, construction and furnishing. It also had to maintain existing branches and to bring to them, or at least, to some of them, the amenities of the twentieth century. Electric light was being introduced, although not all managers' requests to change from gas were approved, and it seems surprising that in 1922 Andover branch was told that a hanging oil lamp could be used to light its strong room. The use of the telephone was spreading but in 1918 whether or not a branch had one was to be decided by the relative general manager; in 1921, in view of a possible increase in charges, the telephone was to be installed only in branches where it was considered essential. Cleanliness was apparently not overrated: the request in 1920 of the manager at Rye for a bath-room in the bank house was turned down, while the following year the manager at Leominster was refused 'a hot water heating apparatus' and his staff had to make do with an anthracite stove. Lavatory accommodation for the women who had come into the bank during the war was often a problem, particularly in small offices, but one hopes there were not many like St. Austell, which in 1921 was told that 'accommodation for the lady clerks should be found somewhere outside the bank'.

In the years after the first world war—indeed, until after the second— there were only two specialised departments: for overseas transactions and for executor and trustee business. The foreign department (later colonial and foreign department, a name which, recognising the decline of Empire, was changed to overseas department in 1950) had been established in 1898, with a handful of staff. The 1919/20 boom brought a sharp increase in business, and record profits, to a level not reached again until the 1950s. In 1921 the bank sent a representative, John Fea, to New York, originally 'for temporary service for six months'—but he stayed until retirement in 1954. For the first six years Fea was mostly occupied in dealing in foreign exchange, only afterwards becoming a representative proper. In 1921 the bank also introduced a world letter of credit, with which, it was claimed, cash could be obtained from 'Helsingfors to Honolulu, from the Canary Isles and Cape Coast Castle to Far Cathay'.

The executor and trustee department started business in 1910, when a clause was added to the bank's memorandum of association enabling it to undertake such work, but it was not until 1933 that the first branch was opened. In the early post-war years there was difficulty in getting suitable clerks, while lack of profit was attributed to fees pitched at too low figures.

Fortunately, this lack of profit was not true of the rest of the bank's operations. Gross profits more than doubled between the two years 1918 to 1920, from over £3m. to nearly £7m., mainly the result of booming advances and high rates. The 1920 figure, a peak not reached again until 1948, equalled just on 1.9% of total resources, the highest rate of return over the whole period covered by this book. In the recession that followed, gross profits slumped to under £3m. in 1922. Net profits (after providing for bad debts, income tax and other adjustments) showed a similar swing but the changes in published profits (after transfers to inner reserves)[14] were much less marked, rising by less than £1m. between 1918 and 1920, and falling by just over £1m. in the next two years.

Board and management

In August 1922 the death occurred, while still in office, of Sir Richard Vassar-Smith, who had been chairman since 1909. Sir Richard's place in the development of the bank and in the affections of his colleagues and staff has already been told[15] and it was little exaggeration for *Lloyds Bank Monthly* to say that 'it is impossible fully to express the regard in which he was held by all in the bank'. The Vassar-Smith Fund, set up as a memorial to help staff and their dependants in need, continues active to this day.

Vassar-Smith was succeeded by J. W. Beaumont Pease, his deputy throughout his chairmanship. Pease, on leaving Oxford, had joined Hodgkin, Barnett, Pease, Spence & Co. of Newcastle upon Tyne and,

[14] Not until 1969 did the published accounts of Lloyds and the other clearing banks show true profits and inner reserves.

[15] R. S. Sayers, *Lloyds Bank in the History of English Banking*.

when this old private banking partnership had joined Lloyds in 1903, he was offered a seat on the board. As a banker, Pease was to the manner born. His father's family had been bankers in the north since the eighteenth century and, as we have seen, he was connected with the Lloyd family through his mother.

Pease remained chairman until 1945, which must be one of the longest tenures of such an office in English banking that there has been. He served four terms as chairman of the Committee of London Clearing Bankers and President of the British Bankers' Association. Against the background of far-reaching economic and financial developments, Pease presided over the changing fortunes of the bank during these twenty-three years with the conservative and orthodox views which had been bred into him when a young man. As a partner in a private bank he must have been accustomed to shoulder responsibility himself and to know what went on in detail and these ways of working, not altogether suited to a large enterprise, he carried over into Lloyds. Board meetings tended to be rubber-stamp affairs, with directors given little opportunity to question or to discuss. The bank acquired something of a reputation for caution. As a man, good-looking with great dignity, Pease was the symbol of integrity and honesty. Although in public somewhat reserved, in private he was genial, kindly, a first-class after-dinner speaker, and a considerable sportsman. In 1936 he became Lord Wardington of Alnmouth in the County of Northumberland.

When Pease succeeded to the chair in 1922, Sir Austin Harris, a member of the board since 1910, became deputy chairman. This was to prove another long tenure, for Sir Austin held this position until 1947, retiring as director in 1949. In 1922, with the board of thirty-four members, Pease inherited one local board and three committees of directors. These were all products of past amalgamations, set up rather to smooth over periods of transition than with the intention of developing a comprehensive system of local centres of control. The local board was in Halifax, a product of the merger with the West Yorkshire Bank; while the three committees were in London (Capital & Counties), in Liverpool (established after the merger with Liverpool Union Bank in 1900) and in Salisbury (the result of the amalgamation with Wilts and Dorset Bank in 1914). The Halifax and Liverpool committees became permanent bodies but by the outbreak of war the Capital & Counties and Salisbury committees had for some time done little. In the meantime, a local committee had been established in 1931 at Birmingham and in 1934 at Newcastle. After the war a start was made on a system of regional committees that eventually was to cover the whole country.

In 1922 the general manager was still Henry Bell, the gifted banker who had come to Lloyds with the absorption of Liverpool Union Bank in 1900 and who, since 1916, had also had a seat on the board. Bell retired as general manager in 1923 but nobody was appointed to replace him as chief executive. The bank was managed by the joint general managers, at first five but later reduced to three, together with one at Birmingham until 1931. This not very efficient system lasted for six years until, in 1929, F. A. (Sir Francis in 1939) Beane and G. F. Abell were appointed as chief general managers. The title of 'joint' general manager was introduced in 1919. In September that year an article appeared in an evening paper by Sir John Ferguson, the London manager of the National Bank of Scotland who had become one of Lloyds' general managers following Lloyds acquiring control of his bank in 1918, which he had signed as 'general manager'. This title apparently stirred some feathers in head office, for Vassar-Smith asked all the general managers except Bell (director and general manager) to sign in future as 'joint' general managers.

Until the early 1930s, district offices were established at Halifax and Salisbury, complementary to the local board committees, while there was a general manager at Birmingham in charge of the district office and a district manager at Newcastle. When head office moved to Lombard Street in 1910 an assistant general manager (later general manager) and a section of advance department remained in Birmingham. On the retirement of the general manager in 1931, the advance department section was brought to London and a district manager appointed. By then, Birmingham was the only place with a district office, the others having been closed down. It continued alone until 1937 when, for three years to 1940, the manager of Liverpool branch became also a local district manager.

What other decentralisation there had been was also largely brought to an end in the 1930s and control centralised in London. In 1920 advance controllers worked in Birmingham, Halifax, Newcastle, and Salisbury, as well as in the main department in London, with authority to sanction individual overdrafts up to £15,000, but by 1930 controllers remained only at Birmingham and Newcastle, and by 1932 these, too, had moved to London. Managers were able to approve loans—their 'discretionary limit' —up to only £100, although at certain branches the limit was higher. This limit of £100 remained the general rule until 1943.

Until 1921 staff control was centred in head office, although some local supervision had been the responsibility of the few district offices and, to a limited extent, the inspectors. Seven staff controllers were now appointed: at Birmingham, Bury St. Edmunds, Cardiff, Croydon, Paignton, Salisbury, and York. In the 1930s, however, as part of the economy measures that then proved necessary, the number of controllers was reduced to three, those at Bury St. Edmunds, Croydon, Paignton, and Salisbury not being replaced on retirement.

Only the premises department maintained its system of provincial offices during the inter-war years. In 1920, besides the chief building inspector in London (a title not changed to architect until 1950) there were building inspectors at Birmingham, Newcastle, Salisbury, and Swansea. By 1930, a colleague had been added at Newcastle and the Welsh office had moved to Cardiff. This was the arrangement up to the outbreak of war.

Staff developments

At the end of 1918 the staff at work in the bank totalled not quite 7,400,[16] of whom some 5,000 were temporary clerks, many of them women, taken on during the war. In the next year or so men were demobilised and women left, and there were also those who did not return—685 Lloyds' men were killed or died. Many young men now joined the bank. In 1921 over 500 juniors were taken on, more than in any other inter-war year, and in the next three years the numbers, though decreasing, were still large. With unemployment high after 1920, there was little difficulty in attracting staff: a letter in 1923 mentions the 'several hundreds of very eligible young men' who had applied for jobs. At the same time, there were too many senior men for the bank's requirements, partly the result of all the amalgamations. The heavy recruitment of the early 1920s inevitably built an imbalance into the age-structure, that took a generation to work through. In 1938, a third of the male staff (excluding messengers) was 30-9 years old; twelve years later, in 1950, a third was now in the 40-9 age-group, while in 1960 only a slightly smaller proportion was fifty years and over. Once again there were too many senior men, with all that implied for the efficient planning of the bank's operations and for dashed hopes of promotion. Moreover, the age-structure was further distorted as a result of the cut-down in recruitment in the early 1930s. This we will come to later.

It was during the first world war that women clerks first appeared in the bank, by 1918 totalling 3,300 (45% of the staff). While the need was clear for their services to replace the men who had left for the war, their presence was apparently viewed not without some qualms, if Cox & Co.'s rule book for 1916 is any guide: male members of the staff were to converse with lady members only on matters of business. General recruitment of women ended in 1920 and they were engaged henceforth only for such work as typing and filing, until the introduction of mechanised accounting

[16] Excluding the 4,000 men on the permanent staff in the Forces.

in 1929 again called for increased employment of young women. In the meantime, the number on the books had fallen from 1,520 in 1924[17] to 1,380 in 1927, to represent just over a tenth of the total staff. Girls had to leave on marriage, but it seems doubtful if it was a unique case when a young lady in 1924 was discovered to have been married for a year. She was promptly given six months' notice.[18]

Among the young men on the bank's staff during these years was Thomas Stearns Eliot. In his last term at Harvard, Eliot, then twenty-six, decided to finish his education in Europe. Awarded a travelling fellowship, he arrived in Germany in the summer of 1914, but left soon afterwards for Oxford, where he stayed until June 1915. In September, for some fifteen months, Eliot turned to teaching. He 'loathed school-mastering but stuck to it'[19] until Christmas 1916, when he gave up his job at Highgate Junior School. Eliot was now married, and in a rather desperate condition was 'hunting for work to stop the gap'.[20] A friend of his wife's family, L. E. Thomas, chief general manager of National Provincial Bank, gave him an introduction to Lloyds Bank, which he joined in March 1917, on the staff of the colonial and foreign department at 17 Cornhill.

One of Eliot's first jobs was tabulating and filing balance sheets of foreign banks, for which his knowledge of French and German proved useful, and there were good prospects of a rise. In 1918 his salary was £270 a year, more than a clerk of his age would normally be earning. A bank clerk during the day, in the evening he was free to write poetry, review books or prepare lectures, and he did in fact believe that his literary work was the better for having a regular occupation.

By 1920 Eliot had moved to information department at head office, dealing alone with debts and claims between the bank and the Germans: 'an important appointment, full of interesting legal questions', and he was kept busy 'trying to elucidate knotty points in that appalling document the Peace Treaty'. His work won him respect from his colleagues, while those more senior in the bank were also aware that here was no ordinary bank clerk.

In the autumn of 1921 Eliot's health broke down and the bank gave him

[17] No continuous series of figures for men and women separately are available before 1924.

[18] But the bank recognised an obligation to the young women who served it: the year before £5 was given to a girl who, when on bank duties, had her costume damaged by a maddened cow—recourse against the owner of the cow was reserved.

[19] Lyndall Gordon, *Eliot's Early Years*, Oxford University Press, 1977, p. 82.

[20] This and other quotations from Eliot's letters are from the introduction to *The Waste Land, a facsimile and transcript of the original drafts*, edited by Valerie Eliot, Faber and Faber, 1971.

three months' paid leave during which, when convalescing in Lausanne, he finished *The Waste Land*. Besides its references to the City, its streets and churches, there are the technical terms Eliot must have picked up during his time in colonial and foreign department:

> Mr. Eugenides, the Smyrna merchant
> Unshaven, with a pocket full of currants
> C.i.f. London: documents at sight

While the two well-known lines:

> One of the low on whom assurance sits
> As a silk hat on a Bradford millionaire

are believed to refer to a customer of the bank.

Eliot's pay in 1922 was £455 a year and there is a note on his staff card that Mr. Harrison, general manager in charge of administration, considered that 'the question of an increase in Mr. Eliot's salary should not be dealt with unless Mr. Eliot raised the question himself'. Whether he did is not recorded but his salary in 1923 was raised to £475.

That Eliot had to earn his living by working in the bank did, of course, restrict the time and energy he could give to his literary work. There was 'no use blinking the fact that it is a crime against literature to let him waste eight hours vitality per diem in that bank' wrote Ezra Pound in June 1920 and speculated about putting together a fund 'to get him out of it'.[21]

Two years later Pound revived his idea, and an attempt to raise money to enable Eliot to resign from Lloyds was organised—though not by Pound—in the autumn of 1922. An appeal was made for contributions to the Eliot Fellowship Fund, but in the end nothing came of it.[22]

In July 1923 Eliot moved back to colonial and foreign department, now at 20 King William Street, to edit a daily sheet of commercial and financial extracts from the foreign press and to write a monthly article on foreign exchange, which appeared (anonymously) in *Lloyds Bank Monthly*. While echoes of Eliot's life in the City can be found in his poetry, it is perhaps understandable that no traces of poetry can be found in these articles. They reported, soberly and factually, on current movements in exchange rates against the background of economic and political developments. In November 1925 Eliot left the bank to join the board of Faber and Gwyer (now Faber and Faber). Frank Morley, Eliot's compatriot and colleague,

---

[21] Valerie Eliot, *op. cit.* pp. xviii, xix. Pound was writing to John Quinn, the New York lawyer, patron, and art collector.

[22] Virginia Woolf was a leading spirit in this 'most muddled appeal ever written' as she called it when sending it to Keynes, see Nigel Nicolson, Ed., *The Question of Things Happening*, The Letters of Virginia Woolf 1912–1922, The Hogarth Press, 1976, p. 590.

believed Geoffrey Faber took Eliot on because he wanted a 'man of business', Eliot having worked in the City, although Eliot himself thought he needed 'a talent scout'. Anyway, Faber offered a much better salary than Lloyds was paying.[23]

Throughout his eight years in Lloyds Eliot got on well with both customers and other clerks, some of whom, now long retired, still remember him as a colleague. One recalls his 'immaculate black jacket and sponge-bag trousers with spats, and his tortoiseshell-rimmed glasses'; another that 'he would often in the middle of dictating a letter, break off suddenly, grasp a sheet of paper, and start writing quickly when an idea came to him'.

Although salary scales for the permanent male staff remained unchanged during the first world war, bonus and special allowance schemes were introduced to mitigate the effects of the rising cost of living. In January 1919 all this was scrapped and a fresh start made, for the permanent staff, with higher salaries, and supplemented, in view of the continued rise in prices, by a new bonus system and payment of income tax. The starting salary for a boy of 17 was raised to £60 (from £40) in London and £40 elsewhere (previously £30), while salaries up to £500 were increased by 20%, reducing to 5% on salaries above. The bonus now became 20% on a salary up to £200 for married men on service or single men in the bank and 40% for married men working in the bank with a salary up to £250, with reducing rates on higher salaries. Temporary clerks (many of whom were women) received a bonus of 30%.

The income tax paid by the bank was that assessed on the salary and bonus for a single man (including pensioners), so that married men were in pocket, as they got a rebate from the Inland Revenue in respect of the allowances to which they were entitled. At once, the ever-watchful Revenue claimed that the bank's payment was an addition to the recipient's income and was liable to tax. The bank then decided that it would also meet this 'tax on tax', but the Revenue did not put in yet a further claim. Income tax was so paid until 1943 when the scheme was abolished, salaries were grossed up and the staff became liable for their own tax.

Salary scales were again improved in 1920, when the normal limit for a clerk became £500 in London and £450 or £375 elsewhere, while in the following year, although limits remained unchanged, starting salaries for juniors (seventeen years old) were raised to £90 in London and £70 elsewhere. The normal annual increase was also raised to £15. It is a striking illustration of the enormous difference between economic conditions in

[23] T. S. Matthews, *Great Tom*, Weidenfeld and Nicolson, 1974, pp. 85–6.

the inter-war years and those after 1945 that these basic salary scales remained unchanged from 1921 to 1946 (except for the reduction in the 1930s of the annual increase to £10 and the grossing-up of salaries in 1943, while staff joining the bank after 1929 came under a new grading scheme).

With the rise in prices in the 1919/20 boom, bonus payments were also increased, in 1921 to 33⅓% of a single man's or woman's salary and 50% of a married man's, with a maximum of £200. Thereafter, with the fall in the cost of living the rate of bonus was reduced, to 21⅔% and 32½% respectively in July 1923, rates which continued unchanged until 1930.

Young men joining the bank in the 1920s received little in the way of formal training. Not until the end of the decade were the first steps taken to devise a scheme of training, and they did not go very far. Only for gaining experience overseas was there any regular system. In 1920 foreign scholarships were introduced, for suitable candidates to spend two years abroad learning methods of business and proficiency in languages. Even so, there was apathy and some antagonism towards the scheme. In all, twenty-nine scholarships were awarded in the period 1921-9, one of which was to G. Y. Hinwood, a chief general manager in the 1950s, who went to South America. No more were given after 1929, no doubt because of the need for economies.

A major development in staff administration in 1921 was the inauguration of a proper superannuation fund for the permanent staff. Men had been retiring at sixty years if they had completed forty years' service but pensions, totalling over £160,000 in 1920, were treated as a current expense. In 1918 W. W. Paine, a brilliant company lawyer in Paines Blyth and Huxtable, had joined the bank as a general manager and legal expert and most of his time at the outset was given to establishing a pension fund on a proper footing. In 1920 a fund was set up to provide annuities for widows and orphans, members of the staff contributing 1% of their salary or pension to a maximum of £15 a year. Then, in July 1921, a non-contributory pension scheme was introduced, for both men and women. This was warmly welcomed by the staff: the rules for pensions, said a circular from the staff representative committee, are 'now based on such considerate and liberal lines that no member of the staff can possibly express anything but the greatest satisfaction with them'. Certainly, Lloyds had one of the best-administered pension funds among the banks.

Paine became interested in the wider financial and economic questions of the day and, needing another lawyer to look after the day-to-day work, E. H. Barchard joined the bank. To help Barchard, a young lawyer, Henry Lawson, was recruited in 1924. Barchard died in 1927 and Paine having

retired in 1925 (but remaining a member of the Board until 1945), Lawson
was appointed principal of the legal department. Sir Henry—he was
knighted in 1963, the first working member of the staff to be so honoured
—had a career of great distinction in the bank and in legal circles outside,
his services being much in demand to prepare evidence, lecture or to sit on
or to chair committees. He retired in 1963 as chief legal adviser and deputy
chief general manager. In 1962 he had become president of the Law
Society, the first salaried solicitor to achieve this position. Sir Henry died
in 1978.

The staff representative committee, whose views on the pension scheme
we noted above, had been established in 1918. The directors, a circular
explained, had considered various methods of increasing co-operation
between the board and the staff and decided to introduce the S.R.C. 'to
confer with them from time to time on matters connected with the welfare
of the staff'. The bank was divided into eight districts, each of which
elected a committee, from which a central committee was formed, and
a constitution was drawn up.

The S.R.C. was not, therefore, an independent initiative of the men and
women in the bank to form a union to protect and further their interests. It
did not result from any frustrated ambitions of the staff for better pay or
conditions. There were no subscriptions, no independently-paid officials.
It was 'an integral part of the Bank's organisation', with a central committee to be 'received by the Chairman and Board of Directors when
occasion requires'. This was hardly the customary language of trade
unionism. But the staff must have seen in the S.R.C. at least an organised
means of presenting their views. In 1918 a circular complained that
anonymous letters were being sent to head office purporting to come from
members of the staff, but also pointed out that they could well have been
signed, since they referred to legitimate subjects for representation or
enquiry. In elections in 1922 and 1924 in the districts or 'constituencies',
as they were now called, some 80% of the staff voted where contests took
place. And there is no reason to suppose that the representatives so elected
put the staff's point of view and argued their case with any lack of force
and zeal. While it was no doubt true, as Beaumont Pease claimed in 1935,
that 'I am able to give them figures and information which I should not
feel justified in divulging to any outside parties', it does not seem that
policy changes affecting the staff were always first discussed with the
S.R.C. There is no record that their views were sought on the staff grading
scheme introduced in 1929. Yet they also knew that they were not dealing
with some skinflint employer intent on grinding down the faces of the

staff. Board and management might have had something to learn about industrial relations but in the hard times of the 1930s, whatever happened to bonuses and annual increases, no member of the staff was sacked or had his or her salary cut, nor was there likely to be, as an S.R.C. circular admitted in 1934, 'any public sympathy for a section of the community who in the main enjoys non-contributory pension rights and exemption from a 4/6 income tax'. The 'outside parties' referred to by the chairman in 1935 were, of course, the Bank Officers Guild, which became the National Union of Bank Employees in 1946. The B.O.G. originated in a meeting in Sheffield in December 1917 to form a new 'combination of bank clerks', and by October the following year the Guild was formally established. Unlike the S.R.C., the B.O.G. had to rely on its members to cover its expenses: the entrance fee was 5/- (25p) and the annual subscription 12/- (60p), half rate for junior members. By 1921 there were 5,400 members in Lloyds, about the same number as in Barclays and Midland Banks but twice as many as in Westminster and National Provincial Banks. Lloyds' membership rose slightly to 1923, then fell each year to 4,100 in 1928, rising again to a peak of just over 5,000 in the early 1930s.

In 1920 the president of the B.O.G., F. C. Clegg, saw Vassar-Smith who, according to Clegg, 'was by no means antagonistic to the Guild, and was quite prepared to accept my assurance that our aims were purely co-operative and conciliatory'. In 1922, however, when National Provincial Bank's staff association suggested working arrangements between the various internal associations and the B.O.G. might be possible, the S.R.C. would not move. Its constitution, it argued, would not permit such co-operation and, in view of the friendly relations between directors and staff, it was not prepared to try to get its constitution changed. It was to be some time before attempts were made to forge a union between the banks' staff bodies and the B.O.G.

The chairman and directors at this time not only wished to establish a closer rapport with the staff over pay and conditions through the S.R.C. but were concerned also to promote the general welfare of the men and women in the bank. In 1919 the bank started to give an annual grant to the sports club they had formed, while in 1920 land was bought in Lower Sydenham, Beckenham, for approximately £10,000 for a sports ground, and a grant given towards the expenses of a golf tournament for head office staff. But the healthy were not the only objects of attention. In 1920 the board staff committee approved the purchase of a bath chair for the use of any temporarily incapacitated member of the staff. How much it was used, and what became of it, is not known.

3

Into the Twenties

The bank thrives

The British economy experienced some recovery in the second half of the twenties from the recession that followed the 1919/20 boom. Output in general (gross domestic product) rose gradually to touch a peak in 1929, nearly a fifth higher than in 1923, while manufacturing production increased by a quarter. But there was much that was dark. The basic industries experienced little growth; with sterling overvalued when the gold standard was restored at the pre-war parity in 1925, the level of exports was below that in the first half of the 1920s. Unemployment remained high: an average of 1,250,000 insured workers were without jobs over the years 1924-9, excluding 1926, the year of the general strike. Interest rates moved relatively little during these years. Bank Rate varied between 4 and 5% from 1924 to 1928, rising to $6\frac{1}{2}$% in September 1929, while the yield on $2\frac{1}{2}$% Consols ranged from an average of 4.39% in 1924 to 4.60% in 1929.

All this ended with a bang with the crash on Wall Street in October 1929. In the U.S.A., industrial production reached a peak in the summer and then turned down. Security prices touched their highest point in September, well over double the 1926 level, then collapsed: by the end of December 1930 the index had fallen by over half. In London, security prices touched the top in spring 1928, then continued on a plateau to January 1929 after which they fell throughout the year.

Against this not very stimulating background, the bank achieved a general increase in business—in advances and numbers of accounts, though hardly in total deposits—reflected in the rise in staff numbers and the expansion of the branch network, and resulting in an upward trend of profits.

Advances rose from £138m. in December 1923 to £204m. in December 1929, a total that was not to be exceeded until 1947. Against an increase in deposits of only £10m. over these six years, this implied a sharp rise in the ratio of deposits represented by loans and overdrafts: from 41% in 1923 to 58% in 1929. This was the highest end-year ratio not only in the inter-war period, but in the half century covered by this study, although it was still somewhat lower than in the years before 1914, when there were ratios of 60% or more. Not until the 1970s was a higher figure touched. Investments, in contrast, declined from £92m. in December 1923 to only £37m. in December 1929, or from 27 to less than 11% of deposits—a ratio as low as this was not seen again until the end of the 1960s.

For the first time, advances were now classified by borrower into thirty-one groups, based largely on a system adopted by the Federation of British Industries. Lloyds was the first bank to publish such figures. In October 1925, the largest group was 'personal and professional', with £44m., a quarter of the total and covering 80,000 accounts, giving an average overdraft of about £550. Farmers borrowed £19m., with an average of £880, while local authorities took £7m. Thereafter, however, few details were given until 1936, when the clearing banks collectively adopted, and published, figures for the classification of advances set out in the report of the Macmillan Committee of 1931.

Lloyds was also the first bank, in 1927, to increase the information given in its balance sheet; in 1930 Keynes remarked that 'Lloyds Bank have been on the whole, I think, pioneers in publishing of full balance-sheets'.[1] In 1918 the Cunliffe Committee had suggested a form of balance sheet for the banks to adopt but, nine years later, Lloyds was the only one to come into line: indeed, as Sir Austin Harris pointed out, the bank had 'actually gone a little way beyond that standard'.[2]

Deposits, as has been noted, increased little in total over this period, from £340m. at end-1923 to £350m. at end-1929. However, there was some shift in their composition, current accounts falling from an average of 50% of the total in 1923 to 45% in 1929, possibly a reflection of the slight upward movement of London deposit rate. For one date only during these years, 31 December 1924, was an attempt made to classify deposits, into four groups.

TABLE 4. *Classification of deposits at 31 December 1924*

	%
Personal and professional	59.7
*Trade	27.7
Finance	8.1
Government and local authorities	4.5
	100.0

* Includes manufacturing, public utilities, and farming.

[1] Qu. 2306, Macmillan Committee evidence, 13 February 1930.
[2] For example, Treasury bills were distinguished from commercial bills.

This classification, particularly for 'trade', is so broad as to be of little value, although it does show that 'personal and professional', the largest single group for advances, was equally so for deposits.

In number, current accounts increased by just over 2% a year in the period 1923–7, to total 774,000 at the end, (see Figure 3). In 1928, with the end of the management period, Cox's figures were now included,[3] resulting in a jump to 848,000 by December. Thereafter, the increase again settled down to a little over 2% a year to the outbreak of war. Deposit accounts, after showing practically no growth at all in 1921–3, then grew at about the same average pace as current accounts to 1927, with an increase of about 4% in 1928–9.

It was in the number of savings bank accounts, however, that, at the end of the decade, the most dramatic increase was seen. In the early 1920s the number was below 50,000 and by December 1927 it had risen to only 62,000. A drive was then begun to increase this business. Managers were encouraged to approach savings asociations and church savings clubs, and to try to get heads of elementary and secondary schools to start school banks. Home safes were introduced, although it was perhaps naïve to believe, as a circular suggested, that these made 'useful presents for Christmas and the New Year'. The campaign was certainly successful in increasing the number of accounts, from 76,000 in December 1928 to 246,000 a year later. Most of these, however, must have represented quite small sums, for total balances rose by only £796,000. A report at this time forecast that savings accounts might 'in course of time become an admirable feeder for the other sections of the Bank's business'. This possibly proved true of numbers of customers but hardly of the volume of funds involved.

Throughout this period London deposit rate was maintained at a margin of 2 points below Bank Rate and country deposit rate generally at $2\frac{1}{2}$%, which was also usually the rate on any current accounts attracting interest. However, managers were often given discretion to offer higher rates for substantial amounts at fixed terms of three, six, and twelve months. In August 1924, for example, when London deposit rate was 2%, increasing competition and high rates made necessary the protection of existing deposits and acquisition of new money. Rates of 3 to $3\frac{1}{2}$% were sanctioned. Moreover, uniformity among branches was sometimes broken: in 1925, to meet local competition, the deposit rate at Cornish branches only was increased from $2\frac{1}{2}$ to 3% for a few months, and in the Newcastle district in 1929 special arrangements were approved.

[3] But not those for the Indian branches. All figures for numbers of accounts refer only to branches in England and Wales. Figures for the distribution of deposit balances among current, deposit, and savings bank accounts also exclude balances with branches in the East.

The second half of the twenties experienced a considerable extension of the branch network, the total number of offices increasing by well over 200 in the six years 1923-9, with another 95 offices opened in 1930, a total for one year not equalled until 1963. In two years alone, 1926 and 1927, expenditure on new branches, covering acquisition of land, building and furnishing, was over £700,000. In 1924 Pease picked out London, Yorkshire, and Lancashire as potential areas for branch extension, noting that all this was 'intimately connected' with the question of further amalgamation. As regards Lancashire, Pease no doubt had a merger with Manchester & County Bank in mind, but this move, as we have seen, was blocked by the authorities.[4]

In respect of London, a report was produced in May 1925 by R. A. Wilson, then an assistant general manager, and L. A. Stanley, deputy chief inspector. They noted that competition by the banks in opening branches was very active, but this had 'not been conceived in any spirit of cut-throat competition but is a perfectly natural business growth'. After considering the possible growth of population and future plans for transport, they drew up lists of places in Greater London where they recommended branches and sub-branches should be opened as soon as possible, with other locations 'to be watched'. In the five years 1926-30 some seventy offices were opened in London and its suburbs. A branch open for only a short time was that at the great British Empire Exhibition at Wembley in 1924-5, the largest jamboree of its kind since the 1851 exhibition. Although all the banks agreed to make a donation, only Lloyds was willing to finance the exhibition's very large requirements. In return for this undertaking, embodied in an overdraft at one time of over £2m., Lloyds was given the privilege of being the only English bank allowed to open an office in the exhibition.

Lloyds acquired a reputation at this time for the architectural merit of some of its new branches, designed by men who often achieved subsequent distinction in their profession. For example, Orpington branch was designed by Edwin Williams, afterwards chief town planning officer of the London County Council, and Notting Hill Gate branch by Edward Maufe, later the architect of Guildford Cathedral.

Architectural quality of an earlier age distinguished the bank's Hereford branch. In 1928 the business was moved to a new office and the former premises, known as the 'Old House', were presented to the City of Hereford. The Old House was a half-timbered structure built in the early seventeenth century to serve as a butchers' guild hall. The city corporation, in the best traditions of municipal philistinism, proposed at first to

[4] See p. 25.

use the building as offices for its rate collector, whereas the bank had
hoped it would house a library or museum. But light prevailed and it
became a museum, which it remains today.

Changes in branches and bank houses continued to reflect those in the
country at large. Electricity was going into more and more branches and
houses, although as late as 1930 it was turned down for Wimborne and the
next year for Torrington, and was sanctioned for Devizes and Attle-
borough 'subject to the charges for electric current being reasonable'.
Stables were being converted into garages, permission given for 'wireless
installations' to be erected and occasionally for central heating to be
installed. In 1929 night safes were first installed in branches, invented and
patented by F. Pritchard, then on the staff, and later manager, of premises
department. Pritchard had demonstrated his invention to the general
managers and board by constructing a model made of Meccano. His night
safes are still in use. It was sometimes difficult to keep the outside of a
branch clear. The suggestion of Brighton Corporation in 1923 to erect
a tram shelter outside one of the Brighton branches was 'absolutely
declined' and objection was reasonably taken in 1924 to a proposal to
install a petrol pump outside Witney branch.[5]

The total number of staff in this period increased by about 1,240, from
11,400 in December 1923 to 12,640 at the end of the decade. An average of
420 juniors was recruited each year. Waiting lists were still long. Indeed,
it was not unknown for headmasters in their annual reports to give the
number of school-leavers who had been accepted by a bank, in the same
way as their counterparts today list those gaining places at university.
Relatively few women, however, joined the staff: the total in the bank in
1929 was no higher than in 1924.

Among the 449 juniors joining the bank in 1925 was a young man who,
like Eliot, was to achieve an international reputation as a poet. This was
Vernon Watkins. In September 1925 Watkins became a clerk at the St.
Helens, Swansea, branch where, most unusually, he stayed until he retired
in 1966. Watkins, born at Maesteg, South Wales, in 1906, and educated at
Swansea, Repton, and Magdalene College, Cambridge, came into the bank
in a spirit of resentment and despair because his father (who was also in
Lloyds and one of the youngest managers ever appointed) would not allow
him, when he came down from university, to live in Italy for a year writing

---

[5] But bank policy was at least consistent with the English love of animals. While the Boy
Scouts of Maidenhead were refused permission in 1928 to place a collecting box for silver
paper outside the branch, a dog's drinking trough had been approved outside Sidmouth
branch in 1925.

poetry—which he had been doing since he was a child. As time passed, however, Watkins came to feel that becoming a bank clerk was, in fact, one of the best things he could have done. He did not aspire to any brilliant career in finance: 'he would never let the bank work interfere with poetry by letting them advance him to a big position'.[6] But, engaged on relatively routine duties—in later years as a cashier, for which he nevertheless had a certain facility (he could add up a five-digit column of figures in his head) —his creative mind was free to follow its true vocation.

Watkins's output was large and widely acclaimed: he had written over a thousand pieces before his work was first printed in Wales in 1936. In 1935 he met Dylan Thomas and they saw much of one another in future years; in 1957 Thomas's *Letters to Vernon Watkins* were published. When he died so untimely in 1967, the year after his retirement from the bank, he was among the few then being considered as a successor to John Masefield as Poet Laureate. It would have been a happy choice *The Times* commented, 'at once a tribute to Celtic genius and to a poet of unusual humility'.

Watkins had great charm, wit and kindness, and was immensely popular with both customers and staff. When he retired from the bank in June 1966, he was appointed Calouste Gulbenkian Fellow in Poetry at University College, Swansea, for 1966-7 and 1968-9. For 1967-8 he was to be Visiting Professor of Poetry at the University of Washington, Seattle, which he had previously visited in 1964, on leave of absence from the bank, and where his gentle character and amiability had endeared him to his colleagues. Watkins and his family arrived from Wales but a few weeks later, on 9 October, he died suddenly while playing tennis.

In a distinctly different field of letters from that of Eliot and Watkins, Basil Boothroyd has earned considerable fame as a light-hearted and witty writer, journalist, and broadcaster. Boothroyd joined the bank in 1927, working for ten years in a number of branches in East Anglia, an experience on which he has drawn for bizarre and entertaining reminiscence. After war service and a spell in Head Office he resigned in 1952 to become assistant editor of *Punch*, to which he had already contributed for some years. In the bank Boothroyd is particularly remembered with affection for his parodies of branch life that appeared in the staff magazine *The Dark Horse* in the misadventures of the staff of the Coggles Bend branch of the Bank of Good Hope.

Salary scales and bonuses remained unchanged during these years. From the second half of 1923 until 1929, however, the staff benefited from a

---

[6] 'Paragraphs from a Letter' by James Laughlin, in *Vernon Watkins 1906-1967*. Ed. Leslie Norris, Faber and Faber, 1970, p. 59.

profit-sharing scheme which, Beaumont Pease claimed, although modest
in dimensions 'in a banking connection also deserves the adjective unique'.
The scheme provided that if the dividend paid to shareholders was not less
than $16\frac{2}{3}\%$—the rate since 1920—then an amount equal to half the
difference between such dividend and 15% would be set aside for
distribution among the staff. From 1926 to 1929, however, rather more
was set aside each year than was produced by this formula. It was left to
the central committee of the S.R.C. to decide how it should be distributed,
subject to the Board's approval. The scheme suggested by the committee
—which declared that such profit-sharing 'cannot fail to intensify the
loyalty and devotion of the staff to the service of the Bank'—was the simple
one of a flat-rate percentage distribution with a maximum payment per
head, and this was approved and adopted. The sum available for the
second half of 1923 was £59,887, distributed at a rate of £1. 18s. (£1·90)
for every £100 of salary, with a maximum of £38. Staff had to pay income
tax on this. For 1924, £119,775 was for distribution, shared out at a
percentage rate of £3. 12s. (£3·60) and the maximum was now £72. The
same sum was available for 1925 but for each year 1926 to 1929 it was
raised to £155,707, while for 1927 to 1929 there was no maximum. For
1930, when profits slumped and economies became necessary, the
dividend was reduced to 15% and the scheme automatically came to
an end. No announcement was made to the staff, which upset the
S.R.C. Although, of course, the rules drawn up in 1923 were quite plain,
it was perhaps optimistic to believe that everybody would remember
them.

Overtime payments were generally abolished in 1924. Such payments
had been first made during the war but, with branches now fully staffed,
late hours should not have been necessary for at least eleven months of the
year. Overtime payments were thus ended, except for the two half-yearly
balance periods. In 1927, however, it was noted that there had been a
tendency for payments for balance work to increase at some branches.
Clerks poor at arithmetic were warned, not too elegantly: 'The clerk who,
through errors by him, is the cause of much waste time, should not himself
receive an allowance in that particular connection'.

After the high figure resulting from the 1920 boom, profits fell sharply to
1922 and then rose gradually to reach another peak in 1929 of just over
£4.5m. Profits of this size were not to be seen again until the war. Total
earnings rose by some £5m. between 1922 and 1929 and outgoings by
£3.4m., to show an improvement in gross profits of £1.6m. The profit
figures published by the bank, as earlier in the decade, moved much less:

£2.54m. were posted in 1929, against £2.07m. in 1922. Reserves were being built up—which were to prove necessary very soon.

The bank did little at this time to present itself in an attractive and interesting light to its customers and the public at large. There were, of course, the accounts and the speech of the chairman at the annual general meeting. But these reached, or were read by, not very many. Advertising was rudimentary and unappealing: perhaps a few figures and the names of the banks with which Lloyds were associated, in a box suggesting mourning. Admittedly, ideas were floated, but often sunk. Proposals to advertise on tramway tickets and on book markers were turned down; in 1924 a suggestion for an electric sign in Leicester Square, in London's West End, was rejected—it was not until 1966 that such a sign was erected in Piccadilly Circus. True, the bank issued a booklet, *How to Use a Bank*, in 1926 but it cost 6*d*. (2½p). In one medium, however, the bank was among the pioneers, and very probably the first among the banks. In 1929, when 'talkies' were just appearing, a seven-minute advertising film with synchronised dialogue was commissioned, and screened in 250 cinemas for six months. Called *The Better Way*, its purpose was mainly to promote the bank's savings accounts and home safes.[7]

Lloyds' review is another field in which the bank can claim to be among the leaders. In 1917 a monthly financial report was started that in time was to develop into the quarterly *Lloyds Bank Review*. At first, it was issued only to correspondents and agents abroad but in 1918 distribution was extended to Britain. From 1920 to 1930 the editor was J. M. Watkins, on the staff of the bank, and from 1930 to 1939 the distinguished financial journalist Norman Crump. During the 1930s, Alwyn Parker exercised a general supervision over the Review and was editor from 1947 until his death in 1951. Parker had joined the board in 1919, after serving in the Foreign Office and diplomatic service. Widely read and cultivated, he brought to the review those meticulous standards of writing and scholarship that did much to establish its reputation and to attract to it writers of international eminence.

A new head office

One of the most important developments in the history of the bank took place in the 1920s, when its head office in Lombard Street was rebuilt.

---

[7] Part of the film was shot in Romford branch. The plot was not very dramatic: a young wife dreams that her savings have been stolen; on waking up, she and her husband go to the bank where, after the strong rooms and safe are pictured, they open an account. Among the players was Bransby Williams, a noted character actor of the day.

The process of planning, demolition and rebuilding occupied nearly the whole decade, from October 1921, when a special board committee first met, to July 1930, when the structure was completed.

By 1910 all head office business had been transferred from Birmingham to 71 Lombard Street. This office was built in 1887, following the amalgamation three years previously of Lloyds with Barnetts, Hoares, Hanbury and Lloyd and Bosanquet Salt & Co., both of which had offices in Lombard Street. The site of this old head office covered seven plots, as shown in Figure 6, of which, by 1921, all the freeholds had been acquired. It had become plain by then that the 1887 building was no longer big enough to house the expanding departments of head office or the thriving business of City Office. Indeed, head office departments had already spilled over into neighbouring premises: colonial and foreign department, for example, had occupied part of 17 (formerly 16-18) Cornhill in 1915, and in 1921 branches stock office had moved into 77 Lombard Street, later taken over by Eastern department.

The decision was taken to rebuild and a small committee of directors was appointed, with Sir Austin Harris as chairman, to plan and supervise. In the summer of 1922, conditions for a competition were drawn up and five firms of architects were invited to submit designs, those unsuccessful to receive an honorarium of £525 each and be entitled to retain their plans. The instructions for the competition specified that the building was to be as high as legally permitted and lighting conditions allowed—as regards light, 'as far as possible the worst light should be given to the customers and the better to the staff'. Growth over the next twenty-five years of 70/75% in the work of head office and of 50% in the business of City Office was to be accommodated, but if 'absolutely inevitable' certain head office departments could be housed outside. The plans were judged and, somewhat unusually, two firms were appointed to work together: Sir John Burnett and Partners for the design and Campbell-Jones Sons and Smithers for the planning. Both already had a number of commercial buildings to their credit: the former, for example, Adelaide House, London Bridge, and the Kodak building in Kingsway; the latter, London Assurance Buildings and the Hongkong and Shanghai Bank in the City.

In July 1924, differences of opinion emerged on several important points between the directors' committee and the architects, who were now asked to prepare two models: of the banking hall (for City Office) and of the Lombard Street elevation. Different plans were drawn up, the first of which the London County Council would not sanction because of the fire risk, since, above the sixth floor, it included a tower of three further floors.

After various amendments, the committee approved the straight roof line which was eventually built. Trollope & Colls Ltd. were appointed as general contractors with, as consulting engineer, Dr. Oscar Faber, who had been consultant for many new buildings, including that of the recently rebuilt Bank of England.

In the meantime, the bank had bought the freeholds of the further plots to be incorporated into the site of the new building, as indicated in Figure 6, except for that of 15 Cornhill (bought in 1926). Of these, the

FIGURE 6. *Lombard Street office*

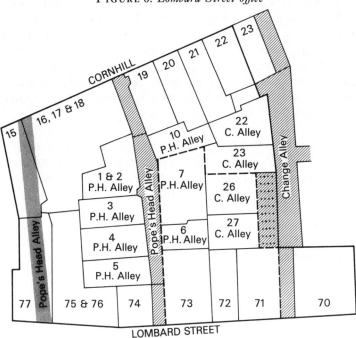

‑ ‑ ‑ Site of Lombard Street office, 1887.
——— Site of head office, 1930. (The Lombard Street frontage was built straight).

largest single transaction was the purchase from the Merchant Taylors' Company in 1921 for £400,000 of the freeholds of 73 and 74 Lombard Street, 21 Cornhill, and 1–7 Pope's Head Alley. The latter alley was, of course, a public right of way and the City Corporation had to agree to its being moved to a new position (marked in the sketch). Similarly, the Corporation's agreement was necessary for the bank's incorporating part of Change Alley into the new building (dotted in the sketch). For these agreements the bank paid £10,000 in consideration. Subsequently, in 1928, the Corporation also agreed to a slight readjustment of the southern part of Change Alley and to its northern end being moved a few feet westwards by the Commercial Union Assurance Co., then occupying 23–7 (now 24) Cornhill. The area of the new building east of Change Alley (formerly 70 Lombard Street) was not all occupied by the bank: the ground and mezzanine floors were leased to Martins Bank.

For work on the new site to proceed, dispersal of some head office operations was necessary. As soon as it had been decided to rebuild, a site was acquired at the corner of King William Street and Gracechurch Street opposite London Bridge, the existing buildings demolished and a new structure put up (it stands today) at a cost of £276,000. In March 1924 the general management and certain head office departments moved to these new temporary premises, while others and City Office remained in Lombard Street. The idea was to complete the new building in two stages, departments moving accordingly, but for City Office to continue throughout in Lombard Street. This was not to be.

The first stage in 1926 and 1927 involved the demolition and excavation of the eastern part of the site next to the Commercial Union Assurance building, which had to be shored up and underpinned and the roadway in Cornhill also strengthened by timbering. To provide three basements, excavations went down fifty feet below street level, some twenty feet beyond the foundations of the Commercial Union's building at 23 Cornhill, and striking a patch of London clay of a dough-like consistency, probably part of the flood-plain of the underground Wallbrook.

During the evening of Saturday, 6 August 1927, the housekeeper at 23 Cornhill noticed a crack in the west wall of his kitchen and immediately informed the police. The outside of the building was examined and a gap about one inch wide was discovered from the street pavement apparently up to the roof. By this time bits of masonry were falling into Change Alley and the excavated site and there were ominous sounds of breaking. The housekeeper and his family got out just before the piers propping up the Commercial Union's building gave way and its western end collapsed. There were no workmen about and no loss of life. But there was considerable damage. The Commercial Union had five floors of offices and the housekeeper's quarters of its building affected and, as work could not be safely carried on in what was left, temporary accommodation had to be found. With commendable speed, business was restarted on 15 August at Adelaide House, London Bridge. Work on the excavations was suspended. Cornhill was closed to traffic until the following February and

Post Office lines and cables and sewers under the street had to be restored to proper working.

The Commercial Union was put to considerable inconvenience, upset, and expense but, in considering the liability of Lloyds Bank for all this, it was loath to institute legal proceedings against another financial institution with which it was on friendly terms. Two directors of Lloyds, Sir Austin Harris and Francis Willey (afterwards Lord Barnby) were also on the Commercial Union's board. The Commercial Union had been forced to move and Beaumont Pease asked right away whether they would be willing to sell their Cornhill property if Lloyds wished to buy. This proposal did not get very far, the Commercial Union board soon deciding to keep the property and to rebuild.[8] However, discussion continued between representatives of the two boards and early in October Paine, for Lloyds, and Alfred Shepherd, a Commercial Union director and friend of Paine's, agreed on an immediate compensation payment by Lloyds of £80,000, with an indemnification against any third-party claims. This arrangement was duly ratified by the two boards.

This settled, and the immediate clearing-up finished, the question to be faced was: who was responsible for the collapse? Builders, architects, consultant? To try to decide the issue Lloyds commissioned a report from two civil engineers, Basil Mott and Ralph Freeman. Mott and Freeman concluded that the collapse was ultimately due to the methods used to underpin the Commercial Union building, and that the responsibility thus rested on Trollope & Colls, to whom the report was then submitted. Trollope & Colls—whose 'whole reputation was involved', wrote Paine, in a long memorandum on the whole worrying episode—thereupon got reports from two engineers of their own choosing: Sir Alexander Gibb and Sir E. Owen Williams. These two reports largely absolved Trollope & Colls and put the blame on the plans and specifications for the underpinning piers prepared by the consulting engineer, Dr. Faber. Faber's reputation, in turn, was now at stake. Thus the experts differed. The quandary was acute. 'One wonders where all this is going to lead', mused Paine, 'and whether we shall not be lost in a maze of technical engineering points, and possibly of litigation, which seems to present opportunities for months, and possibly years, of legal or arbitration proceedings at immense cost.'

Was it wise to try to allocate responsibility? Would it not be better to try by agreement to get 'a fair and equitable settlement of the whole question?' This was the solution finally adopted in February 1929. Trollope & Colls

---

[8] In August 1967 this building was sold to Lloyds for £4,875,000. The bank took possession in October 1969 and, after interior reconstruction, moved in in January 1972.

agreed to pay £65,000 as a contribution towards the cost of the damage, of which the architects and engineer agreed to be responsible for £10,000 and £15,000. However, Trollope and Colls could off-set up to £15,000 of this payment by speeding-up the date by which the new head office was ready for occupation (which they did). Further, a letter was written by Beane to Trollope & Colls entirely exonerating them from any responsibility for the accident.[9]

The cost to Lloyds of the collapse, including the £80,000 paid to Commercial Union, came to just over £112,000, which included payments to the City Corporation for repairing sewers and to neighbouring traders for loss of business. The original plan to rebuild in two stages had to be abandoned and the whole site cleared, which meant that City Office and those head office departments still in Lombard Street in 1927 had to be found temporary accommodation elsewhere in the City. Taking account of the rent for this, but also of Trollope and Colls' contribution, the final net cost of the whole unfortunate business came out at not quite £80,000.

When rebuilding had started the tentative date of completion was put at December 1931. Now, however, that the whole site could be excavated work could be speeded up and the completion date was brought forward a year, to December 1930. In fact, the building was finished five months earlier, in July 1930. As might be expected in excavating such a historic site, a number of items of archaeological interest were unearthed: portions of red Samian ware, of Roman tiles and vases and part of a Roman grind-stone, together with a mammoth's tooth. A Roman wall was also found running north by west under Cornhill, of about three to four feet high at a depth fourteen feet below the present-day street level.

'This building, both externally and internally, is the most monumental of our English banks, not excepting the Bank of England itself', wrote Professor C. H. Reilly, the noted architectural authority of the University of Liverpool, of the new head office at 71 Lombard Street;[10] and the two firms of architects were awarded the bronze medal of the Royal Institute of British Architects for the Lombard Street elevation. Both fronts, in Lombard Street and Cornhill, are of Portland stone on a granite base, rising to a height of eighty feet. The central part of the building on the ground floor is the banking hall for City Office—'the finest banking hall in London', in Professor Reilly's opinion—on the mezzanine walls of which

---

[9] No reputation suffered. Trollope & Colls and the two firms of architects prospered, while Dr. Faber was subsequently consulting engineer for a number of important buildings, including the new House of Commons after the war. He died in 1956.

[10] 'Lloyds Bank New Headquarters', *The Banker*, July 1930.

are sixteen plaques depicting historic coins executed by Miss Honey Harris, daughter of Sir Austin Harris, the deputy chairman at the time. There were many innovations: air conditioning, rubber-covered floors to reduce noise, a conveyor belt for cheques in City Office. The old building had no internal telephones; indeed, external telephones were relatively few. Now, a comprehensive internal telephone system was installed, linking head office with the main London branches. Few banks had such a system in 1930. As a result of the direct link to colonial and foreign department, for example, branches were now able to give a better service than other banks in foreign exchange transactions. Two artesian wells were sunk during the rebuilding but soon began to dry up; a third was sunk in 1934, which continued in use until after the war.

In spite of the greater space available, not all head office departments were under one roof and colonial and foreign and executor and trustee departments continued to operate elsewhere in the City. The cost of the actual building of the new head office came out at a little over £1,032,000. In addition, there were all the fittings, furniture and so on, and also the extra expense caused by the collapse of the Commercial Union's office. Including all these the total bill was £1,275,000, the last item of which was £21 paid in May 1932 for a sloping desk for the chairman's table in the board room.

To mark the occasion, the chairman and directors gave a reception in head office on 23 July 1930, but they decided not to hold a dedication service. For some four years afterwards, the staff of premises department conducted school and other groups on Saturday afternoons on a guided tour of the building.

Two losses

At the end of the 1920s, Lloyds Bank, with other banks in the City, suffered substantial losses resulting from the plight of the Banca Italo-Britannica and from the Hatry crash.

In 1916 Lloyds and London County and Westminster Bank, representing a British financial group, and the Italian bank Credito Italiano, for an Italian financial group, established a British company, the British Italian Corporation, to foster economic relations between Britain and Italy and to promote undertakings in Italy. The corporation became the British Italian Banking Corporation in 1923, among whose shareholders were then Lloyds and two others of the clearing banks and a number of other British banks. The corporation established the Banca Italo-Britannica, which became one of the largest Italian commercial banks, with its head office in Milan and branches throughout the country. The British banks were concerned not only through their interest in the corporation but also as depositors with the bank, with which some also had substantial foreign exchange business. But control of the bank was slack:

there had been irregularities from 1926 onwards, and these had included incompetent management, 'every conceivable method of faking accounts', and the bad luck of those who had speculated with the bank's resources.[11]

Rumours inevitably spread, deposits were withdrawn and closure seemed inevitable unless prompt help was provided. This came in January 1929 when, after consultation with the Bank of England, Lloyds and the other two clearing banks decided to lend the Banca Italo-Britannica up to £2.6m. in equal proportions, and further to make a loan of £1m. to the British Italian Banking Corporation. This was only the beginning. Two weeks later the three banks agreed to another loan of £750,000 to the bank, to cover possible withdrawal of deposits, and this was soon raised to £1.5m. On 1 March the three banks announced publicly that they were supporting the Italian bank, and a scheme for its reconstruction was formulated. However, additional money had to be put in, including £250,000 from the Bank of England, and guarantees given, in the optimistic hope that when confidence was restored deposits would flow back and the bank would be able to repay. The proposal was then tabled to try to sell 49% of the shares in the bank to one of the large Italian banks. Abell pointed out that 'the constant aim of the three banks had been to sever our connections entirely with the Italian Bank', which would not be accomplished by selling 49%. Negotiations were, in fact, later opened in Italy but by the end of the year they had failed. By the summer of 1929 Lloyds' assistance to the bank, either directly or through the corporation, stood at over £2m. A Lloyds' memorandum of this time notes that opinion was very much opposed to liquidation, which would be not only a blow to British finance in Italy, but a most expensive way of getting out of the difficulties. Attempts should continue to find a purchaser for the Italian bank.

In January 1930, a year after the first rescue operation, representatives of the three clearing banks and other interested parties, including the holding company set up in the reconstruction of the previous March, held a meeting with the Governor, Montagu Norman, in the chair. Some definite steps had to be taken and, at a second meeting a few days later, 'Minutes of Decision' were drawn up: the Italian bank's board and management were to be strengthened, unprofitable branches closed and

---

[11] R. S. Sayers, *The Bank of England, 1891-1944*, Vol. 1, p. 260; I have drawn on Professor Sayers's account of this episode for certain details in the preceding paragraph.

policy aimed at such prudent banking operations as would put the concern in a sufficiently profitable position for a substantial part of the shares to be sold within a very few years. In the meantime, the Italian bank would enjoy 'the existing or promised support of the Clearing Banks'.

Within a few months, however, the banks were able to extricate themselves from the quagmire in which they had been floundering, but not without considerable hurt. The interest of the American Blair-Giannini group was stimulated and in October 1930 the Banca Italo-Britannica was sold to this group's Banca d'America e d'Italia. So far as it went this was a successful conclusion to an unhappy venture for, as *The Banker* pointed out,[12] 'owing to the peculiar conditions prevailing in Italy there was little chance for a British bank affiliate to operate there profitably'. It did not, however, go so far as to cover the losses the clearing banks had suffered.[13] Lloyds alone lost the enormous sum of over £1m. (equivalent to around £14m. at today's prices) on the original investment in the British Italian Corporation of £101,000.

Lloyds, with other banks, was involved in the Hatry crash that rocked the City in September 1929, although the ultimate loss to the bank was a good deal less than that suffered from the Italian bank débâcle.

Clarence Hatry, born in 1888, educated at St. Paul's school and on the Continent and clearly with exceptional abilities, had begun his career in insurance. Soon branching out he founded *The Globe*, a London evening paper, and became active in company promotion. In 1923 he lost his whole personal fortune when one of his companies, Commercial Corporation of London, was in trouble, but that did not stop him. In the late 1920s, the solution to the difficulties facing the country's old-established industries, particularly after the return to gold in 1925, was widely held to lie in 'rationalisation'. Hatry became interested in the rationalisation of the steel industry, about which he in fact knew little, and in 1927 established a finance company, Austin Friars Trust, which, among other things, arranged for the amalgamation of several firms producing light castings. This, and another company, Corporation & General Securities, were Hatry's main companies in his plans for co-ordinating the steel industry.

The complex record of deceit, fraud and false dealing that was revealed at the trial in January 1930 of Hatry and his associates has been told often enough and there is no need to go into it in great detail here.[14] In

---

[12] October 1930.

[13] Professor Sayers puts these losses at nearly £3m. *op. cit.*, p. 262.

[14] See, for example, Aylmer Vallence, *Very Private Enterprise*, Thames and Hudson, 1955, and R. A. Haldane, *With Intent to Deceive*, Williams Blackwood, 1970.

essence, loans were obtained from banks and others against security which was unauthorised or spurious, in the form of preliminary documents of title, such as allotment letters and certified transfers. These required a period of time to elapse before definite documents of title could be obtained, when the Hatry group's intention was to exchange them for genuine securities or for further bogus paper. An intricate system of interlocking finance was built up. Corporation & General Securities had a prosperous business handling local authority loans. In January 1929 it arranged for the issue of stock on behalf of Gloucester, Swindon, and Wakefield Corporations and gave bearer scrip certificates to the lenders which were later to be exchanged for stock certificates issued by the corporations. However, not only were the proceeds of these issues to the tune of £822,000 withheld from the corporations but worthless scrip to a nominal value of £795,000 was printed by Hatry and his associates. Hatry had set up Secretarial Services Ltd., to act as a secretary and registrar, and it was through its agency that dud certificates were produced. Another company established in 1929 as part of the steel rationalisation project was Iron Industries Ltd. When promoted, allotment letters for only 300 shares were authorised by the directors. Later, however, letters for over 2m. shares were issued, all unauthorised. A further company was Steel Industries of Great Britain Ltd., for which Hatry raised £4.8m. in 1929 to buy steel shares. But of this, £1.5m. was diverted to Austin Friars Trust, then in difficulties, to pay off debts and to buy the shares of other companies in the Hatry group to support their price.

The crash came on Friday, 20 September 1929 after rumours of trouble in the Hatry companies. One of these, Photomaton, had failed to publish its accounts and by 17 Setember its shares had fallen to 10/- (50p), having previously touched 15/7½ (78p), and two days later they dropped to a nominal price of 2/6 (12½p). Another Hatry company, Retail Trade Securities, had also not produced a report when due. Selling spread to shares of other of his companies. The City, reported the *Financial Times*, was by now a 'hotbed of rumour'. On 20 September the stock exchange suspended dealings in securities of seven of the Hatry companies and in Wakefield Corporation stock.

Hatry and three of his associates were brought to trial at the Old Bailey on 21 January 1930; a fourth, John Gialdini, had fled to Italy when he saw the game was up. At first, they pleaded not guilty to the thirty-nine counts charged against them but on the last (fifth) day of the trial they changed this to guilty. It appeared that the gross liabilities of the Hatry group's main companies, excluding share capital, totalled £29.5m. and liabilities to outside creditors, mainly banks, brokers, and financial houses were

£19.5m. with a deficiency estimated at £13.5m. In passing sentence, Mr. Justice Avory declared that the frauds uncovered were 'far more serious than any of the great frauds upon the public which have been committed within the last fifty years'. Hatry was given fourteen years (of which he served nearly nine), while his associates received terms of seven, five and three years. When released in 1939, Hatry returned to commercial life as a bookseller and publisher, and then set up a group of industrial cleaning companies. He died in 1965.

Lloyds Bank was closely concerned with all this, since it kept accounts for many of the Hatry companies and was principal banker to Austin Friars Trust and Corporation and General Securities. The bank had not, however, helped to promote these companies, except in so far as it believed the interests of British industry were at stake, in particular the process of rationalising the steel industry. The turnover of the accounts of the various companies was about £100m. a year and, almost until the end, there had been no cause to suspect anything was wrong. When the crash came, the total debt outstanding on the group's accounts was £2.2m., against which securities of various kinds were held. There were, the chief general managers, Beane and Abell, admitted in a memorandum to managers, 'many wild rumours afoot'. But any probable loss to Lloyds would be comparatively small and—putting a brave face on it—'apart from its annoyance, not one which will cause us any anxiety or uneasiness'. The position had been safeguarded by taking 'good collateral securities, quite outside the Hatry group of accounts'. Managers could thus 'contradict immediately and definitely any foolish rumours' about the bank's probable loss. To reassure foreign banking opinion, letters along the same lines were sent to twenty-three leading bankers in the U.S.A., and to one in Canada and in Germany respectively.

To cover any loss, £500,000 was set aside out of the 1929 profits and, at the same time, the bank's methods and procedures for handling securities were also examined by a special committee. 'We are quite satisfied that in no case is there any reasonable possibility of that amount being exceeded', claimed Beaumont Pease at the annual general meeting in January 1930. 'On the contrary, we believe that it will be substantially reduced.' This was to prove optimistic. By the summer, after allowing for securities realised, dividends received and guarantees paid, the outstanding debt had been reduced to £1.6m. This process continued gradually in subsequent years and in June 1934 the debt stood at £1.2m. A further 'precautionary sum' of £150,000 was now set aside, in addition to the £500,000 provided in 1930, although it was Abell's opinion that the whole affair 'has turned out far better than was at one time expected'. By four years later, in May 1938, the debt had been reduced to £660,000, but thereafter little more was whittled away. Just after the end of the war, in October 1945, when all the securities held had been realised and there was no likelihood of any further credits being received, the account was finally closed. The debit balance was £621,000.

Other banks also suffered losses but to what extent is not known. Barclays' profits for 1929 would have been 'substantially higher' had it not been necessary to make provision for such loss, which, at the annual meeting in January 1930, the chairman, Mr. F. C. Goodenough, put at possibly £330,000. Westminster Bank increased its contingency allocation by £200,000 but probably not all of this was to cover any Hatry loss. National Provincial made 'adequate provision' for a possible loss, without giving a figure. Midland, however, seems to have been completely uninvolved.

The greater part of the cost of the Hatry crash fell on the banks and other financial institutions and not on small investors, although these were adversely affected indirectly to the extent that the former were weakened. And the ratepayers of Gloucester, Swindon, and Wakefield certainly lost large sums of money. It may be that weak places in the City's safeguards against financial wrongdoing were disclosed and that, at a time of buoyant stock market activity, more could have been done to determine the true worth of borrowers. Yet, it is not always easy to devise procedures that are completely foolproof against rogues, clever and cunning in their deception, who are determined to defraud.

4

Depression and Recovery

The slump hits the bank

The title of this chapter is an apt description of the fortunes of Lloyds Bank during the 1930s, as it is of those of the economy in general. Britain endured the depression of the first part of the decade to experience a revival of activity in the years immediately before the war. Similarly, Lloyds Bank went through as rough a period as it had experienced in its long history to come out into calmer waters in the late 1930s.

The broadest measure of changes in output, gross domestic product, did not, perhaps, show a calamitous fall in the depression years: from 1929 to 1931, the lowest point, the decline was 6%; then came some slight recovery in the next two years, followed by a significant improvement from 1934 onwards. However, manufacturing production slumped by 11% between 1929 and 1931, with the old staples, coal, steel, textiles, shipbuilding, particularly badly hit. Prices fell sharply: at wholesale level by over a quarter between 1929 and 1933. Wage rates were down by only 5% over the same period and, as retail prices dropped by 15%, this implied a marked rise in the living standards of those still at work. There were many who were not. Unemployment soared: the number of insured workers out of a job—a definition not covering all the labour force— averaged 2,829,000 in 1932 and only after 1935 did the figure fall below 2 millions. Externally, the position remained weak throughout the 1930s. Departure from gold in 1931 saw the inauguration of a cheap money policy, with the great $3\frac{1}{2}\%$ War Loan conversion of 1932, and a Bank Rate that, apart from a hiccup on the outbreak of war, remained at 2% from June 1932 to 1951.

The sharpest impact of the depression on the bank was felt in the severe contraction in lending. In December 1929 advances stood at £204m.; four years later, in December 1933, the total had plummeted to £140m., a drop of over 30%. Adjusted for the fall in prices, however, the contraction was somewhat less: by 26% in 'real terms' between 1929 and 1933. As a ratio of deposits, the fall in advances was from 58% to 39%. At the same time, interest rates fell sharply. In 1929 Bank Rate averaged 5.5% and by 1933 had come down to 2%, while the yield on short-dated gilts declined from

5.08 to 2.09%. The combination of a savage cut in advances and some fall in the average rate charged meant that earnings from lending shrank significantly. Deposits, in contrast, rose on balance by £12m. between December 1929 and December 1933, or by 3% (12% in 'real terms'), more than accounted for by the increase in current account balances. In total, the number of accounts grew by 320,000 (18%) over this period, but nearly half these were savings bank accounts opened in 1930 in the drive for savings business. Similarly, investments recovered from £37m. to £99m., or from under 11 to over 27% of deposits, about the same ratio as in the early 1920s.

Before we take this sombre story further it may be useful to pause to consider some of the wider aspects of the fall in lending in the early 1930s. Advances in general fell. Lending by the other nine London clearing banks together in December 1929 was £789m. and at the end of 1933 stood at £600m., a fall of 24%. That Lloyds' advances declined relatively more may possibly have reflected the bank's rather cautious policies under Pease.

We know little of how much various industries and trades were borrowing during these years, either for Lloyds or the other clearing banks. Figures were compiled for the Macmillan Committee but for only one year. These showed that nearly a quarter of Lloyds' lending in October 1929 was for manufacturing industry and rather more than a quarter for 'other production' (agriculture, fishing, mining and quarrying, building and miscellaneous industries, but including retail trade), with a third of the total taken by a category labelled 'other' (mainly the personal and professional group).[1] Industry in general, therefore, with farming borrowed in the region of half the total in 1929. Much of the decline in subsequent years was concentrated on such lending. Could Lloyds and the other banks have in fact done more to help industry? Was the fall in their lending partly their own fault through their insistence on severely high standards and too restrictive criteria?

The latter question need not detain us long. To ask the banks to relax the prudent standards that long experience has shown to be necessary is really to ask them to be less careful with other people's money, although in the 1930s Lloyds may perhaps have erred rather too much on the side of caution. It is also worth remembering that, unlike what happened elsewhere, not a single British bank failed during the depression. Two official investigations at this time found little fault with the banks' arrangements for the finance of industry and commerce. The Balfour Committee on

---

[1] See table on p. 77.

Industry and Trade could not be accused of coming to hasty conclusions for, appointed in 1924, it was not until 1929 that its final report appeared. On the whole the committee considered that

the existing machinery for supplying British industry with financial facilities to meet its legitimate needs is adequate and suitable. Moreover, the evidence available shows that the rates of charge for these facilities compare favourably with those obtaining for similar services in any competing country . . . [Page 48.]

There had, indeed, the committee noted, been criticisms that the banks had been too lavish with their money and propped up firms that in the end collapsed. But this, it argued, was to be wise after the event.

The Macmillan Committee, reporting in June 1931, endorsed this conclusion:

The great English banks . . . use and have used their resources freely, sometimes too freely, in the provision of advances to industry. In general we are satisfied that, subject to the conditions imposed by the necessity of accommodating ourselves to the outside world, our banking system is adequate and satisfactory in the provision of the normal short credits to industry and their distribution. [Para. 391.]

There was, however, what became known as the 'Macmillan Gap'—the lack of facilities for small and medium-sized businesses to raise capital—which was to be filled after the war.

The Macmillan Committee questioned the bank chairmen closely on their lending policies. Beaumont Pease, for example, was quite definite that no industry had been refused help because the bank was short of funds:

I do not know of a single instance where we have turned down a trade advance because we did not think we had the money to lend. When the proportion of advances to deposits has been high—and it is high—when it has been higher than we thought desirable we have granted the trade advance and we have called in other advances which we thought less necessary in the interests of the country, such as Stock Exchange loans, and things of that sort.[2]

While Pease did not think 'any ordinary banker has the technical knowledge to say exactly what improvement should be made' when an industry ran into trouble, he pointed out that the banks could, and did, help in reorganisation schemes, and gave two examples where Lloyds had helped at some sacrifice in terms of liquidity.

The bank had to work within the economic and financial environment in which it found itself, and in such times as the early 1930s necessarily had to pay regard to its liquid resources. It is true that the 30% liquidity

[2] Qu. 2083, 3 February 1930.

ratio[3] was not then the official minimum it became after the war. But its influence on policy was increasing: if the ratio was declining and near to 30% the bank would be more likely to be restrictive in its lending than if it was rising above 30%. Thus, in October 1931, R. A. Wilson, then a joint general manager, suggested that 'we should be as liquid as possible in preparation for possible increased demands from more active trades for accommodation'. Two months later, in December, the liquidity ratio was in fact 31%, compared with 34% in December 1930, giving point to Wilson's argument. Twelve months on, however, at the end of 1932, with depression continuing, the ratio had risen to over 37%, and advances had fallen by £26m. There was certainly no shortage of funds to lend, if the demand was there.

In writing about a bank one is naturally restricted by the rule of confidentiality not to reveal details of transactions with individual customers. Although the period in question is now nearly half a century ago, many customers of that time, in particular companies, remain on the bank's books today. Where, however, they have themselves told what happened, or authorised others to tell the story, one is, of course, free to draw on such disclosures. For example, the relationship in the 1920s and early 1930s between Beardmores, the Glasgow armament and ship-building group, and Lloyds, has recently been revealed.[4]

In the years after the war Beardmores ran into a bad patch, and profits fell away. With liquidity under pressure in 1922, an overdraft of £500,000 from Lloyds was taken up, increased in 1925 to £650,000. Troubles con-tinued, however, and a scheme of reconstruction became necessary in 1928. The Bank of England now stepped in and the Governor worked out a fresh scheme as a condition of official help, with the agreement of Lloyds and two other banks concerned. The financial position was not yet stabilised, however, and in January 1933 Beardmores had difficulty in financing £574,000 worth of Admiralty work: Lloyds and the other two banks agreed to provide a revolving credit of £100,000. Not until rearmament of the late 1930s did the firm really pick up.

Richard Thomas & Co. was another concern that Lloyds helped. In 1936, to finance the construction at Ebbw Vale, South Wales, of an inte-grated steel plant, debentures of £7m. were issued through Rothschilds and a large sum borrowed from Lloyds. But in 1938 financial difficulties arose and the Bank of England stepped in.[5] Lloyds also participated in the

---

[3] The ratio to total deposits of cash and balance at Bank of England, Treasury and other bills, and money at call and short notice lent to the discount market.

[4] John R. Hume and Michael S. Moss, *The History of William Beardmore: A Scottish Industrial Giant*, Heinemann Educational Books, 1979.

[5] R. S. Sayers, *The Bank of England 1891–1944*. Volume 2, p. 549.

Bankers Industrial Development Co., set up in April 1930 to help in the reorganisation of the country's basic industries, and Beane became a member of its advisory council. Its term was originally five years, but this was extended in 1935 and not until 1945 was it finally wound up.

We must now return to consider the profit and loss position of the bank in the depression years. Income from lending fell by over two-fifths between 1929 and 1933. Total interest receipts, from advances, investments, and other sources, exceeded £15m. in 1929; by 1933 they had dropped to under £9m. Earnings from the discount of bills, although not large in total—accounting for only 11% of total receipts in 1929—dropped from about £2½m. in 1929 to less than £500,000 in 1933. Commissions, however, were unchanged at just under £2m. Total earnings fell from about £19m. in 1929 to just over £15m. in 1930, followed by a slight improvement in 1931; but the decline was renewed the next year and by 1933 total income was down to little over £11m., the lowest figure since 1918 and two-fifths less than in 1929. Outgoings, in contrast, were reduced by much less, from £14.6m. in 1929 to £10.4m. in 1933. Well over nine-tenths of this saving came from the lower interest payments on deposit and other accounts as interest rates were cut; deposit balances in total hardly changed on balance between 1929 and 1933. There was a small cut-back in the bill for staff costs but all other outgoings were pretty well the same in total. The net result was that gross profits fell from over £4.5m. in 1929 to about £1.9m. in 1930, then recovered in 1931 and 1932, only to slump to just under £750,000 in 1933. This was little more than half the sum required to pay the dividend to shareholders and the lowest figure since the beginning of the century.

The position was serious, although the record as presented to the world was not quite so depressing. Published profits did fall, but relatively very much less: from £2.5m. in 1929 steadily downwards to £1.4m. in 1933. The accounts were partially sustained by two methods in particular during these years. First, in 1930 and 1931 bad and doubtful debt provisions were absorbed by inner reserves and not set against profits. Secondly, profits on the sale of investments, sometimes substantial, were brought in as a credit. To write down the value of investments, £2½m. were taken from published reserves in 1931.

Economy measures

It was clear that as there was little or nothing the bank could do to stem the decline in its income, cuts were necessary in its expenditure. Economies were planned and enforced wherever possible over a wide range of outlays.

Even so, many of the bank's customers must have been largely unaware of any great change in its fortunes. They might read in the newspapers of a reduction in its dividend or of unhappiness among its staff at having their bonus cut, but business went on much as usual at the local branch. A girl might now be sitting at what looked like a large typewriter in place of a young man on a high stool posting a ledger and a statement might replace a pass-book but there were few other changes. This was, indeed, true of most operations of the bank. The 1930s were not years of innovation and experiments with new forms of business.

One of the first moves was a reduction in the dividend for 1930 on the bank's 'A' shares from 16⅔ to 15%, followed by further reductions for 1931, to 13⅓%, and for 1932, to 12%,[6] a rate that was to remain unchanged for the next twenty years. The vast majority of shareholders appeared to accept this drop in income philosophically, at least to the extent of not complaining to the chairman. In 1931 Pease claimed that, of 65,000 shareholders, only four had written to criticise the reduction; indeed, congratulations had been received 'from various classes of business'. Profits did not warrant a dividend at the former rate; the return on bank shares had wrongly come to be regarded as irreducible and 'immune from the troubles which vex others less fortunate'. There were critical letters from shareholders in subsequent years, some of whom were reminded in 1933 with a kind of grim pride that 'the lead which this bank took in reducing its dividend' had been followed by other banks.

In the search for economy, a thorough review was now put in hand of all aspects of the bank's organisation. It was 'of the highest importance', Beane explained, 'that we should continue a connected and comprehensive programme for dealing with these matters'. A small committee was set up, under the chief general managers, to look at a number of topics, from general expenses, including the cost of running the new head office, mechanisation, loss-making branches, to office re-organisation and stationery and, to show that this was not an inclusive list, Beane's letter asking certain officials to join ended 'etc., etc., etc.'

Various sub-committees were formed and went about their work with great assiduity, sending in reports until well into 1932. So far as the new head office was concerned, at first sight, the relative sub-committee admitted, it looked as if considerable reductions should be possible in expenses running at some £48,000 a year. But close scrutiny revealed that 'no material economy can be effected without impairing efficiency'. They 'unhesitatingly' had come to the opinion that such expenses were

---

[6] The dividend of the 'B' shares remained unchanged at the maximum of 5% from 1926 to 1955.

reasonable and necessary. Higher expenditure was chiefly the result of improvements compared with the former building: better heating, furnishings, lighting, and so on. However, this was not to say that some economies elsewhere were not possible. The sub-committee drew attention to the 'elaborate form' of the bank's monthly review, with a circulation of 12,400 in July 1931, and wondered whether all the banks might not gain if they produced a joint publication. They called for a closer surveillance of postage expenditure. It was recommended that staff control be centralised again in head office. In 1921 a system of provincial staff controllers had been established but time, labour, and expense would be saved if branches dealt once again directly with head office; this recommendation was partly adopted, four staff controllers not being replaced when they retired in the next few years. And candle-ends were not to be ignored: the sub-committee also considered 'the moment opportune to suggest discontinuance of the use of certain expensive brands of soap'.

The mechanisation sub-committee concluded that the introduction of mechanised accounting—which we will consider later—had been 'amply justified by results' and recommended that the employment of women for this work should be continued. There was a cry from one member, however, which has echoed down the years into the age of computers: 'I feel that we are not getting the reduction of staff we should do under a mechanised system'. The report of the sub-committee on staff training can wait until we come to consider this topic, since it was concerned mainly with the organisation of training and had little to say about economy.

It was early decided that any further expansion of the branch network was to be checked and, wherever possible, spending on rebuilding and extensions deferred. One of the sub-committees set up in 1931 had been concerned with the related question of branch profitability. Differences in branch profits, it concluded, were due mainly to variations in the cost of premises and in the salaries of staff and it suggested that each branch should, in effect, be compared with a 'standard branch' and its figures adjusted accordingly, to arrive at their true level. Subsequently, a thorough examination was made of losing branches and in 1935 a formula was devised for selecting those to be closed. Branches had been allowed or charged certain rates each half-year on money they deposited with or borrowed from head office. In 1933 and 1934 the rates allowed had been only $1\frac{3}{4}\%$ for country branches and 1% for London branches, while the rate charged had been $3\frac{1}{2}\%$, which had pressed hard on branches with credit balances with head office. Under the formula adopted, average rates for the previous ten years were taken and certain other adjustments made: probably 'as scientific and accurate a method as can be devised'. On this basis of calculation, of some 350 loss-making branches in 1934, two-thirds would now be in the clear. Of the remainder, it was recommended that a number should be reduced to sub-branch or clerk-in-charge status. Difficulties at some had been caused by heavy spending on premises which it would be impossible to sell except at considerable loss: one small branch in Lancashire had only 260 current accounts in premises which had cost £93,000. There were fourteen branches where the prospects seemed to be hopeless. All but one of these were subsequently closed.

Some of these offices the bank managed to shut on a 'swap' basis with other banks experiencing similar problems. Lloyds closed its branches at Penge and Upper Tooting, in South London, for example, in exchange for Barclays closing its offices at Bourton-on-the-Water, in Gloucestershire, and Honiton, in Devon. Lloyds' customers at the former branches were recommended to transfer to the local Barclays office, and *vice versa* as regards Barclays' customers. The idea had been put forward of a round-table conference of the banks to work out an agreed programme of closures but this was generally turned down in favour of 'unilateral arrangements'. There were occasional difficulties. Lloyds' branch at West Norwood, again in South London, was closed in April 1936, with the suggestion that customers should move their business to the local Westminster Bank branch. Subsequently, Westminster complained that, while credit balances of £3,730 had been transferred to their branch, loans taken over totalled only £160. Lloyds hoped that the position would improve but admitted their branch had 'always been handicapped by paucity of loans, and this matter played an important part in the decision to close the office'.

As a result of these and other closures the number of offices open at the end of 1936 was seventy-four fewer than at the end of 1931, fifty-five of which were sub-branches. Such savings contributed towards the considerable economies on premises that were effected. In 1927 total net expenditure on premises, including acquisition of properties, rebuilding, fittings, and so on, was £733,000. By 1931 this had been reduced to £272,000; while in 1933 the figure was a net credit of £29,000, as proceeds of sales more than off-set spending (which was only £56,000), a position repeated in 1936 with a net credit of £60,000. On buying properties alone, £557,000 was spent in 1930;[7] in 1935 this was cut to less than £7,000. Expenditure on repairs and decoration was trimmed from £115,000 in 1930 to £70,000 in 1932.

[7] None of which related to the new head office, the cost of which was provided for some years previously.

Economies had to be sought in staff costs, accounting in 1930-1 for about two-fifths of total current expenditure. There must be a reduction in the number of male staff and thus in salary costs, Beane emphasised. This was 'a most important consideration, and forms one of the chief avenues for a reduction in expenses'. First, there was a sharp cut-back in the number of young men recruited. The introduction of mechanised book-keeping in 1929 had meant that relatively fewer juniors would be needed, anyway, as more young women were taken on for this work but, to start with, the process was not rapid, and the decrease in male recruitment was much greater than was due to this cause. In 1931 only seventy-three young men joined the bank (excluding messengers) compared with 326 in 1930 and an annual average of well over 400 in the years 1925 to 1929. In 1932 there was a slight increase, to eighty-six, and a further rise in 1933, followed by a recovery in the late 1930s to around 400 a year. Male staff decreased in total by nearly 500 between 1930 and 1933, while the number of women went up by 250, to represent 16% of all staff in the bank. Although after 1933 the number of male staff rose again, the increase was relatively less than that of women staff who, by 1938, made up over 19% of total employees.

This check to recruitment in the early 1930s inevitably distorted the age distribution of the male staff in later years, just as did the heavy intake of juniors ten years earlier. At the time, with retrenchment vital in a bleak economic situation, understandably little thought was given to the problems of staff controllers thirty years hence. The problems of the next thirty weeks were quite sufficient. Nevertheless, the consequences of the decisions of 1931-3 had ultimately to be faced. By the 1960s there was a shortage of men in their forties relative to the number of managerial and other appointments that had to be made. In 1963 men in the 45-9 age-group accounted for less than 5% of the male staff (excluding messengers). On the other hand, reflecting the heavy recruitment of the 1920s, those in the 55 and over age-group made up nearly 13%.

As regards pay, although salary scales were left untouched, the dividend cut to 15% in 1930 had brought profit-sharing to an end and reductions were now made in the bonus. In addition, the normal annual increase a clerk could expect for efficient work was reduced in 1932 from £15 to £10.[8] This was restored to £15 in 1938. The bonus system dated from January 1921 and rates had last changed in 1923, when a single man and

---

[8] For men who joined the staff before 1929. Those who joined after 1929 were on a different scale. In June 1931, 'in view of the general need for economy', overtime payments at the half-yearly balance periods were also stopped. Instead, staff were now entitled to 2s. 6d. (12½p) a night for six days before and after the half year. The S.R.C. agreed with the abolition of overtime, as there had been 'gross abuse of a generous scheme'.

a woman got $21\frac{2}{3}\%$ of his or her salary and a married man $32\frac{1}{2}\%$, with minimum and maximum payments, but young men joining the bank after June 1928 did not receive a bonus. In January 1930 a cut was made in the rates of bonus, although salaries over £500 a year suffered a greater reduction than those below, and any men now marrying continued on the single man's rate. There were two more cuts in 1931 and two again in 1934, by which time the two rates of bonus had been reduced to $8\frac{2}{3}\%$ and 13%, with a maximum of £52 and a minimum of £4. 15s. 4d. (£4·77). No further reductions were then made. In 1929 bonus payments had been £607,000; by 1932 this was reduced to £318,000 and by 1935 to less than £200,000.

These reductions were naturally not made without some resentment on the part of the staff, manifested in protests from the Staff Representative Committee. The S.R.C. do not appear to have been consulted or even given an advance warning and, apart from letters of protest, there was little they could do. When the first cut was made, in January 1930, the S.R.C. agreed that the bonus was given to offset changes in the cost of living but claimed that this had not fallen sufficiently since 1923 to justify the size of the bonus reduction. This seems difficult to substantiate. The bonus was cut by 5%, while the cost of living had already fallen 6% between 1923 and 1929 and was to continue to fall. In 1931, however, the S.R.C. accepted that the drop in the bank's profits meant a cut in the bonus but asked for it to be lessened or postponed. By 1934 the S.R.C. had 'used every argument at their disposal' against the bonus reduction, while agreeing that the bank had been generous in the long years of depression. No one had been sacked or had his or her actual salary cut. The resentment among the staff can also be exaggerated. It was widely realised that the times were bad and that, when millions of their countrymen were without jobs, they were lucky to be in secure employment. Expectations were certainly upset by the cuts in the bonus and the annual increase in salary and, as always, there must have been individual cases of hardship. Yet, by comparison with what was happening elsewhere in Britain, the staff of the bank were not too hardly done by.

For those at work the fall in the cost of living often more than offset any reduction in nominal incomes, so that real incomes increased. This was true in general of the staff of Lloyds Bank. If 1923 is taken as equal to 100, then by 1933 average total remuneration per head in the bank had been reduced to 97.[9] But over the same period the cost of living had fallen to 80, implying an increase in average real income per head of 21%. Average money income per head continued to fall a little during the rest of the 1930s, while the cost of living moved up, so that by 1938 the increase in

---

[9] These are unweighted averages.

average real income per head had dropped to a level only 3% above the 1923 base, much lower than earlier in the decade but still higher than in the mid-1920s. Similar movements in real incomes were true of employees generally in insurance, banking, and finance in the 1930s.[10]

Another measure that appears to have been made partly for economy reasons was the introduction in July 1930 of a contributory pension scheme for male staff. This was back-dated to apply to all those joining the bank after December 1928 and, again, seems to have been formulated without any discussion with, or notification to, the S.R.C. Staff were to pay an annual contribution of 5% of salary, with 7% from the bank (which was subsequently varied from time to time). The retiring age was to be sixty-five, against sixty for the pre-1929 staff, with a pension of 1/60 of the salary at time of retirement for every year of service, up to a maximum of two-thirds of the final salary.

The scheme brought savings on two scores, one of which, however, lay well in the future. First, the bank received a contribution of 5% of salary from all young men now joining. The sums involved clearly were not, at the beginning, on a large scale, since recruitment was low and the salary of a boy of seventeen was £90 a year (which was the same for his counterpart before 1929). But as salaries progressed upwards so staff contributions increased. Lloyds was the only one of the big five clearing banks to bring in such a contributory scheme and, although salary scales and conditions of service were broadly comparable in all five, it was the case that the net starting salary, after pension contribution, of a young man in London seventeen years old, of £85. 10s. (£85·50) was still somewhat above that in the other big four banks. Moreover, jobs were not all that plentiful for school leavers in the early 1930s and there was keen competition to get into a bank. That a boy starting in Lloyds would get a bit less in net salary than he would have done a year or so earlier was often rather less important than the fact that he had landed a job at all.

Secondly, there was the question of the age of retirement. Previously, while most of the staff, particularly those relatively lower paid, retired at sixty years, some senior staff stayed on beyond this age, in some cases to sixty-five. It was apparently decided that the bank would be financially in pocket if staff had to continue to sixty-five, with the possibility, some time in the future, that this might be lowered to sixty. Jumping ahead thirty years, as early as 1962 the effects on staff costs and the pension fund of such a reduction to sixty were considered. When the rules of the

[10] See Agatha Chapman and Rose Knight, *Wages and Salaries in The United Kingdom 1920–1938*, Cambridge University Press, 1952, pp. 152–5.

contributory scheme were later revised, in 1974, the normal retirement age was in fact set at sixty, but that is going beyond the scope of this book. Another event after 1969 that deserves mention originated in the back-dating of the start of the contributory pension scheme to January 1929. Young men who joined in the period from then until July 1930 had their conditions of service changed retrospectively. In the fullness of time they reached sixty but the bank would not agree to their retiring at that age. The issue went to arbitration in January 1972 and was decided in favour of the bank.

For women, a contributory pension scheme was introduced six years later, in July 1936. Members paid 5% of their salary (and the bank 8%, subsequently changed as for the men's scheme) and could retire at fifty-five at a rate of 1/70 of their salary for each year of service. This was improved in 1949 to 1/55, when also, with so many more young women in the bank than in the 1930s, most of whom stayed only a few years, the age at which contributions became payable was raised to twenty-five.

Advertising was another form of expenditure on which it was decided savings could be made and between 1931 and 1932 spending was cut by a third from £31,500 to £21,000, a total which remained virtually unchanged until the oubreak of war. The suggestion was made that advertising could in fact become a source of revenue for the bank if space on its premises was let for posters. Individual cases might be considered but there is no record of any being approved. Any frills were to be trimmed. Bexleyheath and Watford branches were given permission in 1932 to join local tradesmen in flood-lighting schemes 'if it could not be avoided'. But in 1935, when the King's jubilee was celebrated, it was rather cheeseparingly decided not to flood-light head office or the bank's West End offices in St. James's Street and Pall Mall.

Business goes on

By the middle of the 1930s the worst had passed and some recovery was experienced, not only by the economy at large but by the bank, in its business and profitability. An increase in advances and the curb on expenses after the dark years of the early 1930s combined to produce some recovery in profits. From the nadir of 1933, gross profits rose by £1.8m., to nearly £2.6m. in 1937. Of this increase, improved earnings accounted for £1.5m., two-thirds of which came from the greater volume of advances. For the rest, total outgoings in 1937 were about £300,000 lower than in 1933. Interest paid fell by £600,000 over the period, mainly reflecting a decline in deposit balances, but this was partly offset by a rise in staff and other costs. The slight dip in economic activity in 1938 meant profits were set back again, and it was not until the war years that their revival was firmly established.

Throughout the decade Beaumont Pease and Sir Austin Harris continued as chairman and deputy chairman. In 1932 W. L. Runciman (he succeeded as Viscount Runciman of Doxford in 1949) joined the board and was to become deputy chairman from 1962 to 1971. Runciman, an industrialist and shipping expert, had an intimate knowledge of affairs in the North of England which was to prove of considerable value over his long period of association with the bank. In his early days on the board Runciman and one or two young directors recently appointed felt somewhat frustrated by the close control kept by Pease and tried to foster less cautious and more adventurous attitudes, but with little success. For these they had to wait until Lord Balfour of Burleigh became chairman in 1946. In 1936, the new position of vice-chairman was created for Francis Beane on his retirement as chief general manager, which he was to fill until 1947; and in 1937 a link with the distant past was snapped with the death of Charles Edward Barnett. Barnett had been a director since 1884 when Barnetts, Hoares, Hanbury and Lloyd amalgamated with Lloyds.

At the storm centre right through the early 1930s were the two chief general managers, F. A. Beane and G. F. Abell, both appointed in 1929, after the interregnum since 1923. Beane retired in 1935, while Abell continued on his own for the next three years until he too retired in 1938. Beane, the first member of the staff to rise from junior to vice-chairman and knighted in 1939, joined the bank at Longton branch in 1887, becoming manager of the important Collingwood Street, Newcastle upon Tyne, branch in 1906. After a spell in the foreign 'auxiliary' he came to head office in 1920. An outspoken man, he sensed times were changing—he was keen to employ more women—and understood industries' problems during his years as chief general manager. He also realised the importance of delegation and took great care in picking able subordinates. Abell began his career at Bromsgrove branch in 1893 and, after service in the inspection department and at various Midland branches, moved to Lombard Street in 1914. He was a rather cautious banker, conservative in outlook, a good executive and extremely hard-working. On his retirement, Abell became a director 1939–46.

Abell, as sole chief general manager in 1936 to 1938, faced a rather less difficult position than when in harness with Beane earlier in the decade. Although the years immediately before the oubreak of war could hardly be described as a time of great prosperity—unemployment averaged well over 1½m.—yet there was a distinct improvement compared with the slough of depression. Manufacturing production rose by nearly two-fifths between 1933 and 1937, falling off slightly in the mild depression that followed. Coal output improved, steel production increased, shipbuilding was more active, prices started to pick up. As a stimulant to the economy, a significant part was played by the great house-building boom of the middle 1930s that accompanied cheap money: 720,000 new dwellings were completed in the two years 1935-6, compared with 524,000 in the three years 1930-2.

Lloyds' business reflected this recovery. Advances had touched a low point of £140m. in December 1933 (39% of total deposits). The following years saw a rise, accelerating in pace, to £175m. in December 1937 (44% of deposits), then a dip to £168m. at the end of 1938. Throughout this period rates charged remained generally unchanged with Bank Rate stable at 2%.

As was noted earlier, the bank had provided the Macmillan Committee with a detailed classification of its advances for 1929, which were included in the totals for all the clearing banks published in the report. Thereafter, comparable figures for 1936, 1937, and 1938 were published by the Committee of London Clearing Bankers. Table 5 gives the distribution of Lloyds' advances by category for these years, while Table 6 shows Lloyds' share of lending in each category.

The biggest single category for all four years was 'other' which, in fact, was very largely personal and professional borrowing. The share of manufacturing industries dropped sharply during the depression, from 22.9% in 1929 to 14.6% in 1936, concentrated in textiles and food, drink and tobacco. While there was some increase in 1937, the group's share fell back again in 1938. The total of 'other production' can be compared only for 1936 to 1938, since the 1929 figure included retail trade. Of the individual categories, borrowing by agriculture and fishing remained largely unchanged, but the share of building trades increased significantly between 1929 and the late 1930s, reflecting the house-building boom. Lending for 'other' purposes rose from a third of the total in 1929 to over two-fifths in 1937 and 1938.

Table 6 shows that, of lending by all the clearing banks, Lloyds accounted for 18.8% in 1929 and for 16.3/9% in 1936-8. In 1936, however, District Bank became a London clearing bank. Allowing for this factor, Lloyds' share in 1936-8 would be about 17.5%, still somewhat less than in 1929. That an additional bank is covered in the years 1936-8 must, therefore, be remembered when comparing Lloyds' share of the individual

TABLE 5. *Distribution of Advances*

	1929 %	1936 %	1937 %	1938 %
Manufacturing				
Textiles	7.1	4.2	4.6	4.2
Heavy industries	6.7	6.3	8.6	6.3
Food, drink, and tobacco	7.6	3.0	2.9	3.5
Leather, rubber, and chemicals	1.5	1.1	0.9	0.9
	22.9	14.6	17.0	14.9
Other production				
Agriculture and fishing	9.8	9.2	8.7	9.1
Mining and quarrying	2.1	0.9	0.6	0.6
Building trades	2.9	4.9	4.8	4.8
Miscellaneous	11.7*	3.6	3.3	2.9
	26.5	18.6	17.4	17.4
Services				
Retail trade	n.a.	8.7	8.4	8.7
Local govt. and public utilities (excluding railways)	3.1	0.7	0.6	1.2
Amusements, clubs, churches, etc.	1.9	3.5	3.3	3.0
Shipping and transport	3.6	3.3	2.3	3.3
	8.6	16.2	14.6	16.2
Financial	9.2	10.8	7.7	8.2
Other	32.8	39.8	43.3	43.3
	100.0	100.0	100.0	100.0

* Includes retail trade.
Note: data are for October each year.

categories in these years with that in 1929. However, even if this is ignored, Lloyds' lending in three categories—heavy industries, agriculture and fishing, and other (mainly personal and professional)—stands out as above the figures for all lending, and in local government and public utilities as well below.

TABLE 6. *Share of Clearing Bank Advances*

	1929/30 %	1936 %	1937 %	1938 %
Manufacturing				
Textiles	16.2	15.4	16.8	17.1
Heavy industries	19.9	22.6	27.7	21.4
Food, drink, and tobacco	22.5	14.7	14.5	15.3
Leather, rubber, and chemicals	12.2	13.3	9.4	10.0
	18.6	17.4	19.3	17.4
Other production				
Agriculture and fishing	26.6	23.5	23.1	22.8
Mining and quarrying	13.0	7.2	6.2	6.0
Building trades	11.3	11.6	11.2	11.0
Miscellaneous	14.8*	7.8	7.1	6.4
	16.8	13.3	12.7	12.6
Services				
Retail trade	n.a.	21.2	21.0	20.4
Local govt. and public utilities (excluding railways)	11.1	2.0	1.9	3.1
Amusements, clubs, churches, etc.	14.0	12.8	13.7	10.1
Shipping and transport	26.2	20.6	18.4	19.7
	15.5	13.7	12.9	12.7
Financial	12.0	14.5	10.4	11.7
Other	27.8	22.6	23.1	22.5
	18.8	16.9	16.7	16.3

* Includes retail trade.

Notes (1) In 1929/30 there were 10 clearing banks and 11 in 1936–8 with the inclusion of District Bank. (2) Data for 1929/30: October 1929–March 1930; 1936: October; 1937: August–October; 1938: August–October.

Although it is not possible to give details of transactions with individual customers of the bank, an exception can be made for one particular and interesting advance made in the 1930s, which was finally paid off a quarter of a century ago. Keren Hayesod Limited was an English registered company founded in 1920 as the main financial instrument of the Jewish Agency to organise the resettlement of Jews in Palestine, receiving contributions from Jewish communities throughout the world. In 1934 it wished to raise further funds to help Jews fleeing from Germany and approached Lloyds for help. 'If Lloyds Bank make this loan they will *ipso facto* make fifteen million Jewish friends throughout the world' commented a prominent member of the English Jewish community. A loan of £450,000 was made, with a further advance of £150,000 in 1937 to finance irrigation and housing schemes in Palestine. These debts, the bank was assured by Chaim Weizmann, later first president of Israel, 'shall be taken over by the Jewish State as soon as the State has come into being officially'. By 1944 the 1937 loan was all repaid, but part of the original debt was still outstanding. In 1943 a further loan of £300,000 had been made. The position was consolidated in 1945 and the limit now fixed at £900,000. The debt was gradually paid off, a memorandum in 1947 pointing out that 'these reductions have been punctiliously made and all conditions of the advance have been strictly carried out'. The last repayment was made in May 1955.

Total deposits increased by roughly £40m. in the years December 1933 to December 1937, by somewhat more than the rise in advances, and then fell slightly in 1938. In 'real terms', deposits were virtually unchanged between 1933 and 1938. There was a rise in current account balances, partly offset by a decline in deposit money. Deposit balances fell from an average of £169m. in 1933 to £159m. in 1937 and £149m. in 1938. London deposit rate during these years was fixed at the low figure of $\frac{1}{2}$%. For balances elsewhere in England and Wales the rate by 1933 had come down to $1\frac{1}{2}$%. In 1936, because of the continued difficulty of employing money at remunerative rates, $1\frac{1}{2}$% was paid on existing accounts only up to £500, then 1%, the rate paid also on new accounts. This pattern of rates continued until the outbreak of war.[11] When interest was paid on current accounts, $\frac{1}{2}$% was the usual rate in these years.

In number, current accounts increased right through the depression and the rest of the 1930s, from 887,600 in December 1930 to 1,046,000 in December 1938. The total of deposit accounts reached a maximum in December 1932 of 624,000 and then fell steadily to stand at 528,000 in 1938. Not until 1959 was the 1932 total exceeded.

In its final report in 1929, the Balfour Committee had recommended, amongst other things, that the banks should publish figures of the annual

[11] In July 1940 the rate on new country deposits and additions to existing accounts was reduced to $\frac{1}{2}$% (the rate also for London deposits).

turnover of their customers' accounts, that is, the total values of cheques and other items debited. Subsequently, the clearing banks provided monthly figures of the turnover of current accounts for the period January 1930 to July 1939 when, with the outbreak of war, publication ceased. The figures were solely in money terms, with no details of the number of transactions involved, but they provide some indication of the changes in activity on bank accounts during the 1930s and, as one would expect, generally mirror those in the economy at large. Lloyds' figures parallel closely those for the other clearing banks throughout the period. In 1930, turnover on Lloyds' current accounts was about £750m. a month, falling to £600m. at the end of 1931. Turnover changed little in the next three years but then rose gradually to around £770m. in mid-1937 as the economy revived, after which it declined to under £700m. in the summer of 1939.

Related to the total of the banks' current, deposit, and other accounts was the total cash they held in their tills and in balances at the Bank of England. The ratio between these two aggregates was the cash ratio. For many years, going back well beyond 1918, the banks had been in the habit of showing a figure for cash at the end of the half-year in June and in their annual balance sheet somewhat higher than that they maintained during the rest of the year, thus 'window dressing' their cash ratio. When the London clearing banks in 1921 started to publish monthly statements of their accounts, they accordingly extended this practice to the rest of the year. The figures in these monthly statements were the averages of the four, or five, weekly balances made by each bank and each tended temporarily to increase its cash figure on its balance day, and thus the average for the month, above the level it maintained on the other days of the week. The cash ratio, as published, was thus higher than the true average daily ratio the bank maintained. There was one exception: the Midland Bank did not indulge in this practice. The other banks were able to show an inflated figure for cash as they made up their books on different days of the week: for Lloyds it was Tuesday, but no bank balanced on Friday. Each called in loans from the money market on balance day, thus increasing its balance with the Bank of England, and returned the money so called to the market the next morning. The Macmillan Report summed up the result in a well-known passage:

Thus a certain part of the published reserves of the clearing banks in the shape of deposits with the Bank of England is like a stage army, the same liquid resources doing duty four times over in the course of each week. [Para. 368.]

At the end of June and of December, when all the banks made up their books on the same day, the stage army had to be reinforced by extras from the Bank of England. The money market, called upon by the banks to repay loans had, perforce, to turn to the Bank for help.

The Macmillan Report saw no point in all this and suggested it should be ended:

We are not aware that these practices serve any useful purpose. We think that they are not creditable to our banking system; and we recommend that they should be given up at once. [Para. 370.]

They were not given up. Indeed, they continued until the end of 1946,[12] when the clearing banks all moved to the same make-up day each month for their published figures (the third Wednesday, other than June and December) and agreed to maintain a cash ratio of 8% in place of the 10% that had formerly been the rule. The criticisms of the Macmillan Committee were echoed in succeeding years by financial commentators and others: window dressing, it was argued, was stupid and deceived nobody, disturbed the money market to no good purpose, distorted the link between cash and deposits. But there were those who defended the practice, and they were not always in the City: it enabled the banks to adjust to temporary fluctuations in their Bank of England balances, it maintained stability in published cash ratios.

How far did Lloyds Bank window dress its cash ratio? Figure 7 shows the bank's daily balance at the Bank of England for five periods as a ratio of the average balance for the week excluding Tuesday. Tuesday, it will be remembered, was the balance day for Lloyds throughout these years. In 1924-5 and 1930-1, it will be seen that the Tuesday balance was well above that for the other days of the week, and an average of only the Tuesday figures clearly showed an inflated position. In 1933, possibly in response to the Macmillan Committee's criticisms, the Tuesday figure was not nearly so much out of line, but by 1936 and 1937 the old habits had been resumed, although not to quite the same extent.

If the Tuesday figures are adjusted down to the average for the week for the periods shown in the diagram, it is possible to calculate the 'true' cash ratio, as distinct from the cash ratio that was published. In the first two periods the true cash ratio was over a tenth lower than the published ratio, in 1933 it was only 2% lower but by 1936 and 1937 the margin had widened again to 7-8%.

The grading scheme for male staff introduced in 1929[13] has already been

---

[12] From the outbreak of war in 1939 the clearing banks made up their books monthly, not weekly, but still on different days of the week, except for end-June and end-December.

[13] The scheme was actually announced in May 1930 but applied to all young men who joined the bank after December 1928.

FIGURE 7. *Balance at Bank of England*
(*100 = average of 5 days (excluding Tuesday) for period covered*)

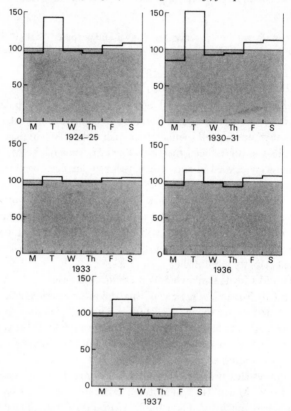

The bold line shows the actual daily balance as a percentage of the five-day weekly average. Data are for various weeks in above years.

TABLE 7.

	Published cash ratio	*'True' cash ratio*
	%	%
1924–5	10.8	9.5
1930–1	10.6	9.1
1933	11.0	10.8
1936	10.6	9.9
1937	10.3	9.5

mentioned in passing but deserves some greater attention, since it marked the first time salary scales were related to differences of ability, and was also associated with an attempt at the reform of staff training. The scheme set up four grades through which men proceeded according to merit and success in the Institute of Bankers' examinations. A young man of, say, seventeen years old was placed in grade A when joining the bank, with a salary of £90 in London, and rose through two successive grades, if all went well, to reach grade D at twenty-eight years, when his salary would be £280 a year. In the country salaries at each step were £20 lower.

Parents were told that their son, when appointed, might have to live away from home, in which event they had to be prepared to supplement his bank pay during the first few years. He should regard himself 'in the light of an articled pupil'. This kind of language served, of course, to reinforce the idea that banking was a profession, comparable to the law or medicine, with its own standards, status and code of conduct. That may have been true of the old private bankers but was hardly applicable to the large commercial institutions banks like Lloyds had become by the 1930s. That it was so, that a bank clerk's status, if not his pay, was superior to that of the great army of clerks at least helped to bolster self-esteem. It is probable, too, that the idea of banking as a profession was partly responsible for the animosity shown by some towards the Bank Officers' Guild. Professional men could not have anything to do with trade unions.

However that might be, difficulties were soon encountered with the grading scheme's salary scales. In 1932, it will be recalled, the normal annual increase in salary for those men who had joined before 1929 was reduced from £15 to £10 as an economy measure. Now the usual increase for the new graders was £15; at one point it was £35 and at another £40. By 1935 a clerk who joined in 1929 (in London) when seventeen years old would overtake men who joined in 1928, but his net pay, allowing for the 5% pension contribution, would still be slightly less. However, looking ahead, he would by 1940 overtake all those who joined in 1926 to 1928, assuming their annual increase remained at £10, even after allowing for the pension contribution. True, years ahead, the limits to the graders' salaries were below those for the pre-1929 staff in London and large provincial branches. Yet clearly, if disharmony was not to grow among the staff, some of the music had to be rewritten. This was put in hand and in 1936 a scheme was introduced to give pre-grade staff extra increases each year. Yet anomalies still remained that were to worry the staff department and to cause resentment among the staff. Another attempt was made in 1941 to remove the distortions but this was still not wholly successful; changes in salary could mean changes in seniority and this, for example, could upset the rota for holidays. Not until 1952, when a new salary scheme was introduced, were all the differences between the pre-1929 staff and later entrants finally removed, other than the 5% pension contribution and the age of retirement.

Some of the staff who joined the bank before 1929 were also affected in the 1930s, or thought themselves affected, by changes in local government boundaries. The salary limits outside London for such clerks were £450 for large towns, with a population of 50,000 and over, and £375 for other, small towns. As a town's population grew so, if it was reclassified, would salary limits be raised. In the 1930s a number of towns ostensibly increased their population by parliamentary power by including neighbouring towns within their boundaries. The staff in branches in such towns were not asleep and usually asked to be upgraded. Sometimes the staff department agreed, sometimes it did not. By January 1939, for example, the urban district council of Rhondda, in South Wales, covered an apparent population of 130,000 by grouping together a number of small towns. But the staff department was not prepared to recognise all these as large towns for purposes of salary limits.

The young men who joined the bank in the 1920s and after 1929 under the new grading scheme usually came from the fifth and sixth forms of grammar and public schools. A limited recruitment of university graduates was now begun.

This was not entirely new. Before 1914 a scheme of sorts had first been drawn up: graduates, rather extraordinarily, had to agree to work for six months without pay and, not so extraordinarily, had to start at the bottom. At the end of six months they were paid a salary of £100 a year, about £20–30 more than their non-graduate colleagues of the same age received. After the war, sixteen graduates were taken on in the years 1920 to 1923 and given special training opportunities (and now paid an appropriate salary when joining the bank), but it was not until the end of the decade that serious thought was really given to recruiting graduates. A memorandum written in 1929 by Alwyn Parker, a director who had taken a keen interest in the question, had some words whose truth the bank did not finally come to admit until many years later:

Indifference and apathy to such [university] education, which has perhaps been most conspicuous in the world of business, was not unnatural in the prosperous past, when self-complacency had some apparent justification; in the difficult future higher intellectual training will be the main hope of business and the chief guarantee of industrial and commercial recovery.

In the next few years two graduates were recruited annually, one from

1. Sir Richard Vassar Vassar-Smith, 1843–1922. Chairman, 1909–1922.
From the painting by Sir William Orpen, R.A.

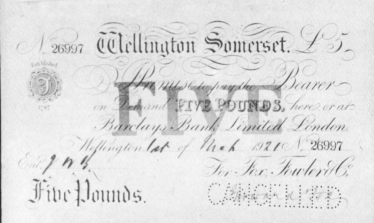

2. Bank notes (*above*) Lloyds Bank, Isle of Man issue, 1961,
(*below*) Fox, Fowler & Co., 1921.

3. The Right Hon. Lord Wardington of Alnmouth, 1869–1950. Chairman, 1922–1945.
From the painting by Sir William Nicholson, R.A.

4a. Stoke Newington branch, 1927.

4b. Bilston branch, 1977.

Change Alley

Pope's Head Alley

5a. Cornhill, 1922.
The buildings along the
dotted line were pulled
down for the rebuilding
of head office 1926–1930.

5b. Head Office,
Cornhill frontage, 1979.

6. Bombay (Hornby Road) branch, 1950.

7. The Right Hon. Lord Balfour of Burleigh, 1883–1967. Chairman, 1946–1954.
From the painting by James Gunn, A.R.A.

8. The Right Hon. Lord Franks of Headington. Chairman, 1954–1962.
From the painting by William Dring, R.A.

9. Sir Harald Peake, 1899–1978. Chairman 1962–1969.
From the painting by Edward I. Halliday.

10a. Foreign exchange dealers, Cox & Co., 1919.

10b. Foreign exchange dealing room, Overseas Department, 1969.

11a. Ledger room. Cox & Co., 1919.

11b. City Computer Centre, 1969.

12. Sir Eric Faulkner. Chairman, 1969–1977.
From the painting by W. E. Narraway, R.P., R.B.A.

Oxford and one from Cambridge. No consistent policy appears to have been adopted on salaries but in the early days most got more on joining the bank than a clerk with ten years' service. One of the graduates who came into the bank in 1932 was Michael Wilson, who had been at Oriel College, Oxford, and was destined to become chief general manager in 1967. By 1939 there were thirty-four graduates in the bank. Not all of them had turned out to be high-flyers. The comments in a report on their work and ability were about what would be said of any other group of clerks: '. . . in no way outstanding', '. . . a clerk of less than average ability'; but also '. . . very intelligent', '. . . a good man'. It was not until the 1960s that Lloyds came to accept that the old ways of recruitment were no longer capable of securing sufficient school-leavers of the right calibre, and that new methods would have to be devised to attract graduates, but not until the end of the decade that a special graduate scheme was introduced with a salary differential.

At the same time as the grading scheme was introduced, a new look was taken at training. In October 1929 it had been announced that men of special merit and ability were to be given opportunities to enlarge their knowledge and experience by transfer to various selected branches and head office departments, while the system of staff reports was to be improved and extended. It was, however, still very much training on the job; what is sometimes known as 'sitting by Nellie'. Beane recognised that more needed to be done. The next month he was writing that 'to young men of spirit and ambition the monotony of Banking routine work in their earlier years of service is very trying' but that it was 'quite possible . . . to make the early years of Banking more interesting and instructive'. As a result, the grading scheme introduced in May 1930 was accompanied by the outline of a course of training during a clerk's first six years in the bank. The onus was put firmly on managers, who 'will be held responsible for the efficient training in Banking duties and general office routine of the young clerks placed in their charge'. Changes in their duties, it was emphasised, would afford welcome relief to clerks engaged on purely routine work.

The next review of training was by the sub-committee of the committee on organisation and economy set up in 1931. The main emphasis of their conclusions was on the provision of sound training for all staff, as opposed to special training for selected men, with the implication that not all managers had assumed with great enthusiasm the responsibilities for training that had been put upon them in 1930. The confidence of the younger staff could not be maintained unless there were 'definite indications that these Head Office views are being carried into effect'. Reports the sub-committee received from regional groups stressed the need for clerks to move from branch to branch to gain experience: there were cases in Wales, for example, where some members of the staff had never moved and where younger men had been allowed to remain as juniors for years.

There were evidently people in the bank, and in the top echelons, who were concerned at the restricted and unsystematic way in which young men were educated to become bankers, but it was not to be until after the war that radical changes were at last made and training was no longer so dependent on the goodwill, discretion and time of managers and senior staff. Yet, the old methods did produce the men who, without having had the benefit of courses and colleges, built up the bank, and their successors who managed it in the often difficult and sometimes novel conditions of the 1950s and 1960s. To some extent, of course, it was a question of luck: having a manager who was prepared to take trouble. E. J. N. Warburton, who joined the bank in 1922 and became chief general manager in 1959, has recalled how managers could find themselves virtually 'thrown in at the deep end' and believes that now they are really trained:

. . . and they are trained in kinds of business which they won't find in their first branch. And if such business emerges they've got the training and the background so they can recognise what they might be faced with and take their chances.

There was no representation of the S.R.C. on the 1931/2 committee on staff training nor does it appear that it was asked for its views. Since it had received scant consultation about the 1929 grading system or the contributory pension scheme, that was not very remarkable. It is perhaps surprising how conciliatory the attitude of the S.R.C. remained. In 1933, an S.R.C. circular stressed that 'the Directors' policy in staff matters is fair and equitable'; in 1938 a letter from the S.R.C. referred somewhat obsequiously to 'any concessions which the Bank are able to give for an increase in remuneration'.

Rather different was the official S.R.C. attitude to the Bank Officers' Guild, which continued to be kept at arms' length. Some staff, however, became disillusioned with their bank-sponsored organisation: in 1934 a meeting of staff in Birmingham and district voted decisively for the dissolution of the S.R.C. and for the bank's employees to 'give allegiance to some more effective organisation to represent their interests'. The S.R.C. central committee rejected this line and argued there was nothing which debarred them from advocating the staff's point of view 'within the ordinary courtesies of debate'.

In February the next year Beane and Abell, the two chief general managers, felt that the 'agitation' of the B.O.G. and its allegations of staff loyalty at breaking point merited a letter to the staff. At that time, Lloyds' membership in the B.O.G. was not quite 4,900, about a third of the total staff, but it was to fall steadily to little more than 3,700 in 1939. Beane and Abell believed the S.R.C. to be 'keen, zealous and fearless in representing the interests and claims of the Staff'. They reminded the staff that the chairman at the annual general meetings in 1932 and 1933 had said that 'the Board of the Bank would not in any circumstances allow the Bank Officers' Guild, a Trade Union Organisation, to intervene between them and the Staff of the Bank' and recommended that, realising all this, the staff should give 'a loyal adherence' to the Staff Representative Committee. The description of the B.O.G. as a 'Trade Union Organisation' suggests that this was not how the S.R.C. was regarded. In an address to the 1912 Club in April 1935, Beaumont Pease confirmed this explicitly: 'It does seem to me out of place that members of a bank staff should be represented by an organisation on Trade Union principles, which were never intended to be applied to employment such as theirs'. All this, and much else, was to change very soon. In 1940 the S.R.C. was to transform itself into the Staff Association, which was eventually to be registered as a trade union, and there were to be proposals for joint action by the Bank Officers' Guild and the Central Council of Bank Staff Associations. This we will come to in the next chapter.

The executor and trustee and colonial and foreign departments remained throughout the 1930s the only two specialist divisions of the bank. In 1933 the first executor and trustee branch was opened in Pall Mall and by 1938 a further eight had been added. Business expanded during this period: 3,090 trusts and wills were administered in 1933, compared with 5,851 five years hence. Staff more than doubled, to 313, between these years.

For the colonial and foreign department it was a decade of growing difficulties and complexities, with the impact of fluctuating rates of exchange, the problem of German debts, the spread of exchange controls and the effects of strife and unrest in Europe and elsewhere. In 1931 foreign exchange business soared with the sterling crisis. In 1935 the Italian invasion of Ethiopia increased the risk attaching to business with Italy and credit lines for Italian banks were withdrawn. After sanctions were lifted in July 1936 (they had been imposed the previous November), facilities were partly restored, to be reduced again in 1937. In 1938, the looming crisis in Central Europe prompted colonial and foreign department to ask Czech and Polish banks to increase their exchange cover against facilities they had been granted.

The Spanish Civil War broke out in July 1936 and soon affected overseas business. The exchange control office in Spain suspended operations, which meant that Spanish banks were unable to get exchange cover for acceptances opened on their behalf. As the war dragged on, so complications grew. By 1938, the republicans held the south-east area of Spain and Catalonia, while the nationalists occupied the rest. Most of the large banks were thus divided, working in two watertight compartments according to their location and each questioning the legality of the signing powers of the other. Each case that arose had to be judged on its merits.

The greater riskiness of overseas business during this period prompted the creation of a special reserve. In 1927, £10,000 had been reserved against possible loss in connection with certain Russian accounts. Further sums were set aside, the total reserve reaching £100,000 by 1931. By now, however, the risk on the Russian accounts was considerably less as facilities had been reduced, and the reserve built up was earmarked for foreign business in general. Provision was subsequently made for a loss on various blocked holdings of securities, such as Hungarian and Chilean Treasury bills, while losses on the sale of 'registered marks' were written off. In December 1937 the reserve stood at £117,000 but during 1938 this was more than wiped out and subsequent losses had to be debited to head office. In the second half of 1938 the loss on registered marks alone was £150,000.

The bank had acquired such registered (or blocked) marks as a result of the successive Standstill Agreements with Germany of the 1930s. The Austrian banking crisis of May 1931 shook confidence in the ability of German banks to meet the considerable obligations they had incurred abroad, in London mostly acceptance credits against which bills could be drawn. The substantial facilities granted by British banks were partly the result of an agreement made with their German opposite numbers after the first world war. In 1914 the German banks ceased business in London and, at the end of the war, they offered to keep their branches closed in return for credit lines from British banks.

In September 1931 the first Standstill Agreement was signed by the German banks and representatives of banking groups in the U.S.A., U.K., France, and eight other countries, aimed at preventing a large-scale withdrawal of facilities by these banks and at providing for some run-down in the total outstanding. London's acceptance credits then amounted to £54m., of which Lloyds' share was £1.2m. In addition, Lloyds had loans of £834,000 outstanding, also subsequently paid off largely in registered marks. R. H. Brand and F. C. Tiarks, a partner in Schröders, headed the British delegation to the negotiations that produced the agreement. W. H. Taylor, chief manager of colonial and foreign department, spent several weeks in Berlin working on the details, with his assistant manager, J. B. Brutsch.

Fresh agreements were signed in following years, with Germany's indebtedness correspondingly reduced, to a significant extent by her creditors being paid in registered marks. These could be sold only at a considerable discount, which widened at times to 50%. Substantial losses were thus incurred on such sales. The outbreak of war froze all German debts and it was not until 1952 that the next attempt was made to clear up the hang-over from the 1931 crisis. Lloyds' interest in standstill debt now stood at £660,000. The 1952 agreement provided for the 'recommercialisation' of debt: in effect, creditors received payment of standstill debts to the extent that facilities of an equivalent amount were granted to German banks. A protocol drawn up in 1954, repeating pre-war procedure, was extended six times. In October 1961, thirty years on, the last standstill debt was paid off.[14]

Mechanisation

From the beginnings of banking in England in the seventeenth century to the 1920s methods of conducting the essential operations of book-keeping and accounting hardly changed. Typewriters and adding machines had appeared behind bank counters before 1914, it is true, but accounts were still kept in ledgers posted by hand, as they had been two centuries previously. Little had altered, except that quill pens were no longer used and standards of calligraphy were not so uniformly high. Machinery came relatively late to banking, but no later than in other service industries. The impetus, as elsewhere, was two-fold: increasing business and rising costs. As always, too, there were those who saw only the difficulties. Were loose-leaf ledgers as secure as bound books?—they could be made to be. Would customers accept statements in place of handwritten pass books?—they could be persuaded to.

By early 1928 a machine had been developed that would post entries on an account and strike a balance. In January the following year Lloyds started to mechanise its book-keeping and a mechanisation department was set up to supervise the change-over and to research into and develop accounting-machine systems. The process continued until the advent of electronic methods after the war; the last branch mechanised was West

---

[14] An excellent account of the standstill agreements as they affected London is given in R. S. Sayers, *The Bank of England 1891-1944* Volume 2, pp. 503-12.

Wickham in December 1962. The original programme was to mechanise branches with a staff of twenty or over, but this limit was soon reduced to fifteen and still lower in later years. In addition to the book-keeping of customers' accounts, 'waste sheets' and other control records were progressively mechanised.

By the end of 1929 City Office and five other branches had switched over and, a year later, the new methods had been introduced at thirty-seven branches. It was clear that mechanisation would pay its way. Machines were being written off over five years, and for these thirty-seven branches net annual savings over this period were put at £24,000 and in subsequent years at £50,000. Six male ledger clerks, it was estimated, could be replaced by five girls working machines, at much lower salaries. Jobs had to be found for the men so displaced. Staff were not needed to man new branches: more branches were closed than opened during the 1930s. But there were always the natural wastage of death and retirement and, as we have seen, recruitment was cut to the bone in 1931–3. On the other hand, girls were now needed to operate the new machines. Women in the bank thus increased from 1,800 in December 1930 to 2,620 in December 1938, the ratio to total staff rising from 14 to 19%.

In the middle thirties, an average of twenty or so branches a year were mechanised, the total at the end of 1938 reaching 218. It was not always easy at first, particularly in the larger branches, to produce a properly integrated system, with all the machines used to their full capacity. There had been an experiment in the early days in which accounts were divided into large and small and mechanisation restricted only to the larger active accounts. As might have been expected, confusion resulted and the idea was soon abandoned. Centralisation schemes were also tested, with a central office doing the book-keeping for a number of branches. But the results were unsatisfactory, branches having to provide too much data and the experiments were ended.

Another experiment made in 1938 was more successful. Since Cox's were taken over in 1923 Pall Mall branch had continued to have a large and important Army connection but, without some radical changes, it looked unlikely to be able to handle the increased volume of business that would accompany an outbreak of war. The use of Powers Samas card tabulating machines was therefore tried and quickly proved its worth. In one operation, for example, they could post a minimum of 800 entries an hour, against only seventy-five if done by hand, while there were also substantial savings in costs. The project was given the go-ahead, but not until 1941 was it fully in operation throughout the branch.

With the outbreak of war further mechanisation came to a halt. In the next few years machines already installed were overworked and their servicing was often poor. By 1946 many of them were due for replacement, but the dollar shortage restricted imports. The total number of branches mechanised in December 1947 had risen to 257, only thirty-nine more than in 1938.

Early in 1949 managers were told that 'the policy of the bank is to mechanise to the full extent that economy and efficiency justify' and by the end of the year the total was up to 364, still only about a third of all full branches. The outbreak of the Korean war six months later, in June 1950, prompted a look at what duplication methods were available to the bank in an emergency and special cameras were subsequently supplied to five large provincial branches. The programme was pressed ahead, however, and by the summer of 1952 some 470 offices were mechanised, a total that increased steadily during the 1950s. The last link with the old traditional handwritten methods was broken in December 1962.

In the meantime, a step had been taken towards electronic accounting with the introduction of 'post-tronic' machines. In 1960 Lloyds became the first English bank to instal such equipment, capable of posting entries on ledger sheets and statements simultaneously by means of a magnetic 'memory sheet'. About 100 of these machines were introduced in 1961/2 at some fifty branches, all of which were withdrawn by the end of 1970. By then all branches had taken a further giant step forward, into the age of computers.

The War

Planning for war

This is not a general history, so that there will be no attempt here to deal in any way with the political and other developments in Europe and elsewhere in the late 1930s. The first organised attempt to consider how to keep the bank functioning if war should break out was made in 1937, when a small committee was set up to study the problems likely to be faced and to suggest ways of meeting them. It soon became apparent that, if the bank were to continue to be able to provide customers with banking facilities, two measures were vital given the probability of air attack: to decentralise certain control functions and to ensure the duplication of key records. On decentralisation, the removal of head office in Lombard Street to elsewhere in the country was not envisaged, except as part of a general move of government, although if head office were so badly damaged as to make it uninhabitable then clearly a shift would have to be made. Apart from this, detailed plans for decentralisation were drawn up.

Much thought was given to the likely consequences of air attack. As early as August 1936 members of premises department had discussed the question and later Pritchard, then assistant premises secretary, began a detailed study. In March 1938 he presented his seventy-three page report, a thorough and carefully documented review of all aspects of A.R.P. By the summer a scheme had been worked out, based on Pritchard's recommendations. Next, arrangements were made for branches in the vulnerable parts of the country in the south, south-east and midlands to send essential and duplicate records to 'custodian branches', in the main those west of a line from the centre of Northumberland to West Sussex, excluding the thickly-populated industrial areas. These branches, thought less liable to suffer from bombing than those in the eastern areas, were normally to be custodian for more than one branch: Witney, in Oxfordshire, for example, was custodian for five branches.

Similar problems, of course, faced most City institutions and discussions were put on foot with the other clearing banks on questions of co-operation and mutual assistance in the event of war. A War Preparations Report was the outcome, covering such topics as the clearings, duplication of records and competition. 'All ordinary competition between Banks', it was decided, 'will cease entirely.' It was also thought that the use of bank offices as public shelters was inappropriate and should be 'discouraged and refused'. A different policy had been adopted in the 1914-18 war when, during air-raids, the banks provided shelter and, indeed, could if they wished keep their counters open. But, of course, the scale of the problem this time was likely to be altogether different. The Bank of England was also concerned, particularly as the note-issuing authority, and the banks were asked in 1938 to provide storage space for emergency supplies of currency in certain towns and suburbs; Lloyds was to supply such accommodation in Norwich, Nottingham, Swansea, and Watford.

In May 1938, Lloyds' staff received a first circular, 'not issued in an alarmist spirit', outlining some elementary precautions regarding staff and records that would have to be taken in what was hoped was 'the very remote contingency of war'. In a short time, however, these precautions were given a trial run in the Munich crisis. In late August work started on duplicating records, numbering accounts and preparing schedules of names, addresses and so on. A month later the full scheme of duplication was brought into operation; daily sheets of entries were sent to custodian branches and other returns were to be sent fortnightly or periodically. All this lasted only a few days, until the return of Mr. Chamberlain from Munich on Sunday 30 September 1938. The scheme was now put on ice. Some 140 staff who had been called-up also returned to the bank.

By early next year preparations to meet war were largely complete. In head office, shelter accommodation was ready for about 1,200 people in the basement strong rooms, where a special ventilation system was now installed; auxiliary lighting plant had been obtained; over 200 people trained in first aid and fire-fighting; and essential supplies had been stored: rubber boots, oilskin gloves, hundreds of buckets, and the rest. In the branches, the custodian system had been tested and had proved itself. All arrangements had been made for the protection of staff, except for provision of gas-proof rooms, but elaborate precautions were not considered necessary for this. Under the Civil Defence Act, 1939, all owners of commercial buildings in specified areas employing more than fifty people had to provide air-raid shelters. In 1938/9 the bank spent some £50,000 on this work, with another £66,000 for other precautions, such as the protection of windows and black-out arrangements. Pritchard's fertile mind invented a ceiling escape mechanism which enabled the bank's strong rooms to be used as air-raid shelters, and fifty were in time installed.

Decentralisation had been arranged and billeting plans worked out. The chief general management was to stay in Lombard Street, together with certain head office departments whose presence was necessary in London—the treasurer and legal department, for example—but the bank's registered office was to be moved to Salisbury. In 1939 there were four joint general managers. One (Gold), responsible for London, was to stay in Lombard Street, while the other three (Cherrington, Johns, and Stanley), together with elements of advance department, were to be stationed in Halifax, Northampton, and Salisbury, to control branches in their respective areas. Administration, staff department and the chief inspector were to move to Swindon. The club-house at the bank's sports ground at Beckenham was to house part of the chief accountant's department, and other staff were to accompany the move of the central clearing house to Trentham, in Staffordshire. Colonial and foreign department had to stay in London, but this was not necessary in the case of the executor and trustee department. This was to move to Ewhurst Place, near Cranleigh, a large medieval-style house built at the end of the nineteenth century that the bank had bought for £2,400.

It says much for the careful thought and planning that went into making these arrangements that in September 1939 they were put into operation virtually unchanged. The general managers, their staffs and other officials left for their war-time homes, and seven large removal vans left the executor and trustee department in Threadneedle Street for Ewhurst Place. The staff of the chief accountant's department did not, however, move to Beckenham. As was to be expected, problems arose over billeting but these were gradually resolved. Clerks leaving London received £5 to cover the cost of their first fortnight's billeting and out-of-pocket expenses, the billeting charge of £1. 1s. (£1·05) being based on the government's figure for a week's bed, breakfast, and supper. If officials who moved to the country had to stay in hotels, then the bank footed the bill for the first few weeks and thereafter they received a weekly allowance. Some, in time, bought or rented houses.

While the main board continued to function in Lombard Street during the war (sometimes in the vaults) three committees of directors were appointed in August 1939 to meet in Halifax, Northampton, and Salisbury. Each had all the powers of the board to manage the current business of the bank in its area, except to grant very large overdraft facilities. However, the Halifax committee met for only a month or so after the outbreak of war, while the Northampton committee subsequently moved to Birmingham, where it overlapped with the existing Birmingham local committee. Of the other local committees, that at Liverpool continued to operate during the war, the Newcastle committee closed down when its two members left for war service, while the old

Capital and Counties and Salisbury committees were now largely nominal bodies.

The bank entered the war with two chief general managers who had only recently taken over the top executive jobs: R. A. Wilson and Sydney Parkes were appointed together when Abell retired at the end of 1938, and elected to the board in 1941. Wilson went on until the end of 1944 when, on his retirement, he was appointed a vice-chairman, until his death in 1955; while Parkes continued on his own for another year to December 1945, when he retired to become chairman of The National Bank of New Zealand. He remained on Lloyds' board until 1955 and died in 1961. The characters of the two men were quite dissimilar, Wilson intellectual and reflective, Parkes dynamic and thrusting, a good combination, as it happened, to lead their staff in the demanding circumstances of war. Wilson in 1898 had joined William Williams, Brown & Co. of Leeds, in which his father was a partner and which merged with Lloyds in 1900. After a career in Yorkshire and the midlands he came to head office in 1924. Cultivated and charming, he was interested in the theory of banking and was president of the Institute of Bankers in 1937-9. Parkes started in Manchester in 1894 at £12 a year with Cunliffe, Brooks & Co., which also joined up with Lloyds in 1900. He was indefatigable, ambitious, and revelled in hard work. He was knighted in 1946 for his work during the war in promoting savings.

The bank keeps going

When the war started A. H. Ensor, then assistant general manager in charge of administration, promised the chairman, now Lord Wardington, that with the help of his two assistants (F. O. Faull and R. T. Fagan) and the premises secretary, F. Pritchard, he would try to keep the business of the bank going. This, with their assistance and backed up by his colleagues, he did. In 1941 Ensor was promoted to be a joint general manager and in 1946 became a chief general manager. When we reach that point in the story will be a suitable time to consider the career of this eminent banker. For the moment, we must return to 1939.

There was no attempt, as in the first world war, to maintain London as an open financial centre. The bank's operations were circumscribed, on the one hand, by exchange control and, on the other, by restrictions on advances. No great importance was attached by the authorities to the interest rate as an instrument of monetary policy. Bank Rate had been raised from 2 to 4% on 24 August but was reduced to 3% a month later and to 2% on 26 October, where it remained right through and after the war. Economic policy was largely effected through budgetary measures and physical controls. This was the general environment in which banks had to operate.

In the spring of 1939 the clearing banks had agreed that, on the outbreak of war, all 'ordinary competition' between them would cease entirely. The day after war was declared Lloyds' managers were advised accordingly. No attempt was to be made to attract business by under-cutting overdraft rates. Routine work was also cut down and various returns branches had to make to head office discontinued. Other changes also became necessary. Hours of business were shortened from 09.00–15.30 to 10.00–14.00,[1] with Saturday morning opening cut by a half-hour. The Bankers' Clearing House moved to Trentham and all the clearing sections (town, metropolitan, etc.) merged into one clearing, branches sending a daily composite remittance. For City branches, however, certain local clearing arrangements were made.

Immediately, men began to be called up, although not in great numbers at first. Under the National Services Act of September 1939 the upper age for conscription was forty-one years (raised in 1941 to fifty-one) but for banking, as for certain other occupations, the Ministry of Labour set up a special scheme to consider the deferment of bank officers whose work was believed to be essential. By December 1939 just over 1,600 Lloyds' men were serving in the Forces. This was the beginning of the rapid recruitment of women. In December 1938 there were 2,620 women on the staff (19% of the total). Over the next twelve months 960 women joined the bank, raising the total to 3,580, just over a quarter of all employees. Managers now had authority to recruit staff themselves, if necessary to keep their branches going, without reference to head office.

In late September 1939 the Chancellor, Sir John Simon, wrote to the Governor, Montagu Norman, pointing out that the prohibition on the export of capital and restrictions on the public issue of new capital for domestic use were aimed at conserving the country's savings exclusively for government purposes. This was not to be frustrated by any increase in bank lending. Simon thus asked for 'the prompt restriction of all advances', except for armament needs, exports (including the mining of more coal) and agriculture. This request was passed on by Norman to the London clearing bankers, who informed him that the policy outlined by Simon would be 'loyally observed'. A month later, in October, a gloss was added, when the banks were asked to grant advances as freely as possible to contractors undertaking essential war work. The speed-up in production by the spring of 1940 meant, for many firms, a sudden increase in their wages bill and managers were instructed that no wages cheque was to be

---

[1] In May 1941 this became 14.30 and in April 1942 was extended again to 15.00.

refused for any customer working directly or indirectly on government account.

It was recognised that, whatever the bank did, some advances would inevitably fall away during the war; office construction and house-building were obvious examples where less finance would be called for. In the spring of 1940 there were vague complaints, particularly from firms in aircraft production, that the banks were not being sufficiently helpful. The firms in question may possibly have not been used to dealing with banks or already had large overdrafts. In any event, managers were reminded that the bank was pledged to support firms on war work 'even beyond the canons of prudent banking practice'. All reasonable support was to be given to customers, and managers were urged to be generous rather than strict. After the long years of depression, of poor earnings or actual losses, some customers were now experiencing 'an unusual feeling of prosperity', which might lead them into extravagance and managers were warned to be on their guard. In the summer of 1940, however, there were other more urgent questions than customers possibly spending too freely.

On 10 May Germany invaded the Low Countries, and four days later broke through at Sedan. The evacuation from Dunkirk soon followed, starting on 27 May, and the next day the Belgian forces capitulated. The French campaign was soon over. On 22 June a new French government under Pétain concluded an armistice with the Germans. Northern France and all her Atlantic coastline was now in enemy hands. Refugees were reaching south coast ports and occasionally presenting branches with unusual problems. Among those fleeing from Belgium who landed at Hastings at the end of May were the managing director and chief engineer of the Belgian National Railways, who deposited two suitcases with Hastings branch said to contain 13.4m. Belgian francs (about £560,000), the property of the Belgian railways. Again, when the Holland-Amerika liner *Volendam* berthed at Tilbury some of her officers wished to open an account at a local branch with the £8,000 or so the crew had between them, pending their hoped-for emigration to the U.S.A. Following the refugees could well be the Germans. An attempted invasion of England looked imminent.

This was clearly a time for concerted action by the banks. By the end of May their representatives were meeting virtually every day in the Lombard Street offices of the Committee of London Clearing Bankers, to consider especially the position of branches in the coastal areas where the enemy was expected to land. On Saturday 1 June there was an all-day meeting at the Bank of England with representatives of the Treasury and other interested government departments, at which Charles Lidbury of the Westminster Bank represented the clearers, and continued on Sunday at the Treasury. A number of decisions were soon put into effect. All bearer bonds, life policies, guarantees, and security deeds were moved from about 290 Lloyds' branches in a band roughly twenty miles from the coast stretching from Portland in the south to Alnwick in Northumberland to more inland branches. In Kent, however, this applied to all branches except eight. Should invasion come, branches in this twenty-mile band might have to be evacuated and 'foster branches' were designated to which they could move. At this time, therefore, such a branch could have four different inland branches to which it was linked: for the custody of duplicate records, of bearer securities, of general securities (sometimes the same as for bearer securities), and to act as a foster branch in the event of compulsory evacuation. Thus, Bognor Regis branch was linked to Port Dinorwic (duplicates), Newbury (bearer securities), Malvern (general securities), and Bedford (foster branch). As regards the Channel Islands, just before the German occupation (30 June), the banks were officially told to burn all their bearer bonds. After discussion, however, the banks agreed to ignore this instruction and all such bonds were shipped to the mainland together with other securities. What happened afterwards in the Channel Islands is told later in this chapter.

On 24 June, with invasion seemingly imminent, official notices were put up in nineteen coastal towns stretching from Great Yarmouth, in Norfolk, round to Hythe, in Kent, telling the inhabitants what to do if evacuation became necessary (of about 90% of their normal population). The clearing banks decided that, in such an event, certain so-called 'remaining branches' would continue to be open, with a quarter of their normal staff. Their business would, of course, be very restricted, not much more than cashing cheques and receiving credits. Eleven Lloyds' branches were so designated: at Birchington, Broadstairs, Dover, Felixstowe, Folkestone, Harwich, Hythe, Margate, Ramsgate, Southend, Westcliff-on-Sea. At the same time, branches of all banks in the nineteen towns were instructed to disperse their business, where possible, to inland areas. Lloyds' managers in these towns, and in a number of other vulnerable parts of the south-east, were told to transfer accounts of customers who had moved away or intended to go. Twelve more towns were subsequently added to the original nineteen. By the spring of 1941, however, invasion had become less likely but, even so, the population of these thirty-one coastal towns remained much reduced. The number of 'remaining branches' was pruned and by the autumn of 1942 Lloyds had only four: at Dovercourt,

Hastings, Margate, and Worthing. There were no further changes until these arrangements were ended in November 1944.

A similar plan was drawn up for overseas business. All exchange transactions were to be concentrated in the best-equipped branch in a particular area, which would be the only one to maintain foreign currency accounts and to undertake foreign exchange business. Of eight centres in which such business was to be concentrated Lloyds was the nominated branch in two: at Bristol and Newcastle upon Tyne.

In the summer of 1940 active Army operations in England seemed a distinct possibility and in June banknotes, usually amounting to £10,000, were sent to a number of Lloyds branches (at first thirty but increased later) to be held as a special reserve as part of a War Office scheme to provide cash for service requirements. Similar amounts were sent to branches of the other big four clearing banks, so that the reserve in each town was £50,000. One bank was selected to be the first Army mobile cashiers would approach for cash—nine of Lloyds branches were in this category—and the War Office was given the names and addresses of local managers so that, in case of need, Army cashiers could contact them after normal banking hours. The country might be invaded but banking hours would be as usual! A scheme to provide funds for the Home Guard, should it be mustered, was also worked out by 1941. Each unit would need to buy food for a few days and to help members who had lost earnings. The banks were thus authorised to open accounts to provide £1 a head for each unit mustering, plus £4 on the fifth day thereafter, the funds to be recouped from the War Office. In 1942 the two payments were combined and slightly increased, and in March 1945 the arrangements were cancelled.

Later in the war the banks were again involved with the expected cash requirements of the Army and this time, with the boot on the other foot, such needs materialised. By the end of 1943 large concentrations of British troops were in certain parts of the country and the banks arranged to open field cashiers' accounts at branches equipped to handle substantial drawings of cash. The first such account with Lloyds was opened at Tunbridge Wells branch in January 1944 and by August another twenty-one accounts had been opened at branches in southern England. In September, with relatively few troops now in England, the scheme was suspended.

Such were the measures the bank took and planned to take to meet the threat of invasion. In a wider sphere, there was the regional civil defence organisation that had been set up in February 1939. Twelve regional capitals were designated and twelve regional commissioners appointed, who were to function only when communications broke down, or central government ceased to operate or martial law was declared. Each had a small staff, among whom was a banking adviser. Of these, two advisers were Lloyds' men: the manager of Collingwood Street branch, Newcastle upon Tyne, for the northern region and the manager of Corn Street branch, Bristol, for the south-west region. If orders had been given to evacuate an area, staff of branches were to pack up, parcel up cash, securities, cheque books, and so on, lock up the safes and report to the regional control office. Special passes were issued, transport earmarked, and emergency petrol coupons distributed. The system was never activated. The regional commissioners never wielded their powers, the two Lloyds' managers were never asked for their advice.

An ordeal, nevertheless, was faced in a few months by the people of Britain. In July and August a few branches were damaged by bombs, mainly their glass and plaster, but it was not until the blitz on London later in the year that losses became severe. At the beginning of the war Lloyds had some 2,000 separate buildings of all kinds, from full branches, clerk-in-charge offices to sundry properties of one kind or another. The first 'incident' recorded was on 19 June 1940 at Millbrook, a sub-branch to Shirley branch, Hampshire, and in all there were to be 1,424 such incidents, of which 641 involved damage or destruction. Thirty-two branches were destroyed, most by fire caused by incendiary bombs, but in only two cases did this include the strong rooms. In all the others, the contents of strong rooms survived in reasonably good condition. Damage to contents, however, was sometimes caused by water, from fire-hoses or burst mains.

In the London blitz an unfortunate chain of circumstances occurred at Belgrave Road branch, which received a direct hit in September 1940. The strong-room walls of reinforced concrete were only slightly cracked, but the explosion caused the water main and drainage sewer in the roadway to burst, the branch basement was flooded and the strong room filled with water and sewage. As a result of unavoidable delay in clearing up, some of the staff contracted skin diseases and other illnesses from the sewage, which lasted in a few cases until well after the war. In the next few weeks, a number of branches in the City and elsewhere in London were very severely damaged or destroyed: Monument, High Holborn, Old Street, Fore Street, Clapham, Lower Addiscombe Road in Croydon, and others. At the last, a safe weighing some seven cwts. was blown about fifty feet and the back came off, scattering £300 of silver; at Fore Street, fire burned for several days; bombs at Park Royal, in North London, completely destroyed the bank's stationery stocks. In head office several hundred people worked, slept and were fed; under a fire officer, two fire squads were on duty every night, each with nine members, and doing a turn of duty every fortnight. Later, in the summer of 1941, representatives of the City Corporation visited head office and, after a survey, concluded that the fire-fighting and other precautionary measures were the best they had seen, and arrangements were made for visits from other firms in the City.

In the meantime, German attacks had now spread to other parts of the country. The cry occasionally heard during the war 'It's one of ours' was certainly true at Parks branch, Liverpool, which in November 1940 got a direct hit from a 500 lb. English bomb that had been captured a few months previously by the Germans in France. In January 1941 the great naval port of Portsmouth suffered extensive damage and branches at Palmerston Road, Southsea, High Street, Portsmouth, and Portsea were destroyed. The premises of the main branch at Commercial Road, Portsmouth, were so badly damaged by fire as to be unusable and, for a time, business was carried on at North End branch and in accommodation provided by Barclays Bank and the local Inspector of Taxes, an example of the ready and willing help that was then everywhere so evident. After the war, new premises were built, opened in October 1955 and designed by Sir John Burnett, Tait and Partners, one of the two firms of architects which had been responsible for the new head office in the 1920s.

March 1941 saw the other great naval base at Plymouth come under attack, in which the main branch in Bedford Street was destroyed. The branch at Stonehouse, however, survived the bombing and, standing in an area of devastation, continued in business throughout the war. It stands today, the oldest bank branch in Plymouth still in its original premises where business started in 1877. With peace, the centre of Plymouth was completely rebuilt and in December 1957 the Lord Mayor opened the new Lloyds' branch on Royal Parade.

In May 1942 the greater part of the business centre of Exeter was similarly destroyed. Fire gutted Lloyds' branch, but business was started in the basement of Rowe Brothers, a local firm, while the administrative section moved to Crediton branch, eight miles away. Again, there was much rebuilding after the war, and in October 1953 a new building was opened to house the branch and the Devon and Cornwall district office.

These cities, Exeter, Liverpool, Plymouth, and Portsmouth, were among the many places where the bank's premises suffered damage or destruction. In all of them, duplication of records and the system of custodian branches proved their worth: customers' accounts could soon be reconstructed. A great help was provided by six portable generators that had been prudently bought before the war. When electricity supplies were cut off, one of the generators was rushed to a branch and light and power soon restored. Much has been written about the home front during the war and of the resilient morale of the people. Lloyds' staff were no exception. Managers faced the extraordinary problems of war-time banking with ingenuity and courage. Some kind of service was provided for customers, somehow and somewhere. There was only one instance where a manager's nerve temporarily gave way as a result of the bombing: he telephoned head office to say he was closing his branch and bringing his staff, cash, and securities to London. He was gently told to think it over for an hour and to telephone again. By then he had recovered his balance. The last branch to suffer damage was at Bognor Regis in December 1945, caused by the explosion of a sea mine.

Under the War Damage Act 1941, the bank was liable to pay premiums on its properties. Business undertakings were compulsorily levied at 10% of the annual valuation as assessed for Schedule A plus an extra premium for moveable assets. Over the period 1941–5 Lloyds paid £274,000 to the War Damage Commission. Although essential repairs to buildings and plant could be done at once, in general compensation was not normally paid until after the war. Lloyds' total claims for destroyed and damaged properties came to about £736,000, together with a further £169,000 in respect of contents, all settled by the beginning of 1964. Actual expenditure during the war on putting damage right had been minimal, only £72,000 over the whole six years 1940–5, and of this half was in 1941. Other premises expenditure, on maintenance, redecoration, and so on, came virtually to a halt. The cost of A.R.P. became less as the years went on: from £140,000 in 1940 to £33,000 in 1943, and by then this was mainly for meal allowances, overtime, and fire-watching expenses.

Deposits and the total number of accounts (apart from a dip in 1940) increased each year during the war. Deposits doubled, from £435m. in December 1939 to £869m. in December 1945, but, with the steady rise in prices, the growth in 'real terms' was less than two-fifths. Most of the increase was in current accounts, deposit balances growing very much less. In 1939 current account balances averaged 55% of total deposits, rising to a peak of 72% in 1945 and 1946.

In number, current accounts increased by 269,000 over these years, while the number of deposit accounts declined by 21,000. In September 1941, in view of rising costs and the difficulties of employing funds remuneratively, managers were asked to examine all allowances on current accounts. It was hoped that customers could be persuaded to accept an end to such allowances or, at least, to agree to keep a minimum monthly balance. Not until December 1945, however, did the clearing banks agree to end all interest arrangements as regards current accounts.

One branch, 6 Pall Mall, accounted for approaching a third of the increase in current accounts for the whole bank, reflecting the war-time expansion in the Army business it had inherited from Cox & Co. Current accounts more than doubled in number, from 51,000 in 1939 to a peak of 127,300 at the end of the war, but that was far fewer than in the first world war when, at one time, Cox's had 250,000 such accounts. Staff increased from 700 on the outbreak of war to a peak of 2,000 in 1941/2, with the pressure on accommodation such that some departments had to move elsewhere. The influx of newly commissioned officers became so great that for several months the Army pay department worked a seven-day week. Much of this work as an Army Agent, shared with Glyn, Mills & Co., was unremunerative and early in 1941 giving it up was considered, which would have ended an appointment first made in 1758. But, on reflection, it was decided to continue. An Army Agent had prestige; the agency was important to the bank in India; and it brought business to other branches of the bank.

Such buoyant activity was certainly not true of lending, the main earning asset. At the annual general meeting in February 1940 Lord Wardington, while recognising the general uncertainty, was 'inclined to think we shall see a greater demand for accommodation in the future'. Twelve months later, however, when advances had gone down, not up, he acknowledged that he had not 'sufficiently foreseen to what a large extent peace-time banking would come to a stop with the outbreak of war'. Lending continued to decline each year, from £176m. in December 1939 (41% of deposits) coming down to £129m. at the end of 1944 (less than 16% of deposits). 'Our deposits go up by leaps and bounds', wrote Parkes, one of the two chief general managers, in 1941, 'our advances go down and our perplexity is to know how to employ our liquid resources.' Lending continued to be restricted, of course, to accord with official policy as set out in the Chancellor's letter of September, 1939. Even farmers, one of the exempted categories, with higher incomes showed no great inclination to borrow more. Customers seriously affected by the war were often treated gently: borrowing rates might be reduced or charges temporarily suspended. In April 1943 the manager's discretionary limit for granting an advance was raised to a minimum of £250 from the figure of £100 fixed in 1920, although there had since been a number of exceptions. This was sensible. More loans approved by managers cut down on paper work at head office.

Government control was pervasive, lending was reduced, risks were less: bad debt provisions in 1942 were down to £27,000 from nearly £100,000 in 1940. In respect of lending, therefore, whatever other difficulties it caused, the war brought a significant lessening in the problems for management. For Parkes, in 1941, 'because of the Government hand in every channel of life, almost in complete control of industry and the main customer of industry, banking is easy'. It was the call-up of staff, the bombing of branches and inflation that worried him. Again, in 1943, 'today we have few problems—lending is easy and the work is light'. This meant acute frustration for a man with Parkes's restless energy—'I sometimes wish I had more to do than I have on many days at present'— which found at least a partial outlet in helping to organise the various City of London Savings Campaigns (Warship Week, Wings for Victory, Salute the Soldier).[2]

The decline in advances over the war years was more than offset by the increase in investments and, especially, in Treasury deposit receipts. The few figures in Table 8 conveniently sum up the net changes.

TABLE 8.

December £m.	1939	1945	Change
Total deposits	435	869	+434
Advances*	176	137	−39
Investments	108	221	+113
:*of which British Government securities*	*88*	*192*	*+104*
Liquid assets	144	491	+347
:*of which TDRs*	—	*290*	*+290*

* Includes items in transit.

Although the investment portfolio more than doubled during the war, as a proportion of deposits investments in 1945 were only fractionally higher, at 26%, than in 1939, at 25%. The really great increase, both absolutely and relatively, was in holdings of Treasury deposit receipts.

T.D.R.s alone, in December 1945, represented a third of deposits and, with other liquid assets, well over half. T.D.R.s were introduced in July 1940, after which the banks[3] were informed each Friday of the amount the

---

[2] In the summer of 1940 over 12,000 of the bank's staff and directors contributed £7,438 towards the cost of a Spitfire, which Lord Wardington asked Lord Beaverbrook, Minister for Aircraft Production, to be named *The Black Horse*.

[3] The London clearing banks, the Scottish banks and two central banks operating in the London market: Commonwealth Bank of Australia and National Bank of Egypt.

Treasury expected to borrow in the following week. They were, in effect, Treasury bills issued on tap only to the banks. Lloyds' actual Treasury bill holdings did, indeed, decline from £63m. in December 1939 to £19m. in 1944, rising smartly to £66m. in December 1945. T.D.R.s had a tenure of 6 months, later for 5 and 7 months also, and earned $1\frac{1}{8}\%$, reduced to $\frac{5}{8}\%$ in October 1945. It was an easy way for the government to borrow, although naturally disliked by the discount houses, as it side-stepped the market. Borrowing could be arranged by a telephone call; one of the reasons for the creation of T.D.R.s was that government needs could continue to be met if invasion in 1940 had resulted in evacuation from the City and a decentralised banking system.

T.D.R.s could be redeemed against subscriptions to long-term government loans and in case of emergency, if repayment was needed to supplement cash, could be rediscounted at the Bank of England. Parkes did try once, unsuccessfully, to invoke the latter provision. Towards the end of December 1944 it looked as if the bank's cash holding would need to be buttressed. Parkes estimated a cash ratio of 10.5% at the end of the year—above the 10% level but, then, window dressing was still going on. He accordingly visited the Deputy Governor at the Bank of England (Basil Catterns) who at first saw no objection to Parkes's request. However, while they were talking, the Chief Cashier (Sir Kenneth Peppiatt) came in and took a different view. There had been only one occasion, he pointed out, when T.D.R.s had been discounted—by a Scottish bank a few years previously—the discount provision applied only to an emergency and he did not consider Parkes's request came in this category. Peppiatt thought window dressing was 'archaic' and, according to Parkes, Catterns told him Lloyds was 'too hide-bound in the matter of these traditional percentages'. In the event, Parkes worried needlessly, for the cash ratio turned out to be 11.4%.

Branches closed during the war not only because of enemy action. A number, particularly sub-branches, were shut because business had fallen off so much as to make their continued opening unprofitable. Bombing, the threat of invasion or changes in local conditions prompted the evacuation of business firms and private customers. Canterbury branch, in Kent, for example, experienced a marked fall in business, as was to be expected, and at Liverpool, with the closing of the cotton market and government control of shipping, lending in 1942 was only half the pre-war level. At Ludgate Hill branch in the City, where many customers were connected with printing and publishing, business decreased substantially as a result of government paper controls. In some cases in 1941-2 loss-making offices were closed on the same swap basis with other banks that had been agreed in the 1930s. In October 1942 the shutters came down on one of Lloyds' most historic branches when it was scheduled for demolition. This was the office, in High Street, Birmingham, to which Taylors and Lloyds, the partnership from which the bank is descended, moved in 1845 from the original premises at Dale End, Birmingham.

Other branches, in contrast, particularly those well away from the south east, saw a considerable expansion in their volume of work. At Cheltenham and at Aylesbury, for instance, there was much greater pressure, while the encouragement of farming was reflected in the considerable increase in business at Ipswich. In June 1942, a great amount of detailed work was accepted by the banks with the introduction of the clothing bank account scheme. To buy clothes required coupons as well as cash and the banks now agreed to operate 'coupon accounts' for retailers, wholesalers, and manufacturers. The Board of Trade paid a small commission for the work. Official restrictions added to the burden of many branches. There was, for example, the work associated with customers' war damage claims or arising from the introduction of foreign exchange controls.

In all, over the years 1940 to 1945, 214 offices were closed and seven opened (all but one sub-branches), making a net total of 207 closures. A number of these were reopened after the war.

The war inevitably also meant a considerable fall in the banks' traditional overseas business: the finance of exports and imports, exchange transactions, foreign security work, and so on. The volume of exports in 1943 was only a quarter of the 1937 level, and import volume was down by a third. 'Foreign business in the old sense of the term has largely, although not entirely, disappeared', reported Taylor, chief manager of colonial and foreign department, in 1942. There was, of course, the work caused by defence regulations but this brought in little income and was regarded as part of the bank's contribution to the war effort. Towards the end of the war things began to pick up. The overseas branch at Birmingham in November 1944 was getting many enquiries from customers wanting to resume business with Belgium and France; at Northampton foreign customers were 'clamouring for goods' from local engineering firms. Elsewhere, however, exchange transactions dropped off at some branches as allied troops moved to the Continent after the Normandy landings: at Tidworth (Americans), Bury St. Edmunds (Poles), Horsham (Canadians).

The bank was still in business in the war years, even if to a degree on a make-do-and-mend basis. Each branch had a salvage officer, responsible for collecting paper and old forms, obsolete rubber stamps (the brass mounts fetched 1/- (5p) per pound in 1940), bits of string, and old pen nibs. But the call to the bank was not always so mundane. In 1943 Whitley-Jones, then a joint general manager, became involved, albeit in a relatively minor way, with the preparations for what was known as *Operation Mincemeat*.

By the beginning of the year the Allies had secured the whole of North Africa and the next obvious target to present itself, to the Germans as to the Allies, was Sicily. But what if the Germans could be deceived into believing that this was not the Allies' next aim but that they planned, instead, to invade Sardinia and Corsica and Greece? The story of how the Germans were in fact so completely deceived has been told by Ewen Montagu in *The Man Who Never Was*, an absorbing account of an operation that 'succeeded beyond our wildest dreams'.[4]

At the end of April 1943 a body purporting to be that of 'Major William Martin', Royal Marines, was floated ashore at Huelva in the south of Spain, carrying specially written letters from Sir Archibald Nye, Vice-Chief of the Imperial General Staff, and Lord Louis Mountbatten which appeared to leave no doubt that an invasion was planned, not in Sicily, but in the Western and Eastern Mediterranean. Major Martin also carried a number of other papers and letters. Among these was the following letter which one of Montagu's group planning *Operation Mincemeat* had obtained:

Lloyds Bank Limited, Head Office, London, E.C.3.

Private   14 April, 1943

Major W. Martin, RM,
Army & Navy Club,
Pall Mall,
London SW1.

Dear Sir,

I am given to understand that in spite of repeated application your overdraft amounting to £79. 19s. 2d. still outstands.

In the circumstances, I am now writing to inform you that unless this amount, plus interest at 4% to date of payment, is received forthwith we shall have no alternative but to take the necessary steps to protect our interests.

Yours faithfully,
(Signed) E. WHITLEY-JONES
Joint General Manager.

---

[4] Lord Ismay, in his Foreword to Mr. Montagu's book, first published by Evans Brothers Limited in 1953.

This letter was drafted personally by Whitley-Jones and typed in his office but it seems rather surprising that he should have signed it and not a less senior official. Would a general manager of a bank really write such a threatening letter to a serving officer for a so comparatively small sum? Montagu in fact raised this question but was assured that, although such a letter was usually signed by a branch manager, it could sometimes come from head office. And, of course, in this particular case the fewer the people in the know the better. However, none of the Germans who subsequently read it apparently knew enough about the ways of English banks to suspect anything unusual. To deceive the German High Command, Montagu concludes, 'was nothing like as difficult as it was to persuade their British opposite numbers that we could do that'.[5]

The call-up of staff was a continuing worry for management. At first, there was only a relatively small decline in the number of men. While over 2,700 left for the Forces in 1940, the number at work in the bank dropped by only 370 as temporaries, pensioners, and others took their place. At the same time, increasing numbers of women were coming in, and during 1940 nearly 1,200 were recruited. By December 1940 women represented about a third of the total staff. In 1941 the pace quickened: the number of men fell by almost 1,000, those serving with the Forces increased to 3,990, while a further 1,300 women joined the bank. There had been some concern at the beginning of the year at the number of men who had joined the Home Guard. So many senior men had signed on that, if there were an emergency and they were called up, some branches would be unable to carry on. The problem was left to managers to deal with.

October 1942 saw the publication of the report of the Kennett Committee, whose objective had been to see how far manpower in banking and finance could be further released. The committee found that already more than half of the pre-war male staffs of the banks had been called up and it had relatively few suggestions for further reductions. Amalgamation of banks was ruled out, as it would take too long to bring much saving in labour; greater mechanisation was impossible, as no new machines could be obtained. On the other hand, further closing of branches was suggested, and yet fewer non-essential returns and statistics, while the committee also recommended that 500 of the 4,350 men of military age in the clearing banks who had been deferred should be immediately released.

For Lloyds, as for the other banks, this meant the call-up of a number of key men. By the end of 1942 over 5,000 Lloyds' men were serving with the Forces. The male staff working in the bank at 7,700 was 1,450 fewer than in December 1941, while a further 320 women had joined, to total 6,380. This marked the peak for the number of women in the bank during the war. In the next two years the number of men continued to fall, to 6,990 in December 1944, when women totalled 6,260, 3,640 more than in 1938. This represented the highest ratio of staff, at over 47%, seen in these years.

Throughout the bank, whether in branches or head office departments, there was thus an increasing dependence during the war on temporary staff who, many of them women, in conditions that were often difficult and sometimes dangerous could be given only the minimum of training. A number took to the work well and helped the bank, in more ways than one: counters became more attractive with the appearance of young women as cashiers. By 1944 the mid-year balance was completed with 'exceptionally few errors', which meant head office's work was thus made 'much less troublesome than it has been for some years'. To a limited extent, the bank was able to draw on the experience of pensioners, over 400 of whom returned to work during the war. There was also some of the staff of the 'auxiliary' who managed to get away from France in June 1940. However, these were only a small offset to the number of skilled and trained men who left for the Forces.

In London, particularly, it was not always easy to get staff. In March 1945 managers of country branches were asked if they could find volunteers willing to come to London from their own staffs, replacing them by temporary men and women recruited locally. Such volunteers could sleep and have breakfast in head office if they could find nowhere else to stay, and get a special allowance of £1 a week and their fare home once a fortnight. This was the fore-runner of a regular system of 'provincial volunteers' that, from 1951 onwards, was introduced to help to ease staff shortages in London.

Salary scales remained unchanged during the war as, indeed they had since 1921, apart from the grading scheme introduced in 1929. Men who had joined the bank before the war under this scheme had been required to pass the Institute of Bankers' examinations to progress from one grade to another but, after 1941, this condition was suspended. Study was difficult in wartime, but some also questioned examinations as a measure of ability. Salaries were grossed-up in 1943 when, this time after discussion with the staff association, the bank stopped paying the staff's income tax. Grants-in-aid, in addition to salaries, were paid to meet the rising cost of living, while men and women who had joined the bank before 1929 still continued to receive the old bonus. There was still no proper system of overtime payment. In 1943, however, a meal allowance of 2/6d. (12½p) was introduced, for work after 1900 hours (and more for work after 2100 hours and on Saturday afternoons), in 1944 increased for more senior staff. After 1943, too, some offices were individually authorised to pay overtime for special work of an urgent nature. Meal allowances continued until 1960, when they were replaced by scaled overtime rates.

The radical changes and upset of received methods and attitudes that the banks experienced during the war did not stop short of relations with their staffs. Early in 1940 the Central Council of Bank Staff Associations started talks with the Committee of London Clearing Bankers to set up a joint body of employers and employees to consult and negotiate on staff matters. Then, in July 1940, the Conditions of Employment and National Arbitration Order No. 1305 was passed, aimed at preventing work being interrupted by industrial disputes, and suggesting the need for some kind of conciliation machinery. The first attempt was now made by the C.C.B.S.A. and the Bank Officers' Guild to set up a joint body to represent bank staffs. By July 1941 they had agreed on a constitution and, with the Committee of London Clearing Bankers, on a constitution for a joint conciliation council. But later in the year a special delegate conference of the B.O.G. refused to ratify the scheme. Not for another ten years was another attempt made to form a united front on the staff side.

In 1940 the Staff Representative Committee was also wound up and replaced by a Staff Association (years later, in 1972, to be registered as a trade union, although not affiliated to the T.U.C.). The association set a subscription for members of 2/6d. (12½p) a year, in 1942 raised to 5/- (25p) for members with twenty or more years of service in the bank. Because of the war, elections to the district committees had to be postponed and not until 1946 was the first 'general election' held. In the meantime, membership of the B.O.G. among Lloyds' staff had shown a marked fluctuation. In 1939 membership had fallen to 3,730. In the next three years, there was a sharp increase to 6,070. Following this peak in 1942, membership steadily declined to no more than 3,620 in the middle fifties.

Looking ahead

In 1943 thoughts were already beginning to turn to the shape of things to come after the war. In September a start was made on reversing the decentralisation programme put into effect in 1939. The district offices at Halifax and Northampton were closed and the respective general managers and advance department staff returned to London. The Northampton board committee then ceased to meet. However, the bank's registered office remained at Salisbury until December 1945, but the evacuated officials and relative staffs stayed at Salisbury until August 1946 (while the board committee continued).

Advances, the traditional mainstay of the bank's income, were at a low ebb and with liquid resources likely to continue to be more than ample the bank would be well placed, when peace came, to meet a brisk revival in borrowing. In his statement to shareholders in January 1944 Lord Wardington acknowledged that 'it is probable that the capital market will remain closed to the general public for a time, as the demands of the Government will not cease immediately after the last shot has been fired'. He had no doubt that the banks would help fully in financing post-war reconstruction and that 'they will also be willing to be more elastic in their views as to what constitutes a legitimate banking loan'.

In July 1944, accordingly, the general management outlined their thoughts on post-war lending for the guidance of managers. It was likely that the bank would be asked to provide finance for such purposes as the replacement or conversion of machinery, rehabilitation of firms, demobilised men starting in business, the provision of new houses. Long-term advances of £5,000 and above falling outside the bank's normal operations would have to be considered separately at head office. For the rest, although policy had been to restrict lending to customers' current requirements, during the reconstruction period 'a broad view' would be taken where facilities were needed for capital purposes, and managers were not to turn down applications simply because they did not conform to standards of pre-war banking. Ex-servicemen were to receive sympathetic consideration. Applications for housing loans were not to be refused. Finally, however, managers were reminded that, while the bank was willing 'to be more elastic in its views . . . no serious departure from sound banking principles is contemplated'. All advances covered by the terms of this circular were to be charged $4\frac{1}{2}\%$ or 5%, plus commission. As it turned out, all the thought and no doubt anxious questioning that went into the preparation of the scheme were to little avail. Although in the immediate post-war years the bank's lending did rise quite considerably, demand for the kind of loans outlined in the scheme did not materialise to any great extent and relatively few such reconstruction advances were made.

Six months later, in January 1945, planning for the peace was taken a step further with the setting-up of a standing committee at head office, backed up by twelve provincial sub-committees, 'to consider and make recommendations in regard to Branch banking development *in all its aspects* with a view to increasing the Bank's business generally'. Meetings were held, discussions took place, projects were canvassed, and in June an interim report was produced. The committee believed that, although it was not possible at present to launch new schemes of business development as the staff was so fully extended, plans should be prepared to be implemented later. These were considered under four headings: getting new business, earnings, savings on expenditure, and new offices. However, the committee's conclusions were hardly of great originality. 'The attraction of new business mainly depends on managerial alertness aided by assistance from Head Office and other branches.' To increase earnings new services needed to be developed but only three were singled out: safe deposits (extension recommended), mobile sub-branches (cannot recommend), personal loans on the American system (unanimously against). Mechanisation results in saving money and should be extended when possible. As regards new offices, 'early information of pending developments is of paramount importance'. The committee was conscious that 'its recommendations do not indicate fresh and hitherto untapped sources of new business'. A second report in September 1946 looked at some other questions: income tax specialists at large branches, scientific costing of the bank's services, effects of nationalisation. There were further periodic meetings until, in December 1947, this particular piece of machinery was scrapped. The central committee was wound up and the work of the provincial sub-committees entrusted to managers' meetings.

The Staff Association had also been deliberating on the future and in September 1944 the central committee produced a report on post-war planning. It urged the bank to work out a rehabilitation scheme for men returning from the Forces (one was). It was concerned with training and proposed a training school and a staff college (both later started). It suggested 'an intermediate minor appointment' (in 1947 introduced in the form of a 'chief general manager's' appointment). However, the committee believed that the marriage bar should remain for women: 'in a business such as banking, the disturbance of staff by inevitable recurring absences for family reasons in itself justifies the Bank's pre-war attitude' (the bar went in 1949).

As regards overseas business, in July 1943 the two chief general managers, Wilson and Parkes, wrote a report prompted by 'recent suggestions that we should expand our business, and take our part in the recovery of our Export trade, by embarking upon the development of business in China and Russia in the first place. . . .' Concerning the first of these, 'we believe the suggestion for China was that we should establish Branches in that country'. This rather fanciful idea had its origin in a misunderstanding. Lord Teviot, a director, had just visited China and reported that the question had been raised if one of the big five banks, or a consortium, would consider entering the banking field in China. In August, however, Dr. T. V. Soong, the Chinese foreign minister, visited the bank during a goodwill mission to London, when it became clear that Soong was really concerned with medium- and long-term credit. There would be 'difficulties' in foreign banks opening branches in China, although possibly an agent might be appointed in Peking after the war. In their report, written before Soong's visit, Wilson and Parkes had nothing at all to say about China, either branches or credits.

As regards the U.S.S.R., Wilson and Parkes were equally non-committal. There had been various ventures in the past. In 1916 Lloyds had taken a £50,000 participation in a £800,000 loan to the 'Holy Synod of the Empire of Russia' to buy wax for use in Russian churches. This stayed on the books until 1929, when the loan was written down to £1. Then, in 1937, an unexpected £1,250 was received in capital repayment, minuted not unrealistically that 'it is unlikely that we shall recover anything further'. In 1919 the bank had taken a small shareholding in the newly-formed South Russia Banking Agency, which came to nothing and went into liquidation in 1925. From 1923 to 1930 Lloyds had been agents of the State Bank of the U.S.S.R., whose account was large and profitable. In 1930, however, some of the State Bank's business was transferred elsewhere in London and turnover declined. There was no recommendation from Wilson and Parkes about any post-war development in the bank's relations with the U.S.S.R.

They pointed out that investments in concerns abroad had been made partly to stimulate overseas business. The return from this investment had not been encouraging. In the years 1906-35 £7.5m. was put into concerns operating in other countries, on which losses totalled £2.1m. (nearly half on the British Italian Banking Corporation) and depreciation £2.7m. This was 'a lamentable financial result'. If policies of expanding Lloyds' presence overseas were to be adopted Wilson and Parkes felt 'it can only be done through a separate company . . . we ourselves possess a good nucleus in the Bank of London and South America and Indian Branches'. This, years hence, was the solution adopted, although not including the Indian branches, for in 1960 Lloyds' Eastern business was sold.

After the unhappy experiences of the 1930s, a welcome increase in profits was experienced during the war years. Gross profits of just over £2m. were recorded in 1939, followed by a slight fall in 1940, but from 1941 onwards there was a steady increase each year, to reach nearly £6m. in 1945. Earnings were up by £5.2m. over the whole period

1939–45,[6] but this was partly offset by a £1.5m. rise in outgoings. Gross profits thus grew by £3.7m. However, a substantial part of this increase was drained off by income tax payments. Net profits rose by under £500,000 between 1939 and 1945, while published profits, allowing for transfers to reserves, were less than £50,000 higher. The profit and loss account now had a more healthy look to it but, even so, the bank did not become liable for excess profits tax. E.P.T. was paid on the excess of actual profit over a 'standard' fixed by reference to pre-war earnings on capital and, so measured, Lloyds' profit did not exceed the standard. In relation to total resources, gross profit in the four years 1942–5 averaged 0.64%. Although higher than in the 1930s, this was well below the ratios achieved in the 1920s. Throughout the war years the dividend was maintained at 12%, the rate that was to last for twenty-one years from 1932 to 1952.

In relation to its business, there was a marked decline in Lloyds' capital funds in these years, as was true of other banks. In the 1930s, Lloyds' capital and published reserves as a ratio of total resources fluctuated about the 6% level, between a peak of 6.6% in 1930 and a low point of 5.7% in 1935. From 1939 onwards the ratio dropped every year. The inclusion of inner reserves raised the level of the ratio but did little to halt its downward slide. By the end of 1943 the board felt that the fall had gone far enough and ought to be checked by the creation and issue of fresh shares, for which, of course, the consent of the Capital Issues Committee would be needed. Wardington then saw the Governor who, while agreeing that the capital structure of the bank needed adjusting, was sure that the C.I.C. would not give its consent to an increase of capital for an individual bank. There the matter rested for another twelve months, when Wardington again saw Norman, whose views, however, were unchanged. So the board had to watch, frustrated, as the bank's capital and published reserves ratio sank even further during and after the war, to touch bottom at 2.5% in 1947. Including inner reserves the ratio was now not quite 4½%, little more than half the pre-war figure. More than ten years were to elapse before a start was made on raising fresh capital, to help to restore a better relationship between the bank's capital funds and its scale of business.

The Channel Islands

Three branches of the bank were overrun by the enemy during the war: Jersey and Guernsey in the Channel Islands in June 1940, and Rangoon, in Burma, in March 1942. German forces occupied the Channel Islands on Sunday 30 June 1940, and communications with the mainland then

[6] While overdraft earnings dropped from 55 to 28% of total income, there was a more than compensating increase in interest receipts on investments and other securities.

ceased. The staff of the branches in Jersey and Guernsey was fifty-four, of whom three were serving with the Forces. In addition, there was one bank pensioner living in Jersey and four pensioners in Guernsey. Twelve men and women managed to escape when the Islands were occupied; of the thirty-nine staff left, four were subsequently interned in a camp at Laufen, in Germany.

Immediately, a Channel Islands department was set up in head office and by the middle of July it had been possible to reconstruct the accounts of the two branches from the duplicate records sent to their custodian branches in England. These showed deposits on 27 June of £2.3m. and overdrafts of £389,000. A complete set of books for each branch was now instituted and accounts conducted on normal lines. Balances on these accounts, whether debit or credit, changed, of course, only by reason of transactions occurring on the mainland. Interest was charged on overdrafts and credited to deposit accounts, even when it was known that the customers were still in the Channel Islands and might be operating their accounts. Dividends, the proceeds of bonds and so on were also being received in London for the credit of such customers, but in July 1942 it was decided on their behalf to invest some of such funds in $2\frac{1}{2}\%$ National War Bonds and 3% Defence Bonds, rather than let them lie idle on their accounts. It was realised that the accounts in the books in London, based on the position at 27 June 1940, and those in the actual books in Jersey and Guernsey would diverge more and more as the war went on. In 1943, therefore, procedures were worked out for reconciling the two sets of books, when that became possible.

Salaries (and pensions) of men and women on the permanent staff trapped in the Islands were paid throughout the war into a special suspense account at head office, together with annual increases on the pre-war scale and, until 1943, income tax. An occasional message was received. In March 1942 A. S. Iles, manager of Guernsey branch, sent a brief note through the Red Cross: 'all well here and carrying on'. In February 1944 C. E. Le Cornu, sub-manager at Jersey, got a message to Ensor: 'You will be glad to hear business continues more or less as usual. Mr. Vaudin [Manager] recovering illness. Remainder staff well. Looking forward reunion'. Then, on liberation in May 1945, came another note from Le Cornu: 'we have had a pretty thin time and are worn out physically and mentally'.

In the Islands themselves, in June 1940 a message had been received from the Treasury that, in the event of occupation, branches of the big five clearing banks should function as normally as possible. For some while, indeed, there was no interference from the Germans; not until February 1941 did two German officers make a round of the branches. In the months that followed, Iles, Lloyds' Guernsey manager, came to be regarded as 'the strong man' of the banking community and he succeeded in maintaining a considerable degree of freedom for the banks with a minimum of restriction. Throughout the occupation, Lloyds' customers whose income came from outside the Islands were allowed to overdraw up to 75% of such known income.

In June 1940 the reichsmark was made legal tender, at a rate of £1 = Rm8. Subsequently, the rate was varied, to between Rm7 and 9.6, but in September 1942 it was fixed at Rm9.36. All the bank's books were still kept in sterling and marks paid in had therefore to be converted. A suspense 'loss or profit on marks' account was opened: the eventual position was a substantial loss for which, however, the Island authorities made themselves responsible. In May 1945, when German currency was called in, there was a rush to the banks to change reichsmarks back into sterling. Long queues besieged Jersey branch for about six days with the St. John Ambulance Brigade providing first aid in the banking hall.

In December 1941 the banks' branches were placed under an Administrator of Enemy Banks, an official of the Reichsbank operating from Paris, to whom monthly reports had to be sent. When Paris was liberated in 1944 this gentleman was captured, still with the reports in his files. In the meantime, the Germans had removed anything of value, such as household silver, certificates, sterling bank notes, and gold. After D-Day and the disruption of communications between the Islands and France, the German Command was unable to bring marks over to pay their troops. They therefore made periodic levies, in Jersey up to Rm4m. a time. The Jersey States borrowed the funds to pay these levies from the big five banks in proportion to the cash balance each held.

Immediately after the end of the war in Europe in May 1945 Ensor flew over to the Islands and was agreeably surprised to find how little the Germans had interfered with the bank's business. Two teams followed him, ten men going to Jersey and five to Guernsey, to undertake the laborious business of reconciling the accounts kept in the Islands with those in the Channel Islands department at head office and to deal with all the many other problems the German occupation left. During the war, when little was known in London of how the branches were faring, a reserve to cover any possible losses was set aside, which by the summer of 1945 had been built up to £478,000. In the event, advances were found generally to be in good shape, with few bad debts. Losses proved trivial:

the Channel Islands department had to write off only £5. In August, the board approved a personal gift to Iles, manager of Guernsey, and Vaudin and Le Cornu, managers of Jersey, as a mark of their appreciation for the excellent services they had rendered to the bank during the years of occupation.

Considerable sums had been borrowed from the banks by the States of Jersey and of Guernsey, amounting at the liberation to nearly £6m. and over £4m. respectively. Of this total of some £10m., Lloyds had advanced £1.7m. The banks, as a gesture of goodwill, agreed to forgo the interest that had accrued on the loans during the occupation and to waive further interest arising before a general settlement was made. After discussions with representatives of the States, the British government agreed to provide a capital sum of £7.5m. (£4.2m. for Jersey, £3.3m. for Guernsey) to be used to help to liquidate the debts to the banks. To cover the balance of about £3m., the banks accepted the States' bonds.

Victory in Europe was celebrated on 8 May 1945. Five days later the Chancellor (now Sir John Anderson) wrote to the Governor of the Bank of England (now Lord Catto) thanking the banks for their efforts during the war:

The banks' contribution has taken many forms . . . the smooth financing of war production, in facilitating subscriptions to war loans of all types, in the administration of the Exchange Control, and in providing the personal needs of the people under the stress of war conditions.

There was a good deal more than this. The banks had seen their business transformed, their branches bombed and run down from years of neglect, their young men called away, their staffs at home, many temporary, keeping things going, hard pressed but undaunted. Lloyds' advances had slumped by a quarter, its liquid assets had risen more than three-fold; over 600 branches had suffered damage, some thirty had been destroyed. Hostilities finally ended in August 1945. More than 5,000 Lloyds' men had served with the Forces, to whom forty-four orders and ninety-four decorations were awarded, and 242 of whom were mentioned in dispatches.

Above all, there were those who did not come back. A total of 344 men and women of Lloyds Bank were killed or died of wounds, including eighteen who lost their lives in air raids. Their names were engraved on the war memorial in the banking hall in Lombard Street, where a simple service of commemoration conducted by Prebendary Holland of St. Paul's Cathedral was held on Armistice Day 1949. Thirty years on, when so many of the hopes of that time have disappeared in disillusion, the truth remains in what the chairman, now Lord Balfour of Burleigh, said in his address:

Look back at the sacrifice these men made; the men whose names stand before you; the old names and the new. 'Brave men, and worthy patriots, dear to God and famous to all ages'. Never let us imagine for one moment that that sacrifice was of no avail, no matter what we see to-day or what we fear. The simple fact is, that if it had not been made in 1914 and 1939 England would not be free to-day. We have to thank them for our liberty. They bought it for us, not counting the cost.

The end of the war marked a fresh beginning, for the bank as for the country. Much had gone, much had changed, much was new. The story of the bank in the years after 1945 stretches from the recovery of the 1950s into the expansion, new ideas, and new hopes of the 1960s. The threshold of this period seems a convenient spot at which to pause and to turn aside to consider the Eastern business of the bank.

6

The Bank in the East

The business acquired

No considered act of policy determined that, in February 1923, Lloyds Bank found itself with branches in Egypt, India, and Burma. The bank had not, of course, confined its interests hitherto only to Britain. There were the investments in various overseas institutions, in the 'auxiliary' in Europe, the London and River Plate Bank, The National Bank of New Zealand, the Bank of British West Africa. All these, however, were other banks, separately managed and organised. This was quite different. Having taken over the ailing firm of Cox & Co. because of official pressure, the bank's business, as a result, was suddenly and directly extended for the first time to places abroad. In Egypt the extension was to last only three years; in India and Burma it was to continue until 1960.

It was owing to its position as an Army Agent that Cox & Co. had set up branches in India. With regiments moving to the sub-continent the bank found there a growing call for its specialised services and in 1905 opened the first office in Bombay, the main port of arrival. Other branches soon followed: Rawalpindi, one of the largest military bases, in 1906; Srinagar, a favourite leave centre in Kashmir, in 1907; and later Karachi and Calcutta and, in 1921, Rangoon. At first, the Army provided the mainstay of the business but gradually commercial connections were built up, centred on the finance of India's external trade. Henry S. King & Co., which merged with Cox & Co. in October 1922, just before the Lloyds' take-over, had also established branches in India: at Bombay, Calcutta, Delhi, and Simla.

In 1919 Cox's had opened a branch in Alexandria, sharing premises temporarily with Cox's Shipping Agency, and in Cairo an office began business the following year, also temporarily with the Shipping Agency. These two branches were geared not to Army business, but to the finance of the cotton crop and of general imports. Cox's also owned two of the best-equipped ginning factories in Egypt, bought in 1920.

This, then, was the position that faced Lloyds in February 1923. From Cox & Co. it acquired six unprofitable branches and two sub-offices in India and Rangoon, with deposits of £2.8m. spread over 16,100 current and 1,780 deposit accounts. Two centres were responsible for most of the business: Calcutta branch had two-fifths and Bombay a third of all deposits. Cox's staff in India and Burma totalled nearly 670, of whom not quite fifty were European, and all of them now became Lloyds' employees. Henry S. King & Co. had only the four branches in India, with deposits of £590,000 and nearly 270 employees, a tenth European. In Egypt, Lloyds took over two branches and the two ginning factories, deposits of just over £1m. held in 2,730 current and fifty deposit accounts, and a staff of 230, of whom thirty were European.

What had now been acquired overseas was largely unknown, prospects were uncertain. It is not surprising that there was some hesitation about what to do next. To get a first-hand assessment of the bank's new interests, W. G. Johns, then an assistant general manager, was promptly despatched to Egypt, while F. A. Beane, also then an assistant general manager, was sent off to India. Their reports would help the board to decide whether or not the bank should remain in these countries. Johns and Beane got back in the summer. First, let us consider the position in Egypt.

Three years in Egypt

Johns left London for Egypt in March 1923 together with Sir Frederick Eley, a director of the Bank of British West Africa, which also had opened branches in Cairo and Alexandria just after the war. Johns soon found methods of doing business that would raise eyebrows in Lombard Street. The entire absence of customers' balance sheets, a lack of knowledge of their other commitments, inadequate or no margins, all these, he wrote to Henry Bell, the general manager, 'strike a newcomer as unsound'. Yet Cox's branches were not alone, as the other banks carried on in the same unorthodox way, and competition was severe.

Alexandria branch, opened in 1919, had moved into permanent premises in September 1921 and three months later Cairo branch, opened in 1920, also moved into new offices. This came in for Johns's criticism: 'the initial mistake here was in building very expensive premises and creating an expensive organisation, before any business had been obtained'. Taking the whole period since they began operations until the spring of 1923 the two branches had shown a substantial loss, of about £120,000. Cairo had just begun to yield a small profit, but losses at Alexandria were increasing. The two ginning factories, fortunately, produced a good return. These were among the best appointed in Egypt and their possession enhanced the bank's reputation among its cotton customers.

Johns was much impressed by the manager of Cairo branch, A. Misrahi. On very good terms with the King of Egypt and those who ran his estates and managed his financial affairs, Misrahi was a very clever man, who had 'a wonderful knowledge of the country and all the important people'. But this had its drawbacks. The branch was a one-man show, with much of its business personal to Misrahi, and Johns was not so happy about its future as he was about that of Alexandria; not, of course, that this looked very rosy. He found the future policy of Lloyds in Egypt difficult to envisage. Johns was convinced from what he had seen that 'we cannot conduct the Bank on English lines, nor can we convert the other Banks to orthodox methods'.

The choices before Lloyds were three: to keep the branches as they were, to try to sell them or to set up a separate company to run the Egyptian business, preferably in association with the Bank of British West Africa. A sale seemed best. In the summer of 1923 Pease accordingly had talks with the Governor of the National Bank of Egypt about a possible sale, which resulted in an offer of £150,000 in cash or shares. Negotiations then broke down, not to be resumed until three years later.

The Bank of British West Africa had started operations in Alexandria in 1918 and in Cairo in 1920, but the record of these two offices had been as unprofitable as had that of the two Cox's branches. In 1921 Sir Frederick Eley and Roy Wilson, assistant general manager, paid them a visit 'and reported on the prospects without enthusiasm'.[1] For the whole period 1918–24 the two branches ran up a loss of £155,000, confirming Johns's belief that, from what he had seen on his exploratory trip, B.B.W.A. would find it difficult to buy out Lloyds' interests in Egypt. In the event, the transaction was the other way round.

Lloyds and B.B.W.A. had developed close and cordial relations and Lloyds certainly lived up to the spirit of the Treaty of Alliance between the two banks when it took over the two unwanted Egyptian branches of B.B.W.A. Under the terms of the agreement made in August 1925, Lloyds were to get two-thirds of the profits, or to shoulder two-thirds of the losses, of the merged business, and B.B.W.A. one-third, but all the assets were to be held by Lloyds, which was also responsible for the liabilities. A separate company was not formed. All the staff of B.B.W.A. was taken over, among whom was a young man Ernest Whitley-Jones, the assistant manager of the Alexandria branch. Whitley-Jones now joined the Cairo branch of Lloyds, and subsequently had a distinguished career in the bank, rising in 1946 to the position of chief general manager.

Before the agreement was formally signed the Bank of England had to be made aware of what was afoot. Pease thus visited the Governor and gave him an outline of the merger proposals. Predictably, Norman did not welcome them. Pease wrote of this meeting:

[1] Richard Fry, *Bankers in West Africa*, p. 97.

The Governor expressed no opinion, except that he would have preferred on general principles that a Clearing Bank should not operate in foreign countries, and if it had been possible he would have liked the Bank of British West Africa to have bought out Lloyds Bank. It was explained that this was not a practicable proposition, as the Bank of British West Africa were unwilling to contemplate this alternative.

Norman's minute was rather more emphatic: 'the arrangement between the two was in utter disregard of every request I had made to Pease'.

The Governor need not have worried, for Lloyds was to remain in Egypt for only a few months longer. Talks were restarted in 1926 with the National Bank of Egypt when, however, the National Bank dropped its offer for the goodwill to £100,000 in cash. Lloyds stood firm at £150,000, the figure originally offered in 1923. The Bank of England now stepped in. Lloyds was in Egypt only because it had been forced to take over Cox & Co., and had taken over Cox & Co. only on the insistence and under the guarantees of the Bank of England. The Bank decided to pave the way to agreement and itself paid the £50,000 difference to the National Bank, to add to its £100,000 on the grounds that 'it would be for the general good as a further step towards the closing of foreign branches of Clearing Banks'. Lloyds thus got its asking price of £150,000, one third of which went to the Bank of British West Africa, under the arrangements made in 1925. For the premises, including the ginning factories, the National Bank paid a further £192,500.

The agreement between Lloyds and the National Bank was dated 24 September 1926. When Lloyds took over Cox & Co. in 1923 it will be remembered that there was a provision under the Bank of England's guarantees for Cox's to be run as a separate concern for a 'management period' ending in 1927. The sale to the National Bank was well before this ended and thus posed some complications. These were whisked away by the Bank of England's convenient assent to the goodwill payment being regarded as if it had been made after December 1927 and thus belonging without strings to Lloyds.

Ensor was sent out to Egypt to assist in handing over the branches and to protect Lloyds' interests following the sale, which, in his opinion, was 'much to the pleasure of those who knew a good deal about the Egyptian business which we had acquired, which was not very profitable and carried considerable risks'.[2] But there was great disappointment in Egypt. The

---

[2] During the years 1925–7 Ensor spent eighteen months at various times in Egypt. Early in 1925 he went out to examine the two branches and cotton agencies and later in the year he was sent to look into difficulties that had risen at Cairo. Then, in 1926–7 he helped with the transfer of the business to the National Bank.

National Bank had never done much commercial banking and the sale was not popular with Lloyds' customers.

India, Pakistan, and Burma

Beane returned to London in the summer of 1923 from his exploratory trip to India and gave the board his report (which unfortunately has not survived) at the end of July. A decision on what to do next was put off for a fortnight. In the meantime, things were brought to a head by an offer from the P & O Banking Corporation to buy the Indian business for £250,000, half in cash and half in shares. The board promptly decided to accept the offer. This bank had been formed in 1920, when Lloyds took 10,000 shares (it was later incorporated into the Chartered Bank of India, Australia and China). In mid-September, however, the P & O Bank withdrew their offer, and the board saw no alternative but to keep the Indian branches for the time being. There were, indeed, Pease admitted to the annual general meeting in 1924, 'prospects of interesting profit'. A scheme for the future control of the branches was therefore drawn up, an Eastern committee of the board established under Sir Seymour King for direction and supervision, together with an Eastern department at 77 Lombard Street for general management and control. In 1927, to save staff and other costs, the absorption of Eastern department into colonial and foreign department was considered, but this was not carried through and a separate Eastern department continued to exist until 1960.

It had been at the urgent request of the Bank of England that Lloyds had taken over Cox & Co. but, right from the start, as we have seen, the Governor was unhappy at Lloyds' acquisition of branches overseas. In 1923 two principles on bank amalgamations had emerged from discussions between Montagu Norman, the Treasury and the Colwyn Advisory Committee,[3] one of which was that there should be no extension by the big five clearing banks of their interests in banks abroad. In March 1923, after Lloyds' take-over of Cox's, the Governor wrote to Sir Basil Blackett, then Finance Member of the Government of India, of his 'vague idea' to combine the Alliance Bank of Simla and Cox's Indian branches into a separate institution, either as a going concern on its own or for sale to one of the existing exchange banks. The Alliance Bank was then in serious trouble, and, as *The Times* reported in April, 'negotiations have been taking place in India and England for the purpose of associating the bank with other and more powerful banking interests in order to re-establish public confidence in the stability of the bank'. The negotiations failed; Norman's idea came to nothing.

[3] See Chapter 2, p. 25.

Norman did not let matters rest. In June 1925, when Beaumont Pease sought the Governor's views on Lloyds' proposed amalgamation with Manchester & County Bank, Norman told him, *inter alia*, that he strongly disapproved of Lloyds' interests in Egypt, India, and South America, and a few days later he minuted, about Lloyds' presence in India: 'less justifiable than any other venture'. Pease soon saw the Governor again and told him that, as regards India, he was 'now willing to sell, at a price', but the time was not right as the branches were losing money: against 'now' Norman minuted 'he was not willing a couple of weeks ago'. Towards the end of June, Pease once more told the Governor that his 'definite policy' in India was to sell if and when opportunity offered.

This remained the objective for some time yet. In March 1926 continuation of talks by Beaumont Pease on the possible disposal of the Indian branches was approved by Lloyds' board, but in September the Governor was telling the Bank's Committee of Treasury that no progress had been made. So things stood for some years. Norman had other pre-occupations; Lloyds found its Indian business now thriving and profitable. But the Governor had not completely forgotten. In November 1934 the deputy chairman, Sir Austin Harris, visited Norman who, during their conversation, asked him whether Lloyds was yet disposed to sell its Indian branches. After looking at the profit and loss account and at the record of the business, the board authorised Sir Austin to tell the Governor the bank was not so disposed. It was to be another twenty-six years before this decision was reversed.

Lloyds Bank in India and, after the partition of the sub-continent in August 1947, in Pakistan, was one of the so-called exchange banks. These institutions, few in number and mostly foreign in origin, made up the oldest and most homogeneous group of banks in India and in 1923, when Lloyds joined this small band, included such names famous in the commerce of the East as Chartered Bank of India, Australia and China, National Bank of India, and Mercantile Bank of India. In 1923 there were eighteen foreign-owned exchange banks in India, by the outbreak of war nineteen and in 1960, after partition, there were sixteen. Their specialised field of activity was the finance of India's external trade, through the opening of documentary credits, negotiation of bills, and purchase and sale of foreign exchange. They also had some part in financing internal trade, in particular the movement of goods between the ports and up-country centres. In addition to their bill transactions, there was also a fairly considerable advances business, for example, to jute mills and tea gardens.

Apart from the exchange banks, and dwarfing them in numbers, were the Indian banks. The largest and most powerful of these was the Imperial Bank of India. Bank amalgamations were not restricted to England. The Imperial Bank was established in 1921 from a merger of the three 'presidency banks': the Banks of Bengal, of Bombay and of Madras. It in fact fulfilled many of the functions of a central bank until the Reserve Bank of India was set up in 1935, and in 1955 it was nationalised as the State Bank of India. Understandably, the Reserve Bank was modelled on the Bank of England, even to the extent of being divided into Issue and Banking departments. It was given the usual responsibilities of a central bank. It had the sole note-issuing rights in British India, fixed Bank Rate, engaged in open market operations, managed the public debt, lent direct to the scheduled banks (those with a certain minimum capital and reserve), fixed the minimum cash ratios these banks had to maintain.

As a scheduled bank, Lloyds' branches in India had to conform to the policies set from time to time by the Reserve Bank. Figures of the Indian branches, of deposits, advances, and so on, were, of course, included with those of the branches in England and Wales for balance sheet purposes. For a time this led to some unnecessary duplication of effort. Until the end of 1946, the bank, in common with the other clearing banks, maintained a cash ratio of around 10% (ignoring any window dressing) of its total deposits, including those with the Indian branches. At the same time, these branches were keeping 10% of their deposits in cash and balances with the Reserve Bank. Thus, Indian deposits of the bank were covered to about 20% by cash and central bank balances. Although a waste of resources, this was not of enormous significance when Indian balances were low: in 1939 deposits were still less than £10m. But during the war, as in Britain, their total rocketed. By 1944 deposits had reached £30m. and it was decided to end this 'belt-and-braces' cash cover. Henceforward cash against deposits of Indian (and later Pakistan) branches was not held in London. Provisions regarding cash holdings were extended in 1951, two years after the Banking Companies Act of 1949 became law. The banks now had to maintain in cash, gold or unencumbered approved securities at least 20% of their demand and time deposits, and assets held in India had to be not less than 75% of local deposit liabilities. The 1949 Act and subsequent amendments covered a number of other topics: the systematic inspection of banks, the issue of policy directions to them, their amalgamation. All this applied to Lloyds' Indian branches.

The branches in Pakistan, after 1947, similarly came under the regulation of the State Bank of Pakistan, established in 1948, and again reflecting Britain's Bank Charter Act of 1844 by being divided into Issue and

Banking departments. It received the customary powers of a central bank: to operate in government securities, to rediscount bills, to control the note issue. The Banking Companies (Control) Act of 1948 considerably widened the State Bank's powers, which became much the same as those of India's Reserve Bank: it was enabled to control bank lending and banks had to maintain in Pakistan assets of at least 75% (later 80%) of their local deposits, with a minimum liquidity ratio of 20%. In Burma, too, the branch at Rangoon came under the control of the central bank, set up in December 1947.

Such, in the barest outline, were the banking systems of which Lloyds' branches formed a part during the bank's thirty-seven years in the East.

In February 1923 the bank unexpectedly added six branches and two sub-branches of Cox's and four branches of King's to its network,[4] and seventy-four Europeans, mostly British, and some 860 Indians and Burmese to its employees. The former were the managers and senior officials, the latter various grades of clerks, servants, bearers and menial staff. Throughout its whole time in India, incidentally, the bank experienced few difficulties because of race or caste. Deposits, Cox's and King's together, amounted to around £3.4m. Cox's business, concentrated in Bombay and Calcutta, was now largely commercial, Army transactions having fallen away after their war-time expansion. King's, in contrast, was rather like an old English country bank. It had Army and personal accounts (including those of the Indian Civil Service) and was busy in local commercial affairs, but took little part in the financing of overseas trade. King's European staff, numbering twenty-seven in 1923, had not taken much comfort from the merger with Cox's in October 1922, for they also had heard the rumours, so that the take-over by Lloyds was warmly welcomed.

There was to be no period of plain sailing for Lloyds to learn to navigate in unaccustomed Indian waters. Early in 1924 there was trouble and confusion at Bombay, where Cox's and King's branches had just merged with a staff of some 450, and which was now responsible for about a third of all the Indian branches' business. Exchange frauds had been committed by one of the staff. Ensor, on the inspection staff and at this time apparently the bank's main 'trouble-shooter' for overseas difficulties, was sent out to investigate with a colleague, H. J. Hutchens. Arriving in May,

---

[4] Cox's branches were in Bombay, Calcutta, Karachi, Rangoon, Rawalpindi, Srinagar, and sub-branches in Murree and Gulmarg. The sub-branch at Gulmarg (of Srinagar branch) was open only during the summer and autumn; at 9,000 feet it was under deep snow for the rest of the year. King's branches were in Bombay (merged with Cox's branch in 1924), Calcutta (merged with Cox's 1927), Delhi, and Simla.

they found the office in a state of chaos. There seemed to be no identifiable departments and Ensor and Hutchens were forced to ask everybody in the branch to write down on paper exactly what they did. Ensor and Hutchens then sorted the papers and in a few days worked out departments, which were immediately established. It took them about three months to clear things up and to be satisfied that the branch was working properly. On the point of returning home, they received a cable from the chief inspector asking them to go to Calcutta to carry out a similar examination and reorganisation. There, to their horror, they found a state of affairs that may possibly have accounted for the Indian branches' profit and loss account coming out in the red: entries in some of the books, such as the cash book and general ledger, were on opposite sides to those in Bombay. To change the book-keeping system was no easy task but, with the help of the branch's Bengali accountant, who put the fear of the gods into his clerks, this was eventually done and things settled down. Ensor and Hutchens were home by Christmas 1924.

Business developed in the next few years and new branches were opened in New Delhi (1927), Lahore and Chowringhee (1928). In 1923, when Lloyds took over the Indian branches, a substantial loss was being incurred, rising in 1924 to £80,000, nearly half at Calcutta. In subsequent years this was sharply reduced and in 1927, the end of the 'management period' for Cox & Co., it was less than £1,000. Next year, 1928, the accounts were in the black with a trading profit of some £20,000. But other troubles had now appeared. The year was marked by a severe loss at Rangoon branch, resulting from a failure of a firm of rice merchants, Beng Huat & Co., run by a prominent businessman and member of the legislative council, Beng Chong. There had been fraudulent juggling with delivery orders. Lloyds was owed £244,000 and the other exchange banks also had substantial loans outstanding. Inevitably, Ensor went out to investigate. He concluded that, though indeed fraud was involved, the position had been made considerably worse by a failure to apply proper banking controls, for which successive managers, inspection staff, the district manager in Calcutta, and the Eastern department in London were all, in varying degrees, to blame. That the other banks, too, had been slack was little excuse or consolation.

This episode illustrated once again that, as Johns had found in Egypt, banking and commercial ethics in the East were not quite the same as in the West: the environment in which business was carried on was rather different in Burma and Bombay from that in Birmingham. The 1935 book of instructions for Indian branches (11″ deep and 3″ thick) recognised that the rules for the bank's branches at home on which it was based could not be wholly applicable: 'it is considered, however, that senior officials will have sufficient discrimination to know when the rules must be observed in the spirit only and when they must be bound by the literal text'. Commercial law and the law relating to negotiable investments were based on English models but Hindu and Muslim laws and customs could raise difficulties. There was, for example, the joint Hindu family, extending not only to the immediate family but to all the cousins and governed by complicated Hindu customs. Responsibility for repayment of an advance could be affected. Land ownership could also present problems. The 1935 rule book pointed out, for instance, that:

All Mohammedan ancestral immovable property is, owing to the doctrine of Waqf, unsafe. At any time the customer or his relations or friends can, by alleging that the property mortgaged or charged to the Bank is Waqf property i.e. that it has been gifted by an ancestor or by the customer to others, attack the Bank's title and, provided the gift (which may have been made verbally) is conclusively proved, impair it.

More was done on trust than in England. To be credible and to carry on business against keen competition local managers had to operate much more on their own, if need be to go beyond any formal discretionary powers. There was no easy and quick reference to district office or head office, as was possible for their counterparts at home. This was true equally of the district (later general/chief) manager in Calcutta, who had the immediate oversight of the Indian branches. Decisions could not always wait on an answer from London. After 1947, moreover, the requirements of three central banking authorities in India, Pakistan, Burma had to be met, as well as those of head office in London.

Personal borrowing was often uncovered, based on managers' close knowledge of their customers. While Europeans tended to turn naturally to Lloyds and other foreign-owned exchange banks, the cachet of having an account with one of these banks also attracted a fairly large personal business from Indians. For Indian companies engaged in exporting or importing there was an advantage that, compared with an Indian bank, Lloyds was bigger, stronger, and had direct connections with London. Lending was customarily by overdraft not loan, as in England, and might be made against railway receipts (a document of title in India) for the transport of cotton, jute, hides or skins. Tea advances were rather different: money was lent at the start of a season against a crop yet to be picked.

Advances, including money at call and short notice, reached their pre-war peak of £3.7m. in 1928, when deposits had risen to £5.5m. from £3.4m. in 1923. The 1930s saw further opening of new branches, although the lack of men of sufficient experience was at first a handicap. An office at Amritsar began operations in 1930 but the next was not until 1935, at Darjeeling, followed by a second office, Princess Street, in Bombay in 1937 and Peshawar in 1938. By then Lloyds had thirteen branches and four sub-branches in India, together with an office at Rangoon. There were ideas of branching out into executor and trustee business but London decided it would be too complicated. By 1939 deposits had increased three-quarters since 1928 to reach nearly £10m. but advances had declined to £2.4m. Profits rose to more than £100,000 in 1934, fluctuated during the next few years, then dropped to just over £70,000 in 1939.

In 1923 there were seventy-four European staff in Cox's eight offices and King's four branches. The majority of these were 'covenanted staff', so-called because of the power of attorney granted by the bank giving a man virtually *carte blanche* powers (necessary when communications were slow), and roughly equivalent to those with a board appointment in the domestic bank. Early in the 1950s the policy was adopted of promoting Indians and Pakistanis to this rank. In 1952, when covenanted staff in the East totalled ninety-six men, six had been recruited locally, and ninety had come from Britain.

Men were picked for the Eastern branches from Lloyds' domestic staff and there was rarely any lack of applicants for the two or three positions to be filled each year. Men selected were trained for four months or so at Eastern department. A young man starting as, say, an assistant accountant in the early 1920s received Rs 500 (£37. 10s.—£37·50) a month, plus outfit and house allowances. He would be expected to pass an examination in Hindustani and in negotiable instruments, for which he would receive an extra Rs 50 a month.

A covenanted officer got six months' home leave (India back to India) after four years' service and although also entitled to local leave this was often difficult to arrange. The 1935 rule book rather grudgingly provided that 'local leave may be applied for each year by members of the Covenanted Staff and, where the exigencies of the service allow, will not be unduly withheld'. They could at least look forward to retiring at fifty-five, having completed thirty years service.

Young men coming out from England usually lived in a 'chummery' and were attended, of course, by the servants to whom few of them were accustomed in England. Their hours might be long: one had a job to do and stayed until it was finished. There was no afternoon siesta. But there were many compensations: the step-up in status, the exotic teeming life of India, the Bombay Light Horse, golf and cricket, the spice of adventure. H. C. Gotts arrived to join Cox's branch in Bombay in October 1921, then a young man just twenty years old, and later to be manager of Peshawar branch during the war and of Rangoon after the war. Here is an extract from his diary for 17 November 1921, when the Prince of Wales was visiting India:

Up at 6.30—short walk and returned to breakfast. Salutes being fired all the morning. Paraded 9/5 with A.F.I. [Auxiliary Force India] in Cruickshank Road and had very good view of Prince. Spent afternoon watching cricket, dressed 7, taxi to Government House reception, met and shook hands with Prince of Wales— home 1. Most beautiful scene in grounds of Government House, lights amongst trees, beautiful uniforms and dresses.

No doubt this was an exceptional day. But how many of Gotts's peers at home, catching a tram to the bank to write up pass books and stamp the letters, could ever hope to experience anything remotely comparable? Of course there were also exceptional days and nights in India of a different kind. On one night in September 1930, twenty-two inches of rain fell on Bombay, flooding the branch record room to a depth of over two feet. And not everyone was always in sparkling good health; sprue, a rather nasty tropical complaint, was fairly common.

Native staff were of three grades: supervisory, clerical, and subordinate (bearers, porters, etc.). The first had an important function in ensuring the smooth running of branches and were responsible for the training of clerks and for discipline. Few women were employed.[5] Industrial disputes were relatively unimportant until the war. But in 1948 there was a notable lapse, when years of indiscipline at Calcutta branch came to a head. In August, with the approval of the West Bengal Government, eleven of the staff were suspended and prosecuted. The rest promptly staged a sit-down strike. The bank insisted on a written declaration of loyalty, none signed and all were sacked. Of these, 474 subsequently applied for re-engagement and 434 were taken back. The dispute about the remaining forty men dragged on through three tribunals, ending in 1958 with their re-instatement and payment of back pay. Disputes were not always about pay and conditions. In 1957 there was trouble at Delhi branch about how many yards of cloth the subordinate staff should receive for turbans.

---

[5] One of the telephone operators at Calcutta for a time in the 1920s was a Miss Estelle Thompson, who later enjoyed considerable success as a film actress under the name of Merle Oberon.

The war brought significant changes, in the volume of business and in the disposition of assets, and culminating in the segregation of certain branches into the new state of Pakistan. Deposits increased four-fold, from £9.7m. in 1939 to over £38m. in 1945, while the number of current accounts nearly trebled, from 23,120 to 67,200. Army business, of course, grew enormously during the war years. At Bombay branch alone a large department was formed merely to deal with the re-direction of letters. Advances slumped to less than £2m. in 1945, but investments and holdings of rupee Treasury bills soared, to equal two-thirds of deposits at the end of the war. All this increased activity was reflected in the growth of profits, from just over £70,000 in 1939 to more than £300,000 in 1945. Considerable pressures were put on the staff. Half the covenanted officers left for the services. All home leave was stopped.

Of all the bank's staff in the East those at Rangoon had the harshest time. At the end of December 1941 the city suffered its first bombing by the Japanese which, continuing into the new year, brought life virtually to a standstill. In February, the government decided upon total evacuation and, as part of this, a special bank train left for Mandalay, taking the staff of the principal banks and essential books and papers. In March, Rangoon fell, Mandalay came under severe air attack and was then destroyed by fire. The staff of the branch now split. J. W. Hyslop, the manager, and A. C. Holmes, his accountant, got away by car, taking branch records and papers with them, and were subsequently picked up by 'plane for Calcutta. The rest of the staff, in company with men from the other Rangoon banks, set out from Mandalay to reach India by, they hoped, boat, train, and air. Boat and train got them as far as Nabha, in the north of the country, but the intended airport further on was now put out of action by the Japanese. There was no alternative but to set out on foot. On 3 May, they all started on the 250 mile tramp, reaching Imphal, in India, twenty-six days later. Terrible hardships had been faced: existence on rice and water and a few odd scraps, intense heat, violent storms, sickness, a climb to 6,500 feet. 'Any amount of writing and speaking', wrote H. S. Aiyer, one of the Rangoon staff who endured it all, 'would not reach one's imagination of how grave and dangerous those days were.'

An office was opened in Lahore where, from May 1942 to December 1945, a skeleton staff reconstructed such Rangoon accounts and records as was possible. Rangoon was recaptured in May 1945 and, with the help of the Army, the banks returned in December, an operation given the code-name 'Operation Shylock'. In charge of Lloyds' contingent and appointed manager was H. C. Gotts, whom we last met shaking hands with the Prince of Wales in Bombay in 1921. The banks' staffs embarked on the

City of Canterbury at Calcutta on Sunday 23 December, reaching
Rangoon five days later with Lloyds' men who had walked out of Burma in
1942 on board. They found the banking hall of the branch quite bare,
except for a short length of counter, while the strong room had been forced
open by the Japanese and the contents burnt. Cleaning-up, repairing and
getting ready occupied the next few weeks and on Wednesday, 23 January
1946 the banks reopened for business.

Peace had not long been restored before the bank had to meet the consequences of independence and partition of the sub-continent into India
and Pakistan.[6] As with the war generally, there will be no attempt here to
cover the causes and wider effects of this momentous event. The transfer
of power to the new states came on 15 August 1947, preceded by widespread communal riots. Commerce was severely disrupted in areas along
the new frontiers. Muslims are not very clerically-minded and most of the
local Lloyds' staff in what was now Pakistan were Sindi Hindus, Goans,
and Parsees, many of whom fled to India. Before partition there had been
some 630 scheduled bank offices in the area now Pakistan. When the plan
for independence was announced the majority of banks shifted their head
office to a location in the new Indian state and, at the same time, there was
a rush to transfer accounts and funds to India. By the end of the year two-
thirds of bank offices had been closed. The scarcity of trained bank staff
was so acute that the Finance and Commerce ministers of Pakistan called
a conference of all interested parties, including the exchange banks, to
discuss how to replace those who had quit. The government itself was
strongly insistent on the banks' employing Pakistanis.

Partition caused many other problems. Accounts in both countries had
to be divided into resident and non-resident (exchange control was strictly
administered), in some cases an advance was in one country but the
security in the other. The control of Lloyds' Eastern branches was still
in Calcutta, to which the Pakistan government raised objections. There
were two solutions if the Pakistan authorities were adamant: to form the
branches in India and in Pakistan into two separate companies or to have
two district offices, in Calcutta and in Karachi. As it turned out, the
structure of control was left unchanged. The Pakistan government was
persuaded of the economies so secured and it recognised that ultimate
control was, in any event, in London, while their respect and high regard

---

[6] Lloyds' branches in India were now in Amritsar, Bombay, Calcutta (two), Darjeeling,
Delhi, New Delhi, and Simla, with a sub-branch at Bombay. In the new state of Pakistan
branches were at Chittagong, Karachi, Lahore, and Rawalpindi and sub-branches at Karachi
and Murree. In Kashmir, there was a branch at Srinagar, with a sub-branch at Gulmarg.

for W. T. C. Parker, then district manager, also helped to swing the argument.

In July 1948 the State Bank of Pakistan started operations. In the meantime, an expert committee had dealt with the ticklish questions of coinage, currency, exchange reserves, and the division of the assets and liabilities of the Reserve Bank of India. In 1949 the National Bank of Pakistan was set up, with a quarter of its share capital provided by the government, and private initiative established two other Pakistan banks. The banking system subsequently recovered and by 1962 the number of bank offices in Pakistan exceeded that before independence.

By the beginning of the 1950s further changes had been made in the branch networks of both India and Pakistan.[7] In the former Lloyds now had ten offices and in the latter seven, and there were still the branches at Srinagar, in Kashmir, and at Rangoon. No particular architectural style distinguished these various offices. There were the elaborate ornamental façades at Chowringhee and Bombay (see Plate 6), the plain frontage of New Delhi, the Ionic columns of Calcutta.[8] And some of the branches must have reminded the English staff of home: Rawalpindi, resembling a branch station from England's Southern Railway; Madras, looking like a smart factory from London's Great West Road; Lahore, in appearance not unlike a pre-war cinema.

The branches in India dominated the business. By the mid-1950s total deposits had increased to £51m., of which the Indian branches accounted for over two-thirds and those in Pakistan for a quarter. Advances had recovered from the negligible figures to which they had sunk during the war and now stood at £18m. Of this total, the Indian branches lent no less than four-fifths and the Pakistan offices practically all the rest. Rangoon's figures were small: only one-twentieth of all deposits. The Army side had virtually disappeared, but was more than offset by the growth in commercial and exchange banking. The decision was now taken to mechanise branch accounting at Calcutta and then, possibly, at other offices. In the event, only Calcutta was mechanised. A number of improvements had also been made in recent years in pay and allowances. Overseas allowance was higher, men with board appointments received a tax-free car allowance, grant-in-aid was raised to meet higher living costs.

[7] In India a branch and sub-branch had been opened in Madras, but the office at Simla had been closed. In Pakistan, there was now a branch in Dacca and another sub-branch at Karachi, but the sub-branch at Murree had been closed. In Kashmir, the Gulmarg sub-branch had also been closed.

[8] Darjeeling branch was distinguished not so much for its architecture, as for the staggering view of Kanchenjunga from the kitchen balcony.

Whatever the expansion in the business of Lloyds and the other exchange banks, this was exceeded after independence by the growth in that of indigenous Indian and Pakistan institutions. Although the figures before 1947 relate to undivided India there seems little doubt that this process had been in train for some years before independence on both sides of the new frontiers. In 1939 the exchange banks held 27% of total bank deposits in undivided India, but by 1952 the ratio had fallen to just over 18% in the new India. Only one new branch was opened after this date, at Khulna, in East Pakistan, in 1954. In both the new states there was, perhaps inevitably, a conscious policy of encouraging and protecting local institutions at the expense of foreign banks. A fine new office was built at Chittagong in the financial centre of the city but Lloyds wished to retain the original branch opened after the war in the port area. The bank was told by the Pakistan authorities that it could not have two branches, so the port branch was closed. Again, a new branch was planned down the coast below Calcutta but permission to go ahead was never given.

The relative decline in the business of the exchange banks continued throughout the 1950s. By the end of the decade their share of total bank deposits in Pakistan had fallen to 41%, compared with 51% only five years earlier. In India, by 1961 the exchange banks' share of total deposits had dropped to less than 13%, against over 18% nine years earlier. The belief that this process was not likely to be halted, that any marked expansion of the bank's business was not possible under the new régimes, was one of the factors that weighted the decision in 1960 to sell the Eastern business.

The branches sold

There were two main reasons for the decision of Lloyds' board to sell the branches in India, Pakistan, and Burma to National and Grindlays Bank. First, the restrictions on expansion just noted; secondly, difficulties of control. Both these problems had been evident for some years before 1960 but it was the offer from National and Grindlays that finally decided the issue.

In the middle fifties the staff in the East sensed the way the wind seemed to be blowing for the exchange banks and had some fear that, as the business was really peripheral to the bank's main concerns, Lloyds would be more willing to quit than would others of the exchange banks, to whom Eastern operations were more important. E. J. Hill, chief general manager, wrote in December 1955 to A. P. Nielsen, chief manager of Eastern department, to allay such anxieties. Lloyds' standing in the world was far higher than that of the other exchange banks and 'the withdrawal of Lloyds Bank would be a measure of great national and international concern'. It would have 'incalculable consequences'. Lloyds was 'far and away the most important Bank catering for the needs of the large British and European concerns operating in India and we have duties to them'. The bank would find it difficult to escape from these 'even if we were disposed to take that course'. This was all very reassuring.

Nielsen himself was optimistic on the prospects for the Eastern branches when he made a tour early in 1958. 'I feel we are in India and Pakistan for many years to come', he reported on his return. 'We have a large, sound business. . . .' There was scope for attractive and remunerative advances 'which at present is almost endless'. Although he was not happy about Burma—where, anyway, the bank's stake was small—Nielsen saw no reason why the bank's business in India and Pakistan should not continue and in fact increase, with good results. 'We have a substantial and profitable business in the East', the board was assured in March 1958. Net profits had reached a peak in 1952 of nearly £500,000 and, after a dip in the following two years, rose again later in the decade. In terms of branch profitability the results were in fact considerably more favourable than those for the domestic bank. For the ten years 1951–60 net profits per branch in the East averaged five times the comparable figure for branches in England and Wales, although the multiple was certainly lower at the end of the decade than it was at the beginning.

Within a year, opinion, at least in London, had swung the other way and prospects were thought to be gloomy, expansion improbable. Nothing had really changed as regards the environment in which Lloyds and the other exchange banks had to operate. Their place in the Indian and Pakistan economies would continue to be hemmed in and restricted, reflecting official policies since independence. This trend, one of the two main reasons for Lloyds' sale in 1960, was evident well before the end of the 1950s but had been largely ignored in Nielsen's report in 1958. To look at the facts on the spot, early in 1959 a tour of the Eastern branches was made by L. F. Andrews, joint general manager in London responsible for this side of the business, and Charles Gardner, now chief manager of Eastern department. Their general conclusion was that, with the political and economic outlook so uncertain, 'it would be unwise to attempt to embark upon any policy of expansion'. The opening of new offices would be very difficult, if not met with outright opposition. In Pakistan, they were told permission would not be granted for Lloyds to open any more offices up-country, but this might be allowed at the ports. In India, there was a non-committal answer to the same question. The impression was that 'we are no longer strictly necessary to the economy' of the sub-continent. In Rangoon, the bank would 'be left sooner or later with no alternative but to close down'. The Burmese government had a 50% stake in all big industrial concerns and all relative banking business had to be channelled through the State Commercial Bank. The branch was not likely to attract any new business.

Early in 1960 this depressing assessment was reinforced by the report of the chief managers in Calcutta that competition in both India and Pakistan was probably 'more intense than at any time during our history in the East'. A weakness in Lloyds' business was that lending was dominated by a few large borrowers, and the effects of the wider branch networks of some of Lloyds' competitors were being felt. Lloyds' share of the business was shrinking.

The second main reason for the sale of the Eastern business turned on the difficulties of control. A separate committee of the board had been established when the branches were acquired in 1923, together with an Eastern department to act more or less as their London head office. The chief managers in Calcutta reported to this department, which canalised all the traffic passing between Lloyds' domestic branches and those in the East and itself operated as an exchange bank in London. Eastern department, and thus the bank's business in India, Pakistan, and Burma, was placed under the executive control of the joint general manager responsible for the London area. In the early days, when the figures were relatively small, branches fewer, and India undivided this system of control presumably worked well enough. In the post-war years, with the growth in business and independence presenting new problems, it does not seem to have been best designed to produce prompt decisions. After their visit in 1959, Andrews and Gardner believed it had to be seriously considered whether the Eastern branches were not over-controlled. The centre of authority was kept in London. In the early fifties the maximum formal discretionary limit for the chief managers in Calcutta was still only £15,000, the same as for a controller in the advance department in head office. London did not always appear to be fully aware of local conditions. Shortly after independence an attractive new building in Calcutta was offered to the bank for £82,500. London turned down the offer, although Chowringhee branch, a few doors away, was bursting at the seams. During the next twelve months the building changed hands several times, the last for £300,000. A year later the bank moved in as a tenant, at a very high rental.

As no real power was delegated to the East it is not surprising that the joint general manager of the day found his Eastern responsibilities increasingly onerous and time-consuming. Moreover, in the nature of things, there was a change in general manager every six or seven years, with each new man coming to the business afresh. For the chief general manager, too, Indian and Pakistan affairs came to take up a disproportionate amount of time.

These, then, were the main reasons prompting Lloyds to sell to National and Grindlays Bank. This bank had more than thirty offices in India, Pakistan, and Burma and eighty elsewhere, with an administrative organisation in London especially designed to control a large number of overseas offices. In India it was the largest of the sixteen exchange banks, with deposits of £44m. in December 1959, a quarter of the total for these banks, against £33m. for Lloyds. Talks took place between J. K. Michie, chairman of National and Grindlays, and Sir Jeremy Raisman, deputy chairman of Lloyds, and agreement was reached, subsequently ratified by the two boards. Sterling reserves for the Eastern business of just over £2m. had been built up by 1960. Lloyds agreed to transfer these reserves, together with the Eastern branches, in consideration for 1,520,700 shares in National and Grindlays, the bank's unissued shares, and giving Lloyds approximately 25% of the total issued capital. Raisman and Lord Lloyd joined the board of National and Grindlays. Representatives of the Reserve Bank of India and State Bank of Pakistan were in London in the spring of 1960 and both approved the sale when told by Raisman. And no doubt the shade of Montagu Norman nodded a vigorous assent.

The interests and future of Lloyds' staff were a particular concern in making these arrangements with National and Grindlays. The total staff in the East was then about 2,520, of whom just over 100 were covenanted officers. There was despondency and some anxiety when the British staff learnt of the sale, and worry about future prospects. They were given the option of staying on with National and Grindlays or of returning home to join Lloyds' domestic staff. Most officers, including John Brough, one of the two chief managers, elected to stay on. Some returned to England, including Eric Tibbetts, the other chief manager, who joined Lloyds Bank (Foreign) as assistant general manager. In London, Eastern department was closed and its staff dispersed either to National and Grindlays or elsewhere in Lloyds.

In 1962 a rights issue increased Lloyds' holding in National and Grindlays Bank to 1,900,875 shares. There was a capital re-organisation in 1966 and in 1969 Lloyds' holding was converted into shares in National and Grindlays Holdings Ltd. which, with other capital transactions, gave Lloyds' 3,500,000 shares. A further purchase of shares in 1971 gave Lloyds 41.4% of the total equity.

Looking back, twenty years later, is it possible to question the decision to end Lloyds' direct association with the three Asian countries? An indirect interest remains, of course, through the stake in Grindlays Holdings (as it is now named). In the light of subsequent developments, however, would it probably have been to the bank's advantage if the business had not been sold? Certainly, Hill's forebodings of 1955 did not materialise. If there were any 'incalculable consequences' they were not very evident. Of the two reasons for pulling out—poor prospects for growth and difficulties of control—the latter could surely have been tackled and new systems devised if this had been an overriding consideration. More authority could have been transferred to the Calcutta chief managers. The idea at the time of independence of two separate companies in India and Pakistan could have been looked at again; although in 1960 the authorities might not have given their approval so readily as they probably would have done in 1947. If business had been booming and prospects bright at the end of the 1950s it is difficult to believe that problems of control would have proved impossible to solve and that suitable administrative machinery could not have been devised.

The answer thus lies in a judgement about the place of the exchange banks in the financial systems and general economies of India and Pakistan—in Burma the banks were nationalised in 1963. For India, where Lloyds had two-thirds of its Eastern business, the belief that the exchange banks would continue to be circumscribed and become increasingly less important has proved right. In 1972 an official banking commission rather dismissed these banks as of little consequence:

As regards the foreign banks, they may be allowed to continue as at present since their branch expansion is in any case limited to port towns and since their share in the total banking business in India is fast diminishing.[9]

By 1977 the exchange banks' share of total bank deposits in India had dropped to just over 4%, about a third of the ratio for 1961 and less than a fifth of the pre-war figure. But the question is not really about these banks as a group but about one particular bank. Would the experience of Lloyds Bank, if it had continued in business, have been different from that of the other exchange banks? National and Grindlays indeed expanded vigorously in the 1960s. By 1975, for example, the bank had fifty-six offices and a merchant banking division in India, fifteen branches and a merchant banking division in Pakistan and ten branches in Bangladesh. In India its deposits increased nearly four times between 1960[10] and 1977 (more than

---

[9] *Report of the Banking Commission*, Government of India, 1972, p. 393.
[10] National and Grindlays and Lloyds figures together.

the rise in prices), but this rate of growth was admittedly far exceeded by that of the indigenous banks.

It is impossible to say if Lloyds could have matched this record. National and Grindlays was geared to overseas business. Lloyds was essentially an English domestic bank. Lloyds might have prospered, even though not improved its relative position, if it had remained as an Eastern exchange bank, streamlined or radically changed its system of authority and continued in one way or another in India and Pakistan—the Rangoon branch would have gone. The international banking group of which Lloyds now forms the British base would thus have had a footing in these two countries, one the largest democracy in the world. Or things might have turned out quite differently. Speculation about 'what might have happened if . . .' may be amusing but that is all. Given the prospects as they appeared in 1960, the decision to sell the Eastern business was clearly right, and it has not necessarily been proved wrong by what has happened since.

7

After the War

New men at the top

With the end of hostilities in August 1945, those who had brought the bank through the war were at last able to step down and to leave to fresh minds the task of tackling the new problems of peace. Lord Wardington had been chairman for an unprecedented twenty-three years, while R. A. Wilson's banking career had covered forty-seven years and Sidney Parkes's more than half a century. A new chairman and two new chief general managers took up their responsibilities in January 1946.

Lord Wardington had been chairman since 1922, from the recession after the first world war and subsequent revival, through the depression and recovery of the 1930s into the strange and dangerous years of war. Indeed, Wardington's experience and memories went back well before 1922, to his days as a partner in the old private bank of Hodgkin, Barnett & Co. By 1945 this was a vanished world; old certainties had been eroded or disappeared, calling for new methods and fresh thinking. There was no obvious successor on Lloyds' board to take over. Sir Austin Harris had been deputy chairman throughout the whole of Wardington's time as chairman and was considered too old. Thought had been given to the succession well before the end of the war and one or two names considered but early in 1945 opinion crystallised on Lord Balfour of Burleigh. He was approached and agreed to his election to Lloyds' board, resigning his directorship of District Bank. Balfour of Burleigh became chairman in January 1946, when a period of office of five years was contemplated. In fact, he went on until 1954. Wardington remained on the board until his death in 1950.

Balfour of Burleigh came from an old Scottish family and had started in the City as a clerk in the Alliance Assurance Co. in 1907. By 1938 he had risen to become chairman of The National Bank of New Zealand and director of other banks and institutions, having on the way spent 'twelve happy years' as an active member of the discount market. Tall and handsome, he was very much the aristocrat, occasionally hot-tempered but friendly, and anxious to play a part in public affairs through his position as a Scottish representative peer in the House of Lords. It was partly for this reason that in 1946 W. Manning Dacey, a noted City economist and editor of *The Banker*, joined the bank as economic adviser. In the early days Dacey acted mainly as a personal assistant to Balfour and helped to draft his annual statement to shareholders which, continuing pre-war practice, was concerned largely with the major economic issues of the moment.

While Balfour's succession invigorated the board, his relations with the two chief general managers, Whitley-Jones and Ensor, were not always without friction. Balfour's interest in economic and financial issues in general was not to the neglect of the narrower questions of bank policy and occasionally there was some resentment, particularly by Ensor, at what was felt to be Balfour's encroachment on the executive function.

One of Balfour's special concerns was to try to bring the bank's staffing policies of recruitment and training more into accord with post-war realities. In his presidential address in 1950 to the Institute of Bankers, for example, he questioned whether traditional methods of recruitment were adequate and saw 'no reason why extended recruitment of graduates, in itself, need introduce any greater stratification than exists in fact at present'. In Lloyds, nevertheless, such extended recruitment would wait for nearly another twenty years. As regards training, however, the bank's procedures were revolutionised during Balfour's term of office. Memories among some of the staff still harked back to the days of 'Capital and Counties' or 'Cox's' and another of Balfour's achievements was to unify loyalties to Lloyds Bank.[1] 'B of B' became deservedly popular with men and women in the bank who, on his retirement from the chair in 1954, subscribed to buy him a motor car.[2]

In 1945, when Balfour of Burleigh joined the board, another election was that of Sir Jeremy Raisman, who became a vice-chairman in 1947 and a deputy chairman from 1953 to 1964. Raisman had had an oustanding career in the Indian civil service, rising in 1939 to become Finance Member of the Government of India, and his expert knowledge of Indian affairs was of great value for the bank's Eastern business. But his counsel and influence were not restricted only to this side of Lloyds' operations.

---

[1] Balfour also started the regular dinners at which the chairman and a few directors and top officials meet small groups of managers for discussion and exchange of views. Balfour had learnt the value of such meetings when he was a director of the old London and North-Eastern Railway, whose top executives were entertained to dinner by the board on the night before the annual general meeting.

[2] This was a Ford Consul convertible, members of the staff contributing a maximum of 1/- (5p) each. After Lord Balfour's death in 1967 the car was lent by Lady Balfour to Lord Montagu's motor museum at Beaulieu. It is still there.

Raisman was intellectually brilliant. His judgements on a number of issues were based on sharp insight and proved of considerable worth in the post-war years. In 1953, when the end of Balfour of Burleigh's term as chairman was in sight, Raisman was sounded out about the succession but decided he did not wish to step into B of B's shoes: for one thing, he thought a younger man was needed (he was then sixty-one); for another, he sensed some anti-semitic feeling still lurked in parts of the City, to its discredit. Raisman remained on the board until 1967 and died in 1978.

Among the other eminent men elected to the board in the immediate post-war years were Derick Heathcoat Amory (later Lord Amory), who was a director 1948–51 and subsequently Chancellor of the Exchequer 1958–60, and the distinguished soldier Lord Ismay (1948–51). An imaginative election in 1950 was that of Sir Frederick Burrows, a director until 1958 and continuing as a member of the South Wales committee to 1962. The son of a Gloucestershire smallholder, his origins were probably the most humble of any on the board. He joined the old Great Western Railway as a goods porter, became president of the National Union of Railwaymen 1942–4[3] and was appointed the last Governor of Bengal in 1945. He died in 1973.

The pre-war system of local committees of the board was re-established and gradually extended. In 1946, as in 1938, there were six: at Birmingham, Halifax, Liverpool, Newcastle, and Salisbury but the Capital and Counties committee, which still existed, was by now largely nominal. In 1947 a committee was established for South Wales, in 1948 for Devon and Cornwall, in 1949 for Pall Mall branch (still having an important Army business) and in 1951 for the Eastern counties. For the rest of the fifties the total remained ten. The Capital and Counties committee was finally wound up in 1958 with the death of Lord Bledisloe, its sole surviving member since 1949, but another committee was formed at Bristol.

On the same day in 1946 that Balfour of Burleigh became chairman, E. Whitley-Jones and A. H. Ensor became joint chief general managers, on the retirement of Sydney Parkes. Whitley-Jones was born at Pwllheli, in a family for many generations connected not with banking or commerce but with the sea, and started his career in the Union Bank of Manchester in 1907. On demobilisation from the Army in 1919 he joined the Bank of

---

[3] Burrows used to say that, while he knew little of such interests of his colleagues on the board as hunting, shooting, and fishing, he was very conversant with shunting, hooting, and hissing. As Balfour of Burleigh said in his statement for 1950, Burrows brought to the board 'a wealth of experience of a kind not previously available to us'.

British West Africa and was sent out to Egypt where he was assistant manager of the Alexandria branch when Lloyds took over the Egyptian business of B.B.W.A. in 1925. His career in Lloyds was rapid. In little more than twenty years, Whitley-Jones reached the highest executive position. Leaving Egypt in 1926, he was appointed assistant manager at Exchange branch in Liverpool and it was not long before his considerable abilities brought him to the fore. In the early 1930s a cotton fraud was discovered at Liverpool and it was Whitley-Jones's investigation and subsequent brilliant report that helped to establish his reputation. In 1933 he came to Lombard Street as assistant general manager, promoted eight years later to joint general manager. Retiring in 1950, he was a director of the bank until 1961. From 1947 to 1964 Whitley-Jones was also a director of his old bank, Bank of West Africa (the 'British' was dropped in 1957) and deputy chairman 1954-64. He died in 1965. Whitley-Jones was devoted to Wales, its people and traditions, and spoke Welsh fluently; outside the bank music and ornithology were among his interests, but his personal life was ever darkened by the death of a young son.

Ensor we have already met a number of times on his forays into Egypt, India, and Burma. He became, in all respects, the complete banker and in the years after 1945 was acknowledged to be one of the most outstanding personalities in Lombard Street. He was president of the Institute of Bankers 1952-4. His whole career was spent in Lloyds, which he joined in 1908 at the new branch at Cape Hill, Birmingham.[4] After war service, in which he was severely wounded, he was appointed to the inspection service and spent a good deal of the 1920s overseas, as we have seen, sorting out various little local difficulties. In 1934 he was appointed chief accountant and in 1939 moved into administration, becoming a joint general manager in 1941. His resourcefulness did a great deal to sustain the bank during the war, while his clear intellect and wide experience of so many aspects of the bank's operations were equally invaluable in the exacting years after 1945. Ensor had a great appetite for work and devoted his considerable abilities unstintingly to the service of the bank. He never forgot his early days and always managed to find time to deal with any matters affecting the staff. Retiring in 1954, he was a director 1954-71 and vice-chairman 1955-63. He died in 1977.

If Lloyds was fortunate in having bankers of the calibre of Whitley-Jones and Ensor at the helm in the difficult years after 1945 it was equally lucky in having its first great administrator in R. F. E. Whittaker. Whittaker joined the Capital and Counties Bank at Islington, North

---

[4] He first applied in 1907 but was turned down because his handwriting was not up to the required standard. Luckily for Lloyds, a second application was better written.

London, in 1911, served in the first war and had an uneventful career in
the inter-war years—he did not pass the Institute of Bankers' examinations until after he became a manager in 1927. He remained in the
territorial army and it was during the second world war that he really
found his feet. By April 1945 he had risen to be a substantive major-
general, a rank never previously reached by a civilian soldier. Whittaker,
demobilised in the following July, seemed to be just the man to handle the
assimilation back into the bank of the thousands of men returning from the
Forces. Appointed assistant general manager, later general manager, in
charge of administration, he was given his head to overhaul the bank's
creaking systems of recruitment, training, and promotion. In 1948 a staff
college was opened, followed in 1950 by a training centre for new recruits.
Whittaker also became interested in mechanisation, and was one of the
original members of the London clearing banks' electronics committee,
set up in 1955 to consider questions of computerisation. An extrovert,
thick-set and in appearance not out of the conventional banking mould,
Whittaker had great energy and drive, power of decision and ability to
delegate. Outside the bank, his great interest was rugby football. He was
appointed O.B.E. in 1938, advanced to C.B.E. in 1945, and appointed
C.B. in 1943. He retired in 1957 and died in 1967.

Early post-war years

The end of the immediate post-war years, so far as the banks were
concerned, may be conveniently taken as November, 1951, when
monetary policy was re-activated with the rise in Bank Rate to $2\frac{1}{2}\%$, and to
4% in the following March, from the level of 2% at which, apart from the
short flurry on the outbreak of war, it had been stuck since 1932. But not
until July 1958 were official restrictions on bank lending lifted, for the first
time since 1939; a freedom, in the event, that was short-lived. In 1958, too,
an important step was taken towards re-establishing London's position as
an international financial centre, when in December that year sterling held
by non-residents was at last made freely convertible into dollars. The
period from the end of the war to the close of the fifties thus divides itself
into two: 1945 to the restoration of Bank Rate in 1951, and 1951 to the
temporary lifting of credit restraint and convertibility in 1958.

Lending by the clearing banks was subject to some kind of official
control or restriction throughout the entire post-war period covered by
this book, continuing war-time restraints, except for two relatively brief
intervals, from July 1958 to July 1961 and from October 1962 to
December 1964. The legal basis for this control was found in the
Borrowing (Control and Guarantees) Act of 1946 and the Bank of England

Act 1946. The controls were of two kinds: qualitative and quantitative. The former changed relatively little over the years, the banks being asked, within their total lending, to give priority to such needs as those of defence, exports, farming, import-saving, and other borrowers from time to time considered to operate in the national interest, at the expense, almost invariably, of borrowing for personal consumption, and speculative and hire purchase purposes. Quantitative controls, in contrast, aimed at helping to curb inflation, became progressively more complex.

The years to 1951 saw a brisk upturn in the economy, punctuated by the 1947 convertibility crisis and devaluation in 1949. Industrial production over the period 1946–51 rose by a third and agricultural output continued its war-time expansion. Steel production in 1951 stood at 15.6m. tons, against 12.7m. in 1946, while electricity generated increased by nearly a half. In two particular respects there was a marked contrast to the pre-war years: prices rose and unemployment fell. Over the five years retail prices went up by about a third, while the unemployment rate dropped to little over 1%.

Against this background it is not surprising that there was a marked increase in advances. Lloyds' total nearly trebled between December 1945 and the end of 1951, from £137m. to £374m. In relation to deposits this implied a rise in the ratio from 16% to 32%, to a level, however, still well below inter-war figures. The classification of advances adopted by Lloyds and the other banks in the British Bankers' Association did not correspond at all closely with the official priority list, except for personal borrowing. The share of such borrowing fell sharply. As will be seen from Figure 8, personal and professional borrowers took 35% of Lloyds' advances in 1946 but by November 1951 their share had been reduced to 26%. Over these years there was a slight rise in the share of manufacturing industries, while that of other production[5] increased from 20% in 1946 to 23% in 1951. Figure 9 shows Lloyd's share of advances by all banks in the five categories. For total advances, the bank increased its share steadily from 1946 to 1949, from 13.9% in February 1946 to a peak of 16.4% in August 1949, but thereafter there was a slight decline to the middle fifties. Throughout these years Lloyds' share of personal and professional borrowing was well above that for all advances, but that of manufacturing somewhat below, except for the early 1950s.

From the end of the war (indeed, from 1939) to November 1951 Bank Rate remained fixed at 2%. The bank's minimum lending rate for

[5] Agriculture and fishing, mining and quarrying, builders and building materials, unclassified trade and industry.

FIGURE 8. *Distribution of advances*

advances was generally 5%, although in April 1946 managers, at their discretion, were permitted to reduce this to 4½%. In 1946, as well, arrangements for dealing with applications for advances were partly revised. The system had remained substantially unaltered for the past thirty years, during which lending had more than doubled. Advance department approved lending up to £15,000, while limits above that figure were sanctioned by the chief general managers and reported to the board. The joint general managers had no discretionary powers at all. Now they were given such powers over the range £15,000–£25,000, but in other respects the previous system continued. Managers' discretionary limits were also raised. The minimum was put up to £500 from £250, but in a handful of large branches, the limit was set much higher. In 1948, a further revision raised the minimum at a number of branches to £750. In

FIGURE 9. *Share of advances by different categories*

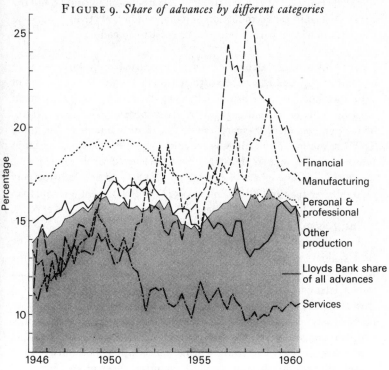

Note: The chart shows Lloyds Bank's share of advances of all banks in the British Bankers' Association.

1955 the general minimum became £750, and in 1958 was raised again to £1,000.

Competition after 1945 woke from its war-time hibernation but its vigour was still curbed to some extent by inter-bank agreements. In part, these reflected the consequences of official wishes on credit restraint; as freedom to lend was restricted, there was not likely to be much profit in aggressive competition for deposits. The clearing banks came to an understanding not to take accounts from one another when advances were refused as being contrary to the criteria drawn up by the authorities. In addition, from time to time they committed themselves to a so-called 'self-denying ordinance' not to compete by way of interest rates or commission charges. In 1953, voicing the general opinion of clearing bankers, Ensor emphasised to managers that there was no intention of reverting to 'conditions of intensive competition' by cutting interest or commission rates, which would, he believed, be contrary to the interests of both the public and the banks. Not until the introduction of 'competition and credit control' in 1971 did such inter-bank arrangements come to an end.

Lloyds' investments remained virtually unchanged in total between December 1946 and December 1950 at around £275m. but at the end of 1951 they shot up to £364m., following the funding of £1,000m. of Treasury bills in November 1951, when monetary policy was revived. This operation made a sharp cut in the bank's liquidity. Including T.D.R.s, the liquidity ratio was reduced to 34.4% of total deposits in December 1951—not far above the conventional 30% level—from 46.4% a year earlier. Government borrowing by T.D.R.s had been considerably reduced after 1945 and by the end of 1951 T.D.R.s stood at no more than £18.5m. in Lloyds' balance sheet (the last time they were to appear), against £290m. in December 1945.

An investment made in 1948 established a formal link with one of the bank's oldest connections, when 2,500 shares were acquired in the Mauritius Commerical Bank, with which Lloyds had previously had an agency relationship. This bank, founded in 1838, had become associated with Barnetts, Hoare & Co., absorbed by Lloyds in 1884. In 1957 an interest was also acquired in Mauritius Commercial Bank Finance Corporation, set up to provide medium-term loans. Over the years Lloyds has provided finance in particular for the production and export of sugar, still, despite diversification, a dominant element in Mauritius' economy.

Deposits in total grew by some £300m. over the six years December 1945-51, from £869m. to £1,172m., an increase of about a third and a much slower rate of growth than during the war. Prices, moreover, also rose by nearly a third, so that in 'real terms' there was hardly any increase at all. Current accounts showed the most growth. With deposit rate fixed at a derisory ½% until November 1951, the proportion of deposit balances remained at historically low levels. By 1951 the ratio had recovered slightly to 30% of total deposits, from 26% in 1945-6, but this was considerably below pre-war ratios—the peak in 1930 was 54%. The number of deposit accounts fell steadily over these years, from 498,000 at the end of 1945 to 427,000 in December 1951, the lowest figure since 1919. Savings bank accounts also shrank in number, from 428,000 to 355,000. However, the increase in the number of current accounts more than offset these falls, so that in December 1951 the total accounts on the bank's books, at nearly 2.4m., were 109,000 more than in December 1945.

At the end of the war the bank faced an enormous back-log of work that needed to be done in its branches and other premises. Apart from the damage caused by bombing, which had been made good so far as possible, general maintenance, decoration, paint-work, and upkeep of fittings had inevitably been reduced to a minimum. Improvements and alterations were also now necessary in many branches. There had been the increase in the staff since 1939, with many more women, requiring lavatories and rest rooms. To eliminate noise, accounting machines needed to be moved from the general office to separate rooms. Heating and lighting had to be modernised. More storage space was needed. Bank houses were often out of date and inconvenient for a manager's family. All this presented a formidable programme and progress was slow at first, since licences were still restrictive and shortages widespread. However, by the autumn of 1948 just on 700 branches had been redecorated and cleaned inside and 580 branches similarly spruced up outside, while work was still in hand on another 430 offices.

During the war some 200 branches had been closed. A start was now made on re-opening them but the process was gradual: in the three years 1946-8 the number of branches increased by only twenty-three. Early in 1946, Whitley-Jones decided that the bank should 'avoid conditions of cut-throat unremunerative branch extension' in the years ahead, a policy which, he believed, Lloyds shared with the other banks. When all the factors appeared favourable then certainly branches should be opened but the general management would want to know very definitely what the prospects were of building up new business in a reasonable period of time. Clearly, the extension spree after the first world war was not going to be repeated.

At the end of the immediate post-war period in 1951, an analysis was made of the main type of business of each branch, divided into six broad categories. The results are shown in Table 9.

TABLE 9.

	%
Personal	28.7
Agricultural	27.2
Industrial	18.8
Mixed	9.7
Sea-side	9.6
Commercial	6.0
	100.0

The main business of over half the branches was either personal or agricultural, and industrial for just under a fifth.

The vital area of staff and administration urgently called for new thinking and new policies with the coming of peace. There were many questions to be faced: the future of the temporary staff taken on during the war, many of them women; the marriage bar for women; the assimilation of returning service men; the recruitment of suitable men for expansion in the years ahead; the proper organisation of training; sufficiently attractive salaries and conditions. Whittaker's dynamic presence and drive came just at the right time.

At the end of 1945 the staff totalled 13,920, against 14,170 in December 1939, a decrease of 250. But there were 2,810 fewer men and 2,560 more women, and women now represented 44% of the total, against 25% in 1939. At the same time, 3,820 men from the bank were still away with the Forces. That the bank had been able to maintain its services to the public so well during the war had depended to a considerable extent on temporaries, and although many now left a number wished to make a career in the bank and joined the permanent staff. Temporary staff made redundant received three months' notice and a gratuity of one week's wages (and grant-in-aid) for each six months' service. In October 1949 the marriage bar for women was finally removed, and they were not required in future to pay pension contributions until the age of twenty-five. The majority were, in fact, under this age. In 1952 three-quarters were under twenty-five, compared with just over half (of a much smaller total) in 1938-9.

The staff of the bank, apart from messengers, were traditionally in one of two categories: clerks, the great majority, engaged on clerical and routine work; and managers and other officials up to the highest rank, whose appointment was subject to formal approval by the board. In 1947 a non-commissioned officer class, as it were, was created between the officers and the other ranks by the introduction of a 'chief general manager's appointment'. To this rank would be appointed, for example, a clerk-in-charge of a small branch or a manager's deputy in a larger office.

A short time later two decisions were taken on staffing requirements which were to form the basis of post-war recruitment policy. First, for male staff (excluding messengers) the objective was set of securing, so far as possible, 250 men in each annual age-group from twenty-five upwards (1960 increased to 350), with women making up the rest of the staff. In few years, however, did the actual pattern correspond at all closely to this ideal. For one thing, changes in social and educational conditions meant that the stream of young men from which, before the war, Lloyds and other banks had drawn the recruits they needed was now significantly narrower. For another, the sharp swing in Lloyds' recruitment between the 1920s and 1930s was still having its effect. The large intake of young men in the 1920s meant that a third of the male staff in 1950 was in the 40-9 age-group. In contrast, the much lower recruitment figures in the 1930s was reflected in well under a fifth of the men being in the 30-9 age-group. Not until the mid-1960s did the large numbers taken on in the 1920s cease to be a problem.

Secondly, the principle of a 'basic staff' was adopted for branches and departments, defined as the number of men and women required to provide the bank's essential services plus a margin of 10% to allow for holidays and sickness. For branches alone, staff requirements had hitherto been roughly assessed on the basis of one member of staff for every 100 current accounts, a ratio that subsequently continued to be more or less generally realised. In 1953 the ratio was 1 : 102, but in 1963 it had deteriorated to 1 : 93. However, this apparent falling off in productivity was explained by a number of special factors: the increase in the numbers of small accounts, the rise in the volume of work handled, the loss of experienced male staff, and the high rate of turnover of female staff.

This high rate of turnover of women, which became even higher later in the 1960s, had been experienced ever since the end of the war. Jobs were plentiful, hours elsewhere might be shorter and, especially, were usually fixed, pay was often more attractive. The bald figures for the number of men and women on the bank's pay-roll give no indication of either rates of turnover or of the quality of staff, particularly young men, being recruited. During 1946 most men with the Forces returned to the bank and at the end of the year not quite ninety were still serving. Between then and December 1951 the total male staff declined by 420 to 10,510 (excluding messengers, by 570 to 9,960), while female staff increased by 2,100 to 7,180 (41% of the total). To achieve these figures, however, meant running faster and faster on the same spot. Female wastage[6] in the years 1949-51 averaged 17%, against only 8% before the war.

Young men were not so attracted to a life-long career in banking as they had been. They might join for a few years but then leave for a better-paid job elsewhere with earlier prospects of promotion. Many of the brighter boys who came into the banks before the war did so because jobs were scarce. Now they were not. Banking had been regarded by headmasters, it was said, as 'designed by heaven as a receptacle for the steady-going lad

---

[6] The number who left during a period as a percentage of the total at the beginning of the period.

who ends up in the upper fifth'.[7] In the post-war years, the steady-going lad either went on to the sixth form and university or could often find other higher-paid or more congenial work. By the autumn of 1951 male recruitment was causing grave anxiety. The intake of young men thought likely to do well in the bank had virtually ceased in some areas, particularly in London and the south-east, the most prosperous parts of the country. If the bank was to attract the young man with high potential for advancement, then it had to offer realistic pay scales. The time was long past when parents could be expected to supplement his bank pay in the early years of service.

The various changes made at the end of the war had clearly proved insufficient. New salary scales had been introduced in 1946, together with a special London allowance and the replacement of the old pre-war bonus and war-time grants-in-aid by a single cash payment. Experience had shown more needed to be done; it was proving impossible to recruit 'even reasonable quality' young men with existing salary scales. In January 1952, therefore, all the male clerical staff were brought on to a common salary scale, the London allowance increased to £50 and A and B scales introduced for young men considered to have high potential. A boy of seventeen joining the bank was initially placed on the C scale at £160 a year. When he was twenty-four years old he would be earning £310 a year, or £350 and £380 if he were promoted to the B or A scales. At the younger ages, girls continued to receive the same salary as men (equality was granted in 1946) but in later years women's pay was only two-thirds. Cash payments continued, equivalent in 1952 to 25% of salary. All this, however, proved to be only the first step towards the recognition that the labour market for the banks had changed fundamentally since the 1930s. Recruitment difficulties soon re-emerged. It was not until the end of the sixties, nearly a quarter of a century after the end of the war, that the bank really at last came to terms with post-war realities of the recruitment of male staff.

Young men and women not only had to be attracted to join the bank but trained once they were on the staff. Indeed, one of the ways of trying to keep them on the staff was to ensure they received adequate and systematic training. Before the war, training had depended mainly on the time and patience of managers and senior staff. Properly formulated schemes of instruction, moreover, should not be restricted to new entrants. Men destined for managerial posts needed a thorough grounding in the essentials of banking techniques and practices and related disciplines.

[7] 'Staffing the Clearing Banks', by a correspondent, *The Banker*, April 1948.

Passing the Institute of Bankers' examinations plus what could be picked up on the way was not enough.

In the early months after the war such training questions were urgently reviewed. The first major development came in March 1948 when the first course started for potential managers at the bank's staff college at Eyhurst Court, Kingswood, Surrey. This was a mock-Elizabethan country house built in 1907, standing in some thirty-six acres of grounds, that was bought for £23,500 in 1946, but needing another £53,000 to be spent on alterations, furniture, and so on. During the war it had been occupied by the Atlas Assurance Company, and part of the underground pipe-line which connected up with PLUTO (Pipe-line Under the Ocean) to the Normandy beaches after D-Day passed through its grounds. M. H. Finlinson, assistant manager at Collingwood Street branch, Newcastle upon Tyne, and later to be general manager of Lloyds Bank (Foreign), was appointed principal with a staff of six instructors. The first course lasted eleven weeks, but was later reduced to nine and then eight weeks. In 1950 a junior course was started, for men before promotion to a C.G.M. appointment, and shorter in length. By 1954 some 550 men had been through a senior course and 320 a junior course. The latter was eventually phased out, after being transferred in 1966 to the Training Centre.

This centre was opened in October 1950. A comprehensive survey made in 1948-9 showed that Lloyds had fallen behind the other banks in respect of pre-entry training schemes, and in the summer of 1949 the decision was taken to establish a residential training school for all new entrants. Boys and girls would be given basic training in juniors' work, machine accounting and other elementary aspects of banking, and it would also be possible at this early stage to weed out those considered unsuitable for work in the bank. The Beacon Hotel, Hindhead, was bought for £32,500, with a further £24,270 needed for alterations and repairs, and the first course of eight weeks began under the principal, R. J. Blanch, previously assistant staff manager, and his twelve instructors. During the following years various changes were made in the pattern of training. By the early 1960s all male entrants were still attending a course of about five weeks, while two-week courses were now in operation for women book-keeping machinists. Other specialist courses, for cashiers, in securities and other work had also been introduced. The advent of computers in the 1960s called for a fresh look at the whole subject of training and in 1966 systems were again radically overhauled.

The end of the war made it possible to gauge what support there was among the staff of the bank for the Staff Association, established in 1940 to replace the former Staff Representative Committee. In 1948, with demobilisation completed and temporaries departed, the association had 11,660 members, 59% of the total staff, including pensioners. The National Union of Bank Employees, as it had become in 1946 on the amalgamation of the Bank Officers' Guild and the Scottish Bankers' Association, counted considerably less than half this number of members in Lloyds: 4,660 (24%). At this time, annual subscriptions differed significantly: N.U.B.E. £2. 2s. (£2·10), Staff Association 5/- (25p) for permanent staff with twenty years' service, 2/6 (12½p) for others. From 1948 N.U.B.E. membership declined steadily until 1954, when there were 3,620, or 17% of Lloyds' staff, in the union.[8] Membership of the Staff Association, in contrast, increased throughout these years and by 1954 had reached 15,030, or 70% of Lloyds' staff. Although membership of the association continued to grow, it picked up again in N.U.B.E., and this was to prove the peak of relative favour among the staff for the Staff Association *vis-à-vis* N.U.B.E.

While the old S.R.C. in the 1930s had tried unsuccessfully to prevent the staff's pay packets becoming thinner, the Staff Association in the 1950s was concerned, but often equally unsuccessfully, to see they grew fatter. An important stage was reached in 1953. In September, the bank and the Staff Association signed an agreement providing for differences regarding terms and conditions of service of the clerical staff which could not be settled by normal negotiation to be submitted to arbitration. This agreement was first invoked by the Staff Association in 1961.

Relations between the Staff Association and N.U.B.E. were no more amicable than had been those before the war between the S.R.C. and the B.O.G. However, a further attempt was now made to sink these differences and to establish a joint body to represent the staff. In March 1952 a meeting of the Central Council of Bank Staff Associations and N.U.B.E. was held under the chairmanship of Sir Walter Monckton, the Minister of Labour, and a working party was set up. But the next month the N.U.B.E. annual delegate meeting reaffirmed its policy of not collaborating with 'internalism'. The vote went the same way in 1953 but was reversed in 1954. Further talks were then held and in November 1955 the C.C.B.S.A. and N.U.B.E. signed an agreement to set up a joint body. Once again, as in 1941, all this came to nothing. The draft agreement was refused ratification by Lloyds' Staff Association and by the Midland Bank's Staff Association, and was also rejected by N.U.B.E.'s annual delegate conference. So matters stood until the mid-1960s.

[8] Most of this decline was in male membership: from 3,490 to 2,590. Female membership decreased only from 1,170 in 1948 to 1,030 in 1954.

Britain's overseas trade revived quickly in the immediate post-war years and by 1950 the values of both imports and exports were more than double their 1946 figures. By volume, exports increased by no less than 75%, against 25% for imports. Invisibles, too, grew during these five years, with an increase in credit items of over half. All this helped to bring a welcome return of activity to colonial and foreign department, whose business had fallen away so much during the war. In 1950 its name was changed to overseas department, a recognition that the world had moved on since it was founded in 1898. Contacts were re-established with banks on the Continent and documentary credit, exhange, and other business resumed, although the foreign exchange market in London was still rigidly controlled. Staff grew in numbers, turnover on current accounts increased nearly three-fold between 1946 and 1950, and a loss in 1946 was turned into a substantial profit by 1950.

In December 1951 official control of the foreign exchange market was relaxed: banks were now permitted to deal among themselves and, in certain cases, with banks abroad, within the spread of exchange rates fixed by the Bank of England, while the Bank also ceased to support forward rates. In effect, this meant the restoration of the pre-war dealing system and the department now had to brush up its techniques. Its success in so doing was reflected in a 50% increase between 1951 and 1952 in earnings on foreign exchange transactions. Business grew briskly during the 1950s. In 1960 the department employed nearly 590 men and women, against some 380 in 1950 and 350 in 1938. Turnover on current accounts not quite trebled between 1950 and 1955, and then increased over four-fold between 1955 and 1960. Gross earnings in 1960 approached five times their 1950 level, while for profits (both gross and net, after provision for bad debts) the increase was seven-fold. In December 1958 sterling convertibility for non-residents was at last achieved and competition in the foreign exchange market became sharper. This market, although important, did not, however, provide the mainstay of overseas department's earnings. In 1960 nearly half its income was earned from loans, while foreign exchange business contributed a quarter. One last statistic illustrates the revival of travel abroad, for business and pleasure: in 1950 the department met 95,000 orders by customers for foreign money. In 1960 the figure was 351,000.

The other long-established department providing specialist services to customers, executor and trustee department, similarly showed a rapid expansion in these years. In 1947 a company was incorporated in Jersey to carry on executor and trustee business in the Channel Islands. More branches were opened and in 1948 numbered twenty-one, double the 1938 total. Nearly twice as many staff were now employed as pre-war, helping to administer 13,140 estates and trusts, against 5,850 in 1938, while the number of will proposals accepted had increased from 19,000 to 63,000 in 1948. Funds under the control of the department were valued at £129m., over double the pre-war figure. By the end of the 1950s all these indicators had moved even further ahead. In 1958, over 20,000 estates and trusts were being administered and will proposals accepted totalled nearly 108,000. There were thirty-two branches open.

The bank's range of services was further extended in 1956, with the creation of a registrar's department, to undertake such work for companies as the certification and registration of share transfers, the payment of dividends, filing of returns, and so on. Hitherto, a certain amount of registration work had been carried out for customers by City Office and by branches stock office, while in the early thirties, for a short period, the secretary's department had been involved. Clearly, it was more convenient for the work to be concentrated in a separate department. It soon made its mark. By the end of 1957 it was dealing with 44,000 accounts and two years later with over 100,000.

The attempt was now made, not before its time, to bring these and other services of the bank to the notice of the public in a manner adopted years earlier by other industries. Advertising no longer consisted largely of the name of the bank, a few figures, and the not very revealing statement that all kinds of banking business were transacted. Advertisements that were more personal, better laid out and with attractive line drawings helped to dispel the idea of the bank as austere and forbidding, remote from the everyday needs of the man and woman in the street. A series in 1945 was concerned with the banking needs of the factory worker and the business girl, as well as with those of the solicitor and architect. That the potential banking market had been enlarged with the increased numbers at university was acknowledged: an advertisement might now consist of a drawing of a couple of students over an imaginary conversation setting out the reasons for opening an account with Lloyds.[9] Other so-called 'prestige' advertisements were aimed at encouraging goodwill towards the bank rather than at selling particular services. Thus, in 1955 there was an interesting series about different British coins and another in 1958 on the export performance of different industries.

---

[9] In 1937 its equivalent in the Cambridge Student's Handbook consisted of no more than the bald statement that 'The services of the Bank are offered to any member of the University desiring banking facilities', and the services listed were current, deposit and savings accounts, world letters of credit, travellers cheques, and open credits.

Controls continue

The revival of monetary policy in November 1951, the month after the return of a Conservative government, did not bring any relaxation of official restrictions on bank lending. These continued in one form or another until the summer of 1958, when the banks enjoyed a respite of just three years, ending in July 1961. And December 1958, it will be remembered, also saw the restoration of sterling convertibility. The nine years from 1951 to 1960, it has been said,

saw a major transformation of the country's economic position. After the recovery from the 1951 crisis, the external environment was kinder to the United Kingdom and balance of payments crises were less frequent. Production continued to expand; and as shortages disappeared, controls were one by one removed. Economic policy thus became markedly less interventionist. Even greater weight, accordingly, reposed on budgetary policy as a means of controlling the economy; and greater use was made of monetary policy—with debateable success. As the first post-war pressure of demand became less intense, something of the old trade-cycle problem re-emerged. The economy showed a distinct tendency to swing between phases of mild recession and of rapid growth and boom.[10]

During these years, despite the occasional alarums of credit policy, the business of the bank continued to thrive: numbers of accounts increased, deposit balances grew, advances rose, more branches were opened, more staff were employed, profits increased. New forms of business were undertaken: in the middle 1950s Lloyds came to the fore in the provision of medium-term finance; in 1956 the registrar's department was established; in 1958 interests were extended to hire purchase business. These years also saw a change of chairman, deputy chairman and of chief general managers.

In 1953 Balfour of Burleigh was seventy years old and had been in the chair well over the five years originally contemplated in 1946. The question of a successor was thus of some urgency. Sir Jeremy Raisman, then a deputy chairman, did not, as we have seen, wish to take on the job; nor did Lord Runciman, the other deputy chairman. Lord Brand, a director, had seen Sir Oliver (later Lord) Franks, who had recently returned to England after spending the years 1948-52 as ambassador in Washington. Brand suggested that Franks, who had already received a number of offers, might be interested in coming to Lloyds if he were approached. He was approached, was interested and, elected to the board, became chairman in November 1954.

[10] J. C. R. Dow, *The Management of the British Economy 1945-60*, Cambridge University Press, 1964, p. 66.

Franks differed from most of his predecessors in the chair: he came from no old banking family, his career had not lain in the City. Pre-war don, war-time civil servant, head of an Oxford college, ambassador, he was distinguished by formidable ability and a powerful mind. Franks was certainly the most brilliant intellect Lloyds Bank had ever had as chairman. Board formalities he conducted with great skill and courtesy, and encouraged discussion. With the general management relationships were easy—Franks had to rely on their technical judgement and experience—though, on one side at least, occasionally tinged with respectful awe. When Franks became chairman Lloyds had been a going concern for approaching two hundred years and a corporate institution for nearly a century and, not so long ago, had struck a bad patch in the early 1930s. He sensed the cautious attitudes that lingered here and there, the conservatism sometimes evident. Franks was keen, for example, to get more graduates into the bank but was unable to make much progress.[11] Innovations were not exactly encouraged anyway by the restrictive environment in which Lloyds, and the other banks as well, had to operate during much of Franks's time as chairman. Yet during these years new ground was broken, new forms of business were started.

With a new chairman there were also changes in the chief general management. Whitley-Jones retired in 1950, leaving Ensor as sole chief executive until January 1953, when he was joined by E. J. Hill. Ensor retired in June 1954 and for the next three years G. Y. Hinwood was also a chief general manager, together with Hill. In 1958 there was again one C. G. M., Hill, until 1959, when he was joined by E. J. N. Warburton, who became sole chief executive the following year. For most of Franks's years as chairman Hill was thus a chief general manager.

Hill had started work in the bank at Romford branch in 1915 and his career was throughout in London and, after 1930, entirely in the City. Elegant and intellectual, Hill was a very proficient banker, decisive and far-seeing. He early realised the need, for example, for medium-term finance as a complement to more traditional forms of lending and, later in the 1950s, was concerned to extend the bank's interests into hire purchase. He retired in 1960, when he was elected to the board. He remained a director until his death in 1964. Hinwood was originally not a Lloyds Bank man. In 1910 he joined the Marlborough branch of the Wilts and Dorset Bank (merged with Lloyds in 1914). Early in the 1920s he was awarded one of

[11] A senior official who was concerned with these matters wrote in 1957 of his firm belief that the majority of the highest executive positions in the future would not be held by graduates and was 'greatly opposed to any policy of introducing special terms to entice their recruitment'.

the first foreign scholarships and spent two years in South America, and in 1928 became the first resident inspector in India. Hinwood perhaps spent too short a time as chief general manager to make any distinctive contribution to the bank's progress. He was technically very accomplished, in all respects the professional banker. He retired in 1957 and died in 1960.

Throughout the 1950s the bank had to contend with the successive shifts of official credit policy. In November 1951, one of the measures to meet the balance-of-payments crisis was to bring the Bank Rate back into use. The extent of the increase, from 2 to 2½%, was not very great but this was of less significance than the fact that an increase had been made at all.[12] At the same time, the banks were asked to intensify their restrictive lending policy, to continue to grant credit only for essential purposes and to give priority to the needs of defence and exports. This was interpreted by Ensor, for the guidance of managers, as requiring an 'orderly and gradual curtailment of less essential lending over a period'. Bank Rate was raised again the following March to 4%, where it stayed until September 1953, when it was reduced to 3½%. Lloyds' advances in fact declined by £54m. during the two years after 1951, to stand at £320m., 27% of deposits, in December 1953.

Qualitative controls continued but in the summer of 1955, with the balance of payments deteriorating once more and the exchange rate under pressure, a cut-back in lending was called for. In July, the Chancellor, R. A. (later Lord) Butler, wrote to the Governor of the Bank of England, C. F. (later Lord) Cobbold, asking for a 'positive and significant reduction' in bank advances. The London clearing banks decided to aim at a reduction of 10% by December, excluding lending to the nationalised industries. For Lloyds, this had a rather paradoxical result. Following the publicity this target received, some customers of Lloyds with generous limits voluntarily offered to cut them by 10% and then borrowed more under the lower limit than before, a 'ridiculous situation' in Hill's opinion. In the event, Lloyds' advances coming within the scope of the official rules fell by £20m., or about 7%, in the eighteen months from June 1955 to the end of 1956.

Although the balance of payments was in better shape by the beginning of 1956, restrictive credit policies were still judged necessary. In February the chief general managers warned that pressure must be maintained to stop advances from rising. A tight rein was necessary for the rest of the year and into 1957.

[12] *The Economic Survey for 1952* described this rise as 'the most significant change in monetary policy since the beginning of the war' (para. 104).

The next flurry of correspondence between the Chancellor, Governor, and the banks came in September 1957. There had been concern over the exchange rate, and a drain on the reserves. Bank Rate was raised to the crisis rate of 7% and, among other measures, the banks were asked to keep the average level of advances during the next twelve months at the same average level as for the last twelve months. Quantitative control was becoming more complicated. This was different from a straight request for a reduction but it did mean that there was some room for manoeuvre: to keep to an average, an increase in one month could be offset by a decrease in succeeding months. 'For the time being new lending will be difficult if not impossible', managers were warned. At the end of the year total advances were £4m. less than in December 1956.

Lloyds kept its advances within the official limit. A fairly rigid attitude was adopted and by the spring of 1958 some accounts had been lost as a result. By then, signs of a modest recession were evident and the authorities now moved cautiously to stimulate the economy. At the beginning of July restrictions on bank lending were lifted and Capital Issues Committee rules relaxed, hire-purchase controls were removed in October, and by November Bank Rate had come down to 4% from 7% in March. At the same time, the clearing banks lifted the curbs on competition that they had imposed upon themselves. This period of freedom from restraint for the banks in their lending policies, the first since 1939, lasted for three years, until July 1961. For many managers this was their first experience of being able to lend solely by reference to banking criteria, without having to consider official attitudes. Although they might know the theory, practice had been lacking. In dealing with the expected increase in lending propositions, Hill reminded managers in July 1958 that the 'first regard should be to observe sound banking principles'. Lending rose sharply from £364m. in December 1957 to £597m. three years later:[13] from 29 to 44% of total deposits.

By the end of the 1950s, an increased emphasis was given to two quite different forms of bank advance: at one end, medium-term lending to finance the export of capital goods; at the other—in the free environment of 1958–60—lending to personal customers to finance, typically, the purchase of cars and durable consumer goods. Lloyds, virtually alone among the big banks, had undertaken a certain amount of medium-term

---

[13] As given in the monthly C.L.C.B. statements for which, during these years, there was a change in the date of compilation: 31 December in 1957 but second Wednesday in December in 1960. Advances as given in the end-year balance sheet rose from £327m. in 1957 to £582m. in 1960.

lending since the war but the way to expansion dates from 1954, when the Export Credits Guarantee Department started to provide unconditional guarantees to the banks to assist the export of capital goods, to 85% of the value of a contract. Such lending was, of course, a break with the traditional banking principle that an advance was repayable on demand, at least nominally, and some of the older generation of bankers had their reservations. The figures built up gradually. In September 1955, although Lloyds had commitments of £42m., only £6m. had actually been borrowed. Five years hence, in 1960, commitments were £76m. and borrowings £50m., while, in addition, the bank had agreed in principle to lend a further £49m. Facilities covered a wide variety of projects: exports of capital equipment for power stations, railways, and steelworks and, in particular, overseas purchases of civilian aircraft.

Personal borrowing had for years been at the bottom of the priority list. It was thus entirely to be expected that, with the lifting of restrictions, a flood of applications would pour into the banks. In August 1958, a month after controls were ended, Midland Bank sharpened the competition with the introduction of a personal loan scheme on American lines, for sums of £50–£500 at 5% repayable over two years. A scheme of this kind had in fact been considered in 1945 by the special committee reviewing post-war business developments, but had been turned down for a number of reasons.[14]

This policy was maintained. Lloyds, it was believed, could meet any new forms of competition through the normal means of lending, with customers offered loan accounts at $1\frac{1}{2}$% over Bank Rate, minimum 5%, against a true rate on a Midland Bank personal loan of nearly 10%. By September 1959 over 48,000 such loans had been made since August 1958, for a total of £8m., half of which was for cars. In December 1960 the total stood at 66,300 loans (£9.5m.) and rose in the following years to a peak of 78,200 loans (£12m.) in September 1964, towards the end of the second short period of lending freedom. Subsequently, numbers and amounts lent declined, to stand at 38,000 (£5.1m.) at the end of the 1960s. By then, credit restrictions had long been in force once more and, indeed, made more severe. In November 1971, after another review of the question and in the new environment of 'competition and credit control', Lloyds finally came into line with the other banks and introduced a flat-rate-repayment personal loan scheme.

We must now return to the end of the 1950s and look briefly at the impact

[14] Principally, that the needs of the small credit-worthy borrower were already catered for, that it would be inflationary and that borrowers 'would probably be persons of poor repute or the improvident'.

on the bank's lending of the first period of freedom in 1958–61. From 1951 until the spring of 1958 the share of manufacturing industries in Lloyds' advances nearly doubled, from 20% to 38%. In the next two years these industries' share dropped, to 30% in May 1960 (see Figure 8). However, this was only a relative decline: in total, borrowing by manufacturing industries actually increased by £35m. over these two years. In contrast, borrowing by the personal and professional category, which had fallen from 27% (£84m.) in 1951 to 16% (£53m.) in May 1958, then increased to 20% (£109m.) in May 1960. Lloyds' share of total advances of all banks changed little over the three years but there were some movements in individual categories. The bank's share of manufacturing advances dropped two points on balance, while a very sharp fluctuation occurred in Lloyds' share of financial advances over the years 1956–9. This was mainly a reflection of the movements of medium-term lending.

Hire-purchase credit in the immediate post-war years was in very small figures and in the early 1950s increased only gradually. It was not until 1958, with the removal of the limits on minimum deposits and on repayment periods, the end of restraint in bank lending and the lifting of the bar against capital issues for hire-purchase companies that the first boom in business was experienced. Total outstanding credit increased from £556m. in December 1958 to £849m. a year later. This was a tempting field for the banks. Already, Commercial Bank of Scotland had in 1954 pioneered banking participation by acquiring a 100% stake in Scottish Midland Guarantee Trust. It was still the only bank with a hire-purchase association in July 1958. There was then a rush. By the end of September, only Coutts, of the London clearing banks, was without a hire-purchase subsidiary. This was a move described by Sir Oscar Hobson, the eminent financial journalist, as 'without doubt, the most important development in English banking for a generation or more'.[15]

In Lloyds there had been discussion some time previously of buying a controlling stake in an established hire-purchase company and in November 1956 Franks had sounded out the Governor, C. F. Cobbold. But no step was taken until two years later. In July 1958 Cobbold set out his views in a letter to the chairman of the C.L.C.B. On broad national grounds, the Governor believed, there was some advantage in the banks participating in this business but management of hire-purchase and banking should be kept absolutely separate and the banks' interests should be only through subsidiary or associated companies. Lloyds acquired two hire-purchase interests in 1958: first, an equity stake of

---

[15] Quoted in *The Banker*, September 1968, p. 815.

approximately 25% in Bowmaker; second, in conjunction with National Bank of Scotland and Commercial Bank of Scotland (which merged in 1959 to form National Commercial Bank of Scotland) a 100% interest in Olds Discount Co. The latter purchase was transferred to a new holding company, Lloyds and Scottish Finance Limited, to which Commercial Bank of Scotland similarly transferred its share holding in Scottish Midland Guarantee Trust. This was a well-placed marriage: Olds specialised in financing consumer goods, while S.M.G.T. confined itself to vehicles and plant. Lloyds thus had a 50% interest in Lloyds and Scottish Ltd. as the holding company became known in 1961.

In the boom year 1959, the bank's earnings on its hire-purchase interests represented a 'satisfactory return', reported the chairman, and were indeed larger than that the resources involved could have earned in ordinary banking operations. In 1960, however, with controls on hire-purchase terms re-imposed, the cost of money higher, increased competition for business, and more bad debts, the return from Lloyds and Scottish was only 'reasonable'. The next year, 1961, was distinctly more unfavourable: lending conditions were 'very difficult', with no growth at all in total hire-purchase credit outstanding in the country. For the rest of the decade there was little further increase: the total at end-1969 was only £128m. higher than at end-1960. In March 1969 Lloyds' interest in Bowmaker was sold to Bowring. That in Lloyds and Scottish remained at 50% until 1970, after which there was a small decrease in Lloyds' share of the equity.

Investments showed relatively little net change during the 1950s: in December 1951 they stood at £364m. (31% of deposits) and in December 1959 at £321m. (24% of deposits). In 1952, however, Lloyds, together with three other clearing banks (Barclays, Midland, and Westminster) made a change in the way the gilt-edged element was treated for balance-sheet purposes. Until 1951 any deficiency between book and market values was covered by a transfer from reserves, to show gilt-edged investments at or under market value. Lloyds and the three other banks now decided to make no further transfers, so that book value could be above market price. Market value for such large holdings as those of the big English banks does not really have much significance. It is improbable that a bank would wish to sell off at one blow a substantial part of its portfolio. From 1952 to 1954 the market value of Lloyds' gilt-edged holdings was, in fact, above book value. In December 1955 and 1956, however, market value was £8m. below book value and in 1957 this discrepancy had widened slightly to £9m. In the period 1958–68 market value once more exceeded book value but in December 1969 there was again a deficiency of £14m.

Liquid assets, the other main group on the balance sheet besides advances and investments, had by the 1950s become the effective credit base in place of cash, in the banks' tills and as balances with the Bank of England. The Bank's formal recognition of the liquidity ratio dates from 1955; and in 1957 the Governor told the Radcliffe Committee that he had made it clear to the clearing banks that he reserved the right 'to make observations' if their ratios fell much below 30%. During the whole of the 1950s Lloyds' ratio fell slightly below this figure on only two occasions.[16] In May 1963 the Bank indicated that it would take a rather less rigid view of the 30% rule and in October lowered the minimum ratio to 28%. To the end of the decade Lloyds' ratio was never once below this level.

The rate of increase of deposits slowed down significantly after 1951. In the six years from December 1951 to December 1957 total deposits grew by only $7\frac{1}{2}$% (and in 'real terms' fell by roughly a fifth). With lending restraints lifted, however, about the same relative increase was recorded in the following two years. Deposit rates tended upwards during these years, particularly after the middle fifties: in September 1957, deposit rate went up to 5% for some six months, the highest level since 1920. This was reflected in an increase in the proportion of deposit balances. In 1951 deposit balances were 30% of total deposits, but rose to 33% in 1957 and to 36% in 1959. The number of deposit accounts increased each year after 1951, from 427,000 to 630,000 in December 1959. Current account numbers also rose from 1,607,000 at end-1951 to stand at 1,860,000 in December 1959. Including savings bank accounts (which shrank slightly in number during the fifties), total accounts increased from 2.4m. in December 1951 to over 2.8m. in December 1959.

In September 1958, soon after lending restrictions were lifted, competition among the banks was quickened with the introduction by Midland Bank of its personal cheque accounts. These were limited to the receipt and payment of cheques, at a cost of 6d. ($2\frac{1}{2}$p) a cheque, (including stamp duty), and customers enjoyed no other services of any kind.[17] Lloyds' reply was swift. 'We in Lloyds Bank', Hill told managers, 'do not believe in the principle of two classes of personal customers.' A simplified and much reduced scale of charges was introduced. For credit personal accounts with an average balance not exceeding £100, up to 100 entries could now be made at a charge of 7/6 ($37\frac{1}{2}$p) a half-year. The new scheme covered the vast majority of personal accounts. A few months later the

---

[16] March 1957 (29.7%), March 1959 (29.5%).

[17] The scheme came to an end in February 1971 with the abolition of stamp duty on cheques. It is understood that it had been only moderately successful.

clearing banks generally introduced what became known as 'I.C.I. terms', since they applied originally to those wage-earners at the Wilton works of Imperial Chemical Industries whose wages were paid by 'traders' credits'. The basic charge was 10/- (50p) a half-year for a maximum of thirty cheques, reduced to 5/- if a minimum balance of £50 was maintained, and to zero for a minimum balance of £100. Later, the terms were amended and the scheme extended to other large companies and government departments.

The branch network was further extended during the fifties, with a steadily rising number of full offices and sub-branches open. The total in December 1959 was 1,851, compared with 1,711 in 1951, but still about thirty fewer than in 1939. In addition to the branch extension programme, much work resulted from the growth in the bank's business generally and the increase in staff. By the end of 1957 modernisation schemes or improvements had been carried out at 750 branches since the end of the war, and similar work was in hand at a further 106 offices.

With the expansion of business more staff were needed. The number of employees increased throughout the fifties, from a total of 17,690 in 1951 to 20,160 in 1959. Of this increase of 2,470, however, 2,320 was in the female staff and all but a handful of the rest reflected a rise in the number of messengers. The number of women rose from 7,180 to 9,500, to represent 47% of the total in 1959. The recruitment difficulties that the bank encountered in the immediate post-war period in no way abated during these years. Indeed, in some respects they were accentuated. To attract suitable staff and to keep them was a constant anxiety that lifted only occasionally. In 1955 a special recruitment manager was appointed, to visit schools and to keep in touch with career masters. Salary scales were increased, cash bonuses consolidated into salaries, London allowance raised. In this improvement, a relatively greater uplift was given to the younger men and women, where the bank was particularly vulnerable to competition from other employers. Thus, the basic salary of a young man of seventeen increased by 94% between 1952 and 1960 (from £160 to £310), while that of a man of thirty-one (scale C) went up by 69% (from £550 to £930). Yet this barely kept in step with changes in the market, and wastage continued at a relatively high level: in 1956, for example, while 184 young men aged 20–4 were recruited, 121 in the same age group left the bank.

Graduates began to come into the bank after 1952, when A and B scales of pay were introduced for young men of promise, but the numbers were not large. In the seven years to 1957 out of 2,500 men recruited only 100 were graduates. They were offered the same terms as other entrants; nothing in particular was done to attract them, no special programme of training was introduced. There was still a reluctance in some quarters to acknowledge that the old ways of recruitment were unlikely to be adequate to bring in the young men of intelligence and promise who would be needed in future to manage the bank.

For managers, in 1953 a change was at last made in the rules governing their insurance agencies. For many years it had been felt that the system needed reform. Managers having large insurance commissions were sometimes unwilling to leave a branch and to accept promotion, and there could be wide variations in the total income of managers not related to differences in responsibility. A committee that had looked into the question before the war suggested that commissions be reduced and phased out. Its recommendations were turned down. It was felt that managers would much resent the reduction in their income, a reaction understandable in the bleak years of the 1930s. Now the nettle was grasped. Commissions were to be restricted to £200 a year, with anything more to go to the bank. The new system lasted until 1971, when it came to an end with the creation of the bank's insurance department.

Among female staff wastage continued at a high rate for most of the fifties, and by the end of the decade was running at nearly 20% a year. In London, particularly, difficulties were often acute and in 1951 the first 'provincial volunteers' were recruited. These received a special allowance and regular free travel home (the scheme was later extended to male staff for work in London branches). In 1957 the relationship of older women's pay to that of men was improved: a woman doing work comparable to that of a man now received four-fifths of his pay, instead of two-thirds. The majority of women in the bank were machinists, typists or engaged on routine clerical work. A number of them found counter duties congenial, to the satisfaction of the bank's customers, and in the mid-1950s there were about 600 women cashiers. By 1968 nearly half the 6,000 or so cashiers were women.

In 1948 the first woman had received a board appointment and in 1950 the first woman received a chief general manager's appointment, but in 1955, out of 7,900 women in the bank, only two had board appointments. The number of such women increased only gradually. In 1968, of over 15,000 female employees, only eight had board appointments—four in head office departments—while another sixty-four had chief general manager's appointments. Not until 1970 was a woman appointed as a branch manager.[18]

[18] At Bath Road, Cheltenham, branch. Barclays Bank had appointed a woman as branch

Gross profits rose steadily after the war and between 1946 and 1958—the year when the brakes on lending were taken off—increased by some £11m., from about £5½m. to nearly £17m. This was the result of an increase in total earnings of £40m., combined with a rise in outgoings of around £29m. Over a third of the improvement in earnings came from increased overdraft receipts, reflecting the revival of lending and, in the later 1950s, higher rates of interest. In 1959 and 1960, with a jump in lending, overdraft earnings went up by a further £13m. and gross profits increased by nearly £9m., to stand at over £25m. in 1960. There was thus an increase of 377% in profits between 1946 and 1960. In 'real terms', however, the increase was considerably less, at 158%.

These figures, of course, take no account of such off-sets as income tax and provision for bad debts. Net profits between 1946 and 1958 increased by £5m., less than half the rise on the gross basis, while published profits, struck after allowing for transfers to reserves, went up by just over £1m. However, in the next two years, 1959 and 1960, net profits improved by a further £4½m. and published profits by rather less than £2m.

In 1953, as 'a matter of simple justice to the shareholders', as the chairman put it, the dividend paid was raised to 14% from the level of 12% at which it had been maintained since 1932.[19] But the net return to a shareholder after tax was still less than before the war, and before making any allowance for inflation. Lloyds' shares, however, could now be regarded once more as an equity rather than as a form of fixed-interest security, and subsequent years saw further improvements in the dividend.

Besides justice for shareholders, there was also the need to build up capital and reserves in relation to the bank's business. Inner reserves had been strengthened during the war and by 1947 were nearly double their 1937 level. This husbandry proved its worth, for in the early post-war years the bank's reserves had to meet such calls as the heavy backlog of expenditure on property maintenance, rebuilding, and re-equipment. But in relation to total resources, capital and reserves—published and inner combined—stood at not quite 4½% in 1947, little more than half the ratio ten years earlier. It was one of Franks's prime objectives when he became chairman to raise this ratio and this he achieved. In December 1952, the year before he joined the board, paid-up capital stood at £15.8m. (unchanged since 1926), published reserves at £16m., and inner reserves

---

manager in 1958. It must be remembered that relatively few women chose a life-long career in the banks and, of these, not a great number prepared themselves professionally for senior positions. In 1968 only a quarter of the women in Lloyds were aged twenty-five years and over. But a change may be occurring: by 1976 the proportion had risen to over a third.

[19] On the 'A' shares.

at nearly £27m. Capital and reserves combined thus approached £59m, or just under 5% of the bank's total resources. In 1955 paid-up capital was increased by £3.6m. by drawing on general reserves, in 1956 there was a capital reorganisation and in 1958 and 1959 further capital changes, including a rights issue. By December 1959 paid-up capital had been raised to £34.8m. published reserves to £25m. and inner reserves to over £48m. Capital and total reserves were now nearly double the 1952 level, at £108m., and equal to $7\frac{1}{2}$% of total resources. This was not quite back to the ratios of the twenties and thirties but, nevertheless, was a marked recovery from the war-time deterioration.

8

Expansion in the 1960s

Years of growth

The 1960s were years of growth and new ventures, for Lloyds as for the other banks, following on the various changes ushered in by the end of credit restraint in 1958. 'The developments in British banking during the past decade', said the president of the Institute of Bankers in 1965, 'have been on a scale never seen before in its long history'.[1] Lloyds' business expanded at a much faster rate than at any time since the war, against a background of recurrent balance-of-payment crises—in 1961, 1964, and 1967—and of a continued rise in prices, but also of an average increase in the country's output of some 3% a year. Not only was there growth in such traditional indicators as deposits and number of accounts. There were also new interests, new methods of operation, and new services. All this was in spite of the fact that for most of the decade advances business was inhibited by official restriction. The first phase of freedom came to an end in July 1961; the next lasted from October 1962 to December 1964. Thereafter, lending continued to be cramped and controlled until the new methods of 'competition and credit control' were introduced in 1971.

Towards the end of the decade, in 1968, Lloyds tried to follow some of the other clearing banks along an old road to expansion. If the bank had gone that way it would have been the greatest change since it was founded two centuries previously. A merger with Barclays and Martins Banks, if it had been accomplished, would have been not so much a new development as the extinction of Lloyds as a separate and independent institution, with the probable disappearance of many of its distinctive traditions and ways of doing business. But this was not to be. The government accepted the conclusion of the majority of the Monopolies Commission's members that a merger of Barclays and Lloyds would be against the public interest, and Martins was subsequently acquired by Barclays. The bank's progress this way blocked, it was not long before, under the dynamic leadership of a new chairman, Eric Faulkner, a new route ahead was mapped out, whose destination was a properly organised world-wide Lloyds Bank Group.

[1] D. W. Stirling, presidential address, 19 May 1965.

Franks became chairman in 1954 and had been in office just six years when, early in 1961 he announced, to the board's surprise, that he had decided to return to Oxford. As in 1952, when Franks had returned from Washington, a man of his outstanding ability and unrivalled experience was not lacking offers of distinguished and worth-while jobs. He chose to accept the position of Provost of Worcester College. Franks and his immediate predecessor as chairman, Balfour of Burleigh, had both come from outside the bank and there was now a feeling among the board that, for the next chairman, it would be preferable to choose one of themselves. There were then at least three directors on any short list, from whom Harald Peake was elected to succeed Franks and he became chairman in February 1962.

Peake, a director since 1941 and a vice-chairman since 1947, came from a coal-mine-owning family in Yorkshire and had followed a varied career in business. He had been chairman of the Steel Company of Wales 1955-62, and was a director of Rolls Royce and of a number of other companies. He was, however, no trained banker and did not pretend to any profound knowledge of credit policy or financial questions. The bank's affairs in the main were left to the general management to deal with, although Peake wished to be consulted, and convinced, about major issues. One of Peake's main objectives was to improve communications, particularly with shareholders and staff, and in this he largely succeeded— he had been Director of Public Relations in the R.A.F. 1940-2 and Director of Air Force Welfare 1942-3. Peake was also instrumental, together with another member of the board, Sir Roy Matthews, in arranging the purchase in 1967 of 24 Cornhill from the Commercial Union Assurance Company, which provided much needed space for head office expansion. Peake's term as chairman will probably be remembered especially for the attempted merger with Barclays and Martins, in which he was one of the prime movers, and in this he met failure. The proposal was made without any previous study or analysis and this, it could be argued, showed a certain lack of judgement and unawareness of how mergers come about, although it is also to be remembered that the subsequent case made out for the merger was by no means negligible.

At the beginning of 1967 Peake told the board that he wished to step down at the annual general meeting in 1968 to make way for a younger man—he would then be sixty-eight—and Sir Reginald Verdon-Smith accepted the invitation to succeed him. Verdon-Smith, chairman of Bristol Aeroplane Company and a director of other companies, had become a director of Lloyds in 1951, vice-chairman in 1963 and deputy chairman in 1967.[2] In July 1967 a report of the Committee of Public Accounts was highly critical of Bristol Siddeley Engines and the excess profits the company had made on official contracts, of which firm Sir Reginald had at the time been chairman. Subsequently, the government appointed a committee under Sir Roy Wilson Q.C. to enquire into the affair and, in the circumstances, Sir Reginald decided to withdraw from the prospective appointment as chairman.[3] Peake thus continued in the chair until February 1969, when he was succeeded by Eric O. Faulkner, chairman of Glyn, Mills & Co. Peake remained a director until 1972, was knighted in 1973, and died in 1978.

The system of local committees of the board was extended early in the 1960s. In 1961 the number was increased from ten to thirteen, with the establishment of district committees, as they were now called, at Aylesbury, Guildford, and Nottingham, while the next two years saw two more established, for Greater London and for the South-East (at Tunbridge Wells). In 1968 the name was changed once more, to regional board. Regional boards have proved to be a most useful part of the bank's organisation. The five or six members are chosen for their local standing and knowledge of regional affairs, with the chairman of each board a member of the main board in London. Good relations are fostered with customers, board members' visits and interest boost managers' morale, and awareness of what is happening and likely to happen locally is often a considerable help in planning the bank's policy.

Development of district (in 1968 regional) offices also went ahead. In 1946 seven district offices were in existence, and ten years later there were nine. At the beginning of 1956 Franks noted that 'our policy in this matter does not make sense . . . at present there are large omissions'. There was, for example, no district office for the home counties, as it was argued that customers in these areas looked to London. A committee then examined the question and recommended that the whole country should be covered by district offices, except for London and the home counties. Subsequent years saw this policy carried out, but branches in the home counties were included, while in 1962 a Greater London district office was set up. By then district offices and board local committees matched completely,

---

[2] Together with the chairman, Sir Oliver Franks, Verdon-Smith was a member of the 1957-9 committee on the working of the monetary system, under Lord Radcliffe as chairman.

[3] He remained as deputy chairman. The Wilson Committee exonerated Sir Reginald of any intention of misleading the C. P. A. about the actions taken by Bristol Siddeley regarding government contracts. However, he was dismissed from all his public positions, a move that was widely condemned as victimisation.

except for the special case of the board local committee for Pall Mall branch. This was absorbed in 1968 into a new regional board, established together with a regional office, to cover some eighty branches in Central London, hitherto controlled by head office. In 1969 the regional office in Birmingham was divided; one office to cover Birmingham and another the West Midlands, but both sharing the same regional board. Similarly, in 1970 the Greater London regional office was divided into an office for North London branches (and, incidentally, those in the Channel Islands) and another for South London branches, again both coming under the same regional board. There were now fifteen regional boards and seventeen regional offices.

This structure of regional offices has proved as equally valuable as that of the regional boards, which it complements. The regional general manager is the local representative, as it were, of the general management and is able to explain and discuss policy and other developments through regular meetings with managers in his region, to whom he is always available for advice and help. He also keeps in touch, together with the regional board, with local customers and with regional commercial and other conditions. Until 1957 a regional general manager had no power to sanction overdraft limits. He was then given authority to sanction limits in the range £15,000–£25,000. In 1966, however, this authority was rescinded, but the R.G.M. was now to receive loan applications over £30,000 for the subsequent approval of higher authority.[4] This change meant a welcome reduction in the paper work of the regional general managers, who thus had more time to get out and about in their areas.

There were few further moves in the 1960s to decentralise any other head office functions. In the late thirties there had been three staff controllers outside London, in Birmingham, Cardiff, and York, while during the war staff control was centred in the evacuated staff department at Swindon. Soon after 1945 seven, later eight, regional staff controllers were established, a system that remained unchanged until 1970. It was then decided to appoint a regional staff controller at each regional office, except for London, while the Birmingham and West Midlands regions were to be treated as one area for staff purposes. The number of premises department building inspectors outside London—or staff architects, as they were called after 1950—was five in 1938, four in 1945, still four in 1960, and six in 1969. In the 1970s, premises department, like staff control, came to be represented in each of the regions of the bank.

---

[4] Other sanction authorities were also changed. In 1957 the limit for a joint general manager was raised from £25,000 to £50,000 and in 1964 to £100,000, while in 1966 the limit for the advance department was increased from £15,000 to £30,000.

Two chief general managers spanned the expansion and new developments of the 1960s: E. J. N. Warburton from 1959 to 1966 and Michael
Wilson from 1967 to 1973. Warburton joined the bank in 1922 at Brighton
in what had been a branch of the Capital and Counties Bank. In 1931 he
moved to the chief inspector's department, and received his first board
appointment as sub-manager of Aldwych branch, London, in 1936. The
war brought much and varied experience as personal assistant to Whitley-
Jones, then a joint general manager, and Sydney Parkes, one of the two
chief general managers. Appointed a joint general manager in 1953,
Warburton became deputy chief general manager in 1958 and, together
with Hill, chief general manager the following year. Hill retired in 1960,
when Warburton became the sole C.G.M. The only two periods of
freedom from lending restrictions in all the years from 1945 to 1971 thus
came during Warburton's time as chief executive. It was a testing
experience, through which he brought the bank unscathed.

Warburton was another of the all-round professional and gifted bankers
whom Lloyds has been fortunate to have as chief executive. Extremely
able and ready to accept responsibility, Warburton rose to the needs of the
time when lending restrictions were lifted. He also saw the benefits of
closer relationships with the press and other media. A year before his
retirement in 1966 Warburton was elected to the board, the first chief
executive to become a director since Henry Bell in 1916, if one excludes
R. A. Wilson and Sydney Parkes, who became directors in 1941 in the
exceptional days of war. In 1966 he was awarded a C.B.E. for his work as
deputy chairman of the City of London Savings Committee. Warburton
continued on the board until 1975, and was a vice-chairman 1967–75.

Michael Wilson succeeded Warburton as chief general manager in
1967. Wilson joined the bank after coming down from Oxford in 1932
under the scheme started a short time earlier to recruit graduates. Apart
from a brief spell in the thirties at Newcastle upon Tyne and at Reading
his entire career had been in London branches and head office. The war
years Wilson spent in various units of A.A. Command and, later, on the
staff in Britain and India, and was awarded an M.B.E. He became assistant
chief general manager in 1961 (a new position), deputy in 1963 and chief
general manager in 1967.

In addition to his day-to-day duties, Wilson had to deal during his years
as chief executive with a number of complex and demanding issues that
affected Lloyds, either as an individual bank or as a leading clearing bank:
the investigation of bank charges by the National Board for Prices and
Incomes in 1967, the attempted merger with Barclays and Martins in
1968, the disclosure of true bank profits in 1969, the launching of Lloyds

Associated Banking Co. (LABCO) in 1970, the new methods of 'competition and credit control' in 1971. All these added very considerably to an already heavy volume of work. Yet throughout, Wilson, a first-class banker and a man of considerable charm, remained urbane and unruffled. He was elected to the board in 1968 and became a vice-chairman on his retirement in 1973. In 1975 he was knighted for his work on the Export Guarantees Advisory Council, of which he had been chairman since 1972.

The growth in the size of the bank during the late 1950s and 1960s, the changing methods of operation and the increasing diversity of its services produced the need for certain important functions to be represented at general management level. From the end of the war until 1953, there were four joint general managers, each responsible for the bank's business in one of the four areas into which England and Wales were divided. In 1954 general managers were appointed also for administration and for the executor and trustee department, who were joined in 1960 by general managers for organisation and for the overseas department, and after the end of the decade by general managers for other specialised aspects of the bank's work.[5]

There was faster expansion of the bank during the 1960s than in any comparable peace-time period in the years covered by this study. Deposits in the ten years 1959–69 rose by a half, against less than a fifth in the years 1949–59. In 'real terms', the contrast was even more marked: a rise of nearly a tenth in the period 1959–69, against a fall of over a fifth in the years 1949–59. Advances increased by more than four-fifths. It is true that during the period 1949–59 there was the same proportionate growth in advances but most of this was concentrated in the years 1958–9, when lending restrictions were lifted: between 1949 and 1957 advances grew by less than a quarter. The advances ratio thus rose to approach the levels touched in the late 1920s and early 1930s. From 41% of deposits in December 1959 advances rose to 54% in December 1964, to fall back to 50% at the end of the decade. The second half of the 1960s was almost all a period of tight credit restrictions, with the imposition of 'ceilings' on advances. Investments, in contrast, declined by nearly £100m. over the decade to £224m. in December 1969, when they equalled just 11% of deposits, against 24% in December 1959.

The first post-war period of freedom from lending restraints was near

---

[5] Although all the general managers are of equal standing, the 'banking' joint general managers have tended to attract to themselves a certain slight air of superiority, possibly because they occupy traditional long-standing positions by comparison with the more recently-created appointments of their colleagues.

its end in April 1960, when the first call for special deposits[6] was made and controls re-imposed on hire-purchase agreements. There was now a need, the chief general managers informed managers, for 'selectivity and some restriction in the Bank's lending', although it was hoped to avoid more stringent measures. These became necessary the following year. In 1961 the balance-of-payments crisis prompted a rise in Bank Rate to 7%, a further call for special deposits and strict qualitative guide-lines for lending. The bank's policy was now to curb the rate of increase in advances, and the total in December 1961 was in fact cut to slightly below the December 1960 level. The economic position mended and by the summer of 1962 'a significant, though small, change in climate' meant, Warburton believed, that a modest increase in lending was possible. In October all official lending restrictions were once again removed and the aim was set 'to make the utmost use of our present easier position to promote the long-term interests of the Bank'. However, with the investment ratio down to under 20%, compared with 30% in 1957, there was not the room for an expansion in advances on the scale of 1958–9.

Even so, lending increased smartly and Warburton was surprised at the size of the pent-up demand that came forward. Fortunately, the potential for growth was raised somewhat in 1963 when, as was noted earlier, the Bank of England reduced the minimum liquidity ratio for the clearing banks from 30 to 28%. But in February 1964 the first sign that the end of lending freedom was not far off came with a rise in Bank Rate to 5% as an 'amber light'. Once more, the payments position deteriorated and confidence in sterling slumped. In November Bank Rate was back to 7%, and the next month lending again came under official controls. The increase in advances now had to be reined in, made even more imperative by pressures on liquidity.

From 1965 until the end of the decade, except for a few months in 1967, Lloyds and the other clearing banks (and then all commercial banks) came under a series of official 'ceilings' for lending. Such ceilings became more complicated, to mix metaphors in the official style, when adjusted for seasonal factors; and the height of the ceiling was not always the same. At the end of 1967, for example, the banks were asked to keep their lending at or under the total reached in November, allowing for seasonal movements, but excluding lending to the nationalised industries, local authorities, and for export transactions and, 'within the ceiling', to give priority to finance for production and investment, to foster exports, to save imports, and to promote invisible earnings. Then, just as the banks had settled down to try to meet this 'request', the rules were changed. In May 1968, the ceiling

---

[6] Details of the special deposits scheme had been announced in July 1958.

became 104% of the total to the private sector in November 1967 but now including export finance. Presumably, the bureaucrats believed that advances could be turned on and off like a tap. In spite of the bank's efforts, it was sometimes not possible to keep advances within the limit set: while in the first half of 1968 Lloyds' advances were under the ceiling, in the same months of 1969 they were somewhat above.[7] Not until 1971, with the new system of 'competition and credit control', were ceilings pulled down.

Finance for exports was always a top priority and one particular form, medium-term lending, increased significantly during these years. Lloyds' total rose from £50m. in 1960 to over £140m. in 1969. Lloyds continued to be the front runner among the clearing banks in this field and in the late 1960s still accounted for about a third of all the clearers' medium-term export finance. Such lending, although made against the security of E.C.G.D. guarantees, was foreign to the banks' traditional practices and there were limits to the extent to which they would wish so to commit themselves. In 1961, therefore, a scheme was agreed with the Bank of England whereby the Bank agreed to re-finance a certain proportion of the banks' medium-term loans, thus improving their liquidity commensurately; these procedures were extended in 1965 and 1969. In January 1962 the banks announced a special scheme to provide medium-term finance for exporters at a fixed rate of $5\frac{1}{2}$%, the average blue-chip rate for the previous five years. At the time this was a realistic rate but as the years went by and rates generally tended upwards it became increasingly out of line with market conditions. In 1969 Lloyds' lending under this and other export finance schemes was in fact costing the bank nearly £4m. a year.[8] Not until October 1970 was the rate raised to 7%.

Figure 10 shows the distribution of Lloyds' advances during the 1960s. The classification adopted by the banks did not correspond with official qualitative criteria, as has been mentioned before. However, manufacturing industries, much of whose production was exported, accounted for an increasing share of Lloyds' advances from the end of 1964 onwards, and particularly after 1968. The drop in 1962-4 was only relative: actual advances to manufacturing rose by £45m. In contrast, the shares of the personal and professional and financial categories declined steadily after 1964, when lending restrictions were reimposed. Lloyds' share of all

---

[7] In November 1968 the ceiling had been changed again. Lloyds was not alone in not being able to get its advances in 1969 under the ceiling. In June 1969, as a penalty, the rate of interest paid on special deposits of the clearing banks with the Bank of England was halved. It was restored the following April.

[8] The difference between what the funds committed to these schemes could have earned if lent at market rates and what they actually produced.

FIGURE 10. *Distribution of advances*

Note: In 1967 there was some re-classification of individual categories of advances.

banks' lending changed little during the decade (see Figure 11) but it was of course at a somewhat lower level after the change in coverage in 1967. However, a very sharp drop occurred in Lloyds' share of all financial lending: from 14% in February 1967 to under 7% in November 1970. This was the result of a significant contraction in advances to hire purchase and property companies.

Deposits, as was pointed out above, increased by half in the ten years 1959–69. The greatest relative growth was in deposit account balances, partly reflecting the upward movement in rates during the decade. Deposit money represented 36% of liabilities to the public in 1959 and increased to 42% by 1969, the highest ratio since the outbreak of war. While less than a third of total deposit balances in 1969 were in accounts of under £1,000, such accounts represented nine-tenths of the total number of deposit accounts. These had more than doubled between 1959 and 1969, against an increase of little more than a half in the number of current accounts. The total number of accounts, including savings bank accounts, grew from 2,806,000 in 1959 to 4,626,000 in 1969. This increase, in ten years, was slightly greater than that in the whole forty-one years from 1918 to 1959.

Deposit rate throughout the period, under the clearing bank cartel of which Lloyds was a member, remained at 2% below Bank Rate for money at seven days' notice. In 1963 the clearers examined schemes for an extension of deposit accounts, with the introduction of rates for balances at fourteen, twenty-one, and thirty days' notice, and linked to some increase in lending rates. However, the latter met with official disapproval and the proposals came to nothing. In 1969, the government made clear its view that 'the public interest would not be served, at any rate at the present time, by urging the banks to abandon their agreement upon deposit and lending rates'.[9] Another two years were to elapse before the agreement came to an end, with the introduction of the system of 'competition and credit control'.

The branch network was further extended during the 1960s, with more offices opened than in any period since the twenties. The total of branches and sub-branches increased by 456, to stand at 2,307 in December 1969. The rebuilding of Colmore Row branch in Birmingham, finished in 1967,

---

[9] This followed the suggestion for such changes made by the National Board for Prices and Incomes in its 1967 report on *Bank Charges* and the comments by the Monopolies Commission in its 1968 report on the proposed merger of Barclays, Lloyds, and Martins Banks.

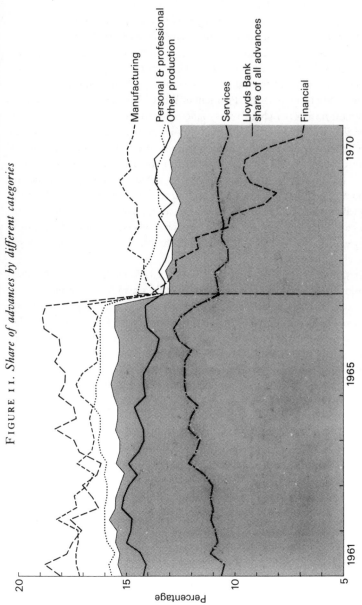

FIGURE 11. *Share of advances by different categories*

Manufacturing

Personal & professional

Other production

Services

Lloyds Bank
share of all advances

Financial

20

15

10

5

Percentage

1961

1965

1970

Note: The chart shows Lloyds Bank's share of advances of all banks in the British Bankers' Association, 1961–6, and of all banks in Great Britain, 1967–70.

was the largest such project undertaken by the bank since the rebuilding of head office in the 1920s.

Some of these new offices were opened in anticipation of the increase in business that was thought likely to result from a reform in the way wages could legally be paid. In 1959, when a committee under Mr. David Karmel Q.C. was set up to consider the operation of the Truck Acts, the government decided to deal separately with the limited question of how wages could be paid. By the Payment of Wages Act 1960 payment of wages by credit transfer or cheque was made legal. Much more work, the banks thought, would now fall on their branches and clearing departments through an increase in the number of cheques drawn, and pressure on counter space was likely to be greater. But there was also the prospect of more personal accounts being opened. A survey of Lloyds' branches in 1960 revealed that a quarter expected no material effect, while half could absorb any likely increase in business resulting from the Act. For most of the rest, alterations of premises would be necessary. New offices were suggested in 258 locations, in which, as a first step, it was decided to open branches in eighty-four.

In the event, the 1960 Act turned out to be rather a damp squib. Neither employees nor employers showed much enthusiasm for changing existing methods of wage payment and there was no great rush to open more personal bank accounts.[10] This might possibly have been expected. The Truck Acts did not apply to Scotland, and there had been no material differences between England and Scotland in how wages were paid. Of the eighty-four new branches planned in 1960, fifty-five had been opened by 1966, but twenty-seven had been abandoned, and work was proceeding at two.

Overseas and executor and trustee departments both experienced an upsurge in business and all-round growth in their figures. At overseas department, turnover on current accounts increased nearly five-fold between 1960 and 1969, while forward exchange contracts outstanding rose from £75m. in December 1960 to £748m. in December 1965, and to a

---

[10] The great majority of weekly-paid employees are still paid in cash. A survey in 1976 of methods of payment in Britain showed the following:

Workers paid	Cash	Paid by Cheque	Credit transfer	Other
	%	%	%	
Weekly	86	7	6	1
Monthly	6	22	70	2

Peter Hirsch and John Railton, 'Cash Rules U.K. O.K.?', *Journal of the Institute of Bankers*, April 1978.

peak of over £2,000m. in the devaluation crisis of 1967. Gross earnings in 1969 were nine times the 1960 level, profits more than double and the number of staff up by over half. In addition, earnings by branches on overseas business, which for some, of course, were fairly small, in total added up to a respectable figure and more than trebled between 1960 and 1970.

The executor and trustee department not only achieved a growth of its traditional forms of business but started to widen its range of facilities. In 1960 an investment management service was launched and in October 1966 the department introduced its First Unit Trust, a balanced equity fund for capital and income growth. Lloyds thus became the first of the London clearing banks to take on the management of a unit trust and the first to sell units of any trust over its counters. At the end of the year 14.5m. units were outstanding, increasing to 53.4m. by December 1969. A Second Unit Trust followed in November 1968, aimed mainly at capital growth, of which 36.5m. units were outstanding in December 1969. A life assurance savings scheme was also introduced in 1968, in conjunction with the Royal Insurance Group, under which policies issued were linked to units.

For the bank to make its way in the increasingly competitive environment of the 1960s the legitimate public interest in its affairs and policies could not be disregarded. Advertising, it is true, had been brightened up. Yet, little had been done actively to present the bank as an up-to-date efficient enterprise and the press and other media were generally kept at arms' length. 'We are really very amateurish in our approach to public relations and advertising', a paper in 1960 admitted, 'the old fashioned conservatism will no longer be enough.' In 1961 the first step was taken with the appointment of a public relations officer,[11] with his own department to handle advertising, relations with the press, and so on. Most of the bank's promotional booklets were now rewritten. Advertising was not restricted to telling the public about the bank's services—'Lloyds Bank is helping this policeman's wife to save money safely'—but was now aimed also at getting some of the public to join the bank's staff—'I *did* enjoy my first day'. In 1966, more than forty years after it was suggested for Leicester Square, a large electric sign, representing a Lloyds Bank cheque book, was erected in Piccadilly Circus.

New interests

In spite of the credit restrictions that were in force for most of the 1960s,

[11] He had been a manager of a provincial branch. Not until 1972 was a trained professional appointed to head the bank's public relations department.

during these years the bank introduced new facilities and undertook new ventures. It is indeed surprising, given the cold hand of restraint, that so many flourished. Some have already been mentioned: medium-term export finance, unit trusts, an investment service. In addition, there were extensions of the bank's interests in other financial institutions. One development of enormous significance—the introduction of computers— deserves a section of its own.

Lloyds itself established a specialised institution: Lloyds Bank Property Company. This was set up in 1963, with an initial capital of £100,000 and wide borrowing powers, to carry out property develop- ment schemes incorporating branch premises. Many of the bank's branches were established when land was cheap and building costs low, an advantage shared also, of course, by other clearing banks with extensive branch networks. Post-war development and high and increasing rents had brought new problems. Various ideas were canvassed to enable the banks to co-operate in the modernisation of town centres. Lloyds property company was one solution: to undertake building schemes involving operations larger than the bank's own requirements justified. The first property acquired was in 1963 at Nottingham, where planning permission was given for a large development scheme, to include the rebuilding of the bank's old-established branch. This was completed in 1968. Many other development schemes have followed.

In 1965 and 1966 the bank's interests in overseas business were extended on two fronts.

First, the bank acquired a 25% share in Exporters' Refinance Corporation. This had been established in 1961 by S. Japhet & Co. Ltd., Hongkong and Shanghai Banking Corporation and National & Grindlays Bank to provide credit to help British manufacturers to sell abroad and overseas governments and others to buy capital goods in Britain. Lloyds put in further capital in 1966, 1967 and 1969 to raise its stake to 75.6%. E.R.C.'s business expanded rapidly, and it made a name for itself in providing specialised financial services for exporters, to supplement the bank's own medium-term facilities. However, in 1971, after this study ends, lending irregularities came to light and Lloyds and the other shareholders had to make certain provisions against loss. Business was run down and, as Lloyds had the majority shareholding, it was decided that the necessary financial adjustments would be easier to make if E.R.C. became a wholly-owned subsidiary of Lloyds, which it did in 1975.

Secondly, in 1966 The National Bank of New Zealand, in which Lloyds had first invested in 1919, became a wholly-owned subsidiary.[12]

In July 1967 Lloyds acquired another bank, with the purchase from Martins Bank for £3.2m. of the share capital of Lewis's Bank. This institution, founded in 1928, had been owned since 1958 by Martins, which offered it for sale on the acquisition by Sir Charles Clore, a customer of Lloyds, of the ten department stores in which it had branches. Lewis's head office was in Liverpool and it had no other offices outside these stores. In 1967 it had deposits of about £12m., lending of £830,000, 68,000 customers, and some 180 staff. Lewis's is thus something of a curiosity among banks but has provided first-hand experience of the problems of providing in-store banking.

In the summer of 1967 there were discussions among certain of the banks operating overseas about the creation of some kind of link or association. These crystallised in September, when the formation of Intercontinental Banking Services was announced by Lloyds and six other banks.[13] One of these was Barclays; for Lloyds and Barclays to work together in this group foreshadowed the attempt to forge an even closer union in 1968.[14] The prospects for I.B.S. looked bright, at least on paper. Its activities were to be 'diverse within the fields of economic survey, viability study, and the provision of finance upon an almost world-wide basis in most currencies'. It might be able to compete with the World Bank in Washington as a source of finance. The seven owners had world-wide connections, deposits exceeding £7,000m., and over 8,000 branches. Capital was £350,000, each bank subscribing for 500,000 shares, 10% paid. Eric Woolgar, recently retired as general manager (overseas) from Lloyds, was appointed general manager.

Unfortunately, Intercontinental Banking Services was launched at just the wrong time. In November 1967 sterling was devalued and bank advances came under a new ceiling. Any money placed with I.B.S. by its parent banks as advances was thus subject to this restriction; and any lending in sterling by I.B.S. itself was limited by a ceiling of no more than £500,000. Operations in sterling were thus virtually impossible and business consisted chiefly of lending in Euro-currencies at medium-term.

[12] For details of this transaction see Chapter 2, p. 29.
[13] Australia & New Zealand Bank, Bank of London & South America, Barclays, Barclays D.C.O., Chartered Bank, National Bank of New Zealand.
[14] Sir George Bolton, chairman of BOLSA, remarked that this was '. . . the first time that we have had two major clearing banks, Barclays Bank and Lloyds Bank, publicly showing every possible goodwill towards co-operating in this overseas banking field'.

The story of I.B.S. after 1969 is outside our scope. In brief, although it made a profit, the parent banks came to question the role of I.B.S. If, in time, it was able to expand, it would increasingly compete with operations they themselves carried out and its provision of economic intelligence to some extent duplicated their own facilities. In the summer of 1970 doubt hardened into certainty and I.B.S. was put on a care-and-maintenance basis. Woolgar left, business was run down and the company ceased to trade after March 1976. Barclays Bank International (as Barclays D.C.O. had become) bought out the other shareholders and in September 1976 Lloyds received back its original stake of £50,000.

Another venture with which Lloyds was associated was the introduction of a cheque card. In 1966 Lloyds and eleven other banks, excluding the big four, issued a card to customers guaranteeing the payment of cheques up to £30. This lasted three years. In 1969 the major English, Scottish and Irish banks agreed on a standardised card to replace the existing individual cards.

The growth in business, innovations, and new interests of the 1960s had their impact on the bank's profitability. Our glance at this, however, will extend no further than 1968. For the accounts of Lloyds (and the other clearing and Scottish banks) were for 1969 and subsequent years published on a new, fully-disclosed basis and were thus not comparable with those for previous years.

Gross profits in the nine years 1960 to 1968 improved from over £25m. to nearly £37m., or by 44% (but in 'real terms' by only 11%). The increase in advances and the upward movement in rates over the period raised interest earned on loans and overdrafts from 46% of total income in 1960 to 55% in 1968. On the other hand, the growth in deposit balances and the rise in rates meant a not quite three-fold increase in interest allowed. The bill for salaries and pensions, the other major element in costs, also went up considerably: by three-quarters between 1960 and 1968.

Gross profits thus rose by some £11m. during these years. As a return on total resources the peak was touched in 1965, when the ratio of gross profits rose to just over $1\frac{3}{4}$%, the highest figure since the boom year 1920. After allowing for income tax, bad debts, and other charges, net profits increased by about £9½m. between 1960 and 1968. Profits as published— the net figure after allowing for transfers to reserves—rose by nearly £8½m.

The bank's paid-up capital almost doubled in these eight years, increasing from £34.8m. in 1960 to £64.9m. in 1968. In 1961, 1962, and 1964 there were capital re-organisations, involving scrip and rights issues, which raised the total to £61.3m. Then, in 1966, the purchase of the outstanding shares of The National Bank of New Zealand by the issue of eleven Lloyds' shares for every ten N.B.N.Z. shares added a further £3.6m. to issued capital, making the total £64.9m. Reserves were also strengthened, with published and inner reserves combined raised from £73m. in December 1959 to £189m. in 1969 (now all published). As a ratio of the bank's total resources, capital and reserves rose by half: from 7.5% to 11.3%. In this fundamental respect, the bank was thus now more secure than at any time in the whole period covered by this study.

The computer revolution

In October 1970 Lloyds Bank became the first British bank to have transferred its entire branch network to a common computer accounting system, and thus to hit a target date set four years previously. The other clearing banks were, of course, also similarly engaged but none of them matched Lloyds' achievement.

The characteristics of bank accounting—a multiplicity of entries combined with the relative simplicity of the processes involved—made it an ideal field for the application of automation.[15] The advent of computers marked a much more fundamental change than the switch to mechanisation a generation earlier. Not only was the speed of operations enormously faster but other aspects were revolutionised: ledger sheets no longer existed; an electronic box, getting smaller as the years went on, took the place of machinists; automation was not restricted only to book-keeping.

A number of reasons were responsible for the move to computers by Lloyds and the other banks during the 1960s. There was the growth in the number of accounts and the volume of transactions;[16] the difficulty and expense of attracting and keeping staff, particularly in London—rather more than half the staffs of the clearing banks were engaged, directly or indirectly, in clearing cheques—and the high cost of premises to house book-keeping machines and those operating them. Once the decision had been taken to switch to computers a deadline was set of February 1971, by

[15] In 1927 Keynes was remarkably accurate in his forecast that the banks of the future would have 'physical bodies of wonderfully contrived mechanism, almost everything of routine being done by machinery . . .' Talk to Cambridge Centre of Institute of Bankers, *Journal*, November 1927.

[16] The number of debit items handled by the London Bankers' Clearing House increased as follows: 1950 321m., 1960 438m., 1969 752m. The credit clearing, started in 1960, expanded even faster: 1961 64m., 1969 196m.

which time it would be highly desirable, at the least, for all branches to be on the new system. For this was the date, announced by the government in March 1966, for the introduction of decimal currency. In the event, Lloyds—and only Lloyds—beat the deadline, by four months.

Just as in the years after 1945 the needs of the hour in respect of staff recruitment and training called forth the man, R. F. E. Whittaker, so on this occasion the bank was fortunate that one of its senior staff, C. B. Howland, as general manager in charge of organisation from 1960, was ready and able to direct its move into computers. The great progress made in this novel undertaking owed much to Howland's drive and understanding of what had to be done.

Pressures on the capability of the banks to handle the mounting volume of paper resulted not only from the increasing number of accounts but also from the entries they produced. In other words, automation had to be applied to the clearings as well as to the accounting. This was realised very early. Indeed, in 1945 there was discussion of the possibility of special machinery for 'electric-eye' sorting and a few years later a prototype sorter was demonstrated, based on photo-electric principles. Although enthusiasm for this particular example varied among the banks, they soon recognised their common interest in these emerging new techniques and in 1955 the Committee of London Clearing Bankers set up a special electronics sub-committee. As things developed, both the clearings and branch accounting were automated in parallel.

The C.L.C.B. sub-committee decided that automatic sorting would need some common machine language expressed in figures. Three type-founts became available. One of them, called E-13B, the American Bankers' Association had helped to develop, and in 1958 the association adopted it for inter-bank use in the U.S.A.[17] Before the C.L.C.B. made their choice among these three founts, Lloyds with foresight went ahead in March 1960 and ordered an automatic sorter-reader using E-13B to handle 1,500 cheques a minute, the first such equipment to be ordered by a British bank. Nine months later, in December, the C.L.C.B. adopted E-13B. Other problems besides that of magnetic type-founts had to be faced. There had to be sorting code numbers for branches: a new system was introduced. The paper hitherto used for cheques was too soft to stand up to mechanical handling at high speeds: with the help of two research organisations a suitable paper was eventually produced. Staff had to be chosen and trained.

[17] The development and standardisation of E-13B has been called 'one of the great commercial romances of all time'. J. D. Cowen, 'Electronics in Banking: The Phase of Action', *The Banker*, January 1961.

In the meantime, in 1956 Howland, then chief accountant and responsible for the bank's clearings, and a colleague, L. Temple, had visited the U.S.A. to see accounting machine manufacturers and to find out what was happening in American banks. In their report they recommended that a study should be made of the feasibility of computer accounting at Pall Mall branch, where in 1939-41 Howland had supervised the transfer of book-keeping to Powers Samas machines, now coming to the end of their working life. A thorough study was put in hand, which indicated that automation would indeed produce considerable savings. With some 60,000 current accounts in 1960, Pall Mall was an ideal branch for the bank's first essay in computer accounting. Three computers were ordered, the first of which was installed and started operations on 1 January 1962. The initial loading was 2,000 accounts but by April this had risen to 15,000, with further increases in subsequent months. Pall Mall was fully computerised by the summer of 1963.

The computers at Pall Mall were not, however, being used to capacity and the accounts of five other West End branches were now added. This, too, went well and by the spring of 1964 about 70,000 accounts had been loaded. Experience was being built up and routines evolved for the computerisation of branch book-keeping. The Pall Mall installation was converted into a West End Centre, a second centre opened in the City and a computer systems department established, under Howland, to plan the change-over of branches to computer methods. More branches were now taken on by the two computer centres.

The extent to which the two centres could handle further branches was limited at this time by the physical difficulties of passing vouchers or paper each day between branch and centre. A major break-through was made in 1965, when a means of transmitting work—or, in the jargon, paper tape input—became available on an economic and practicable basis. In principle, this and other changes now made it possible to extend computer accounting to about two-thirds of the bank's branches. The problem of the remaining one-third branches, more remote from the two centres, remained. This, too, was overcome in 1967 with the production of suitable terminals, which could print output as well as accept input.

By the autumn of 1966 some 385,000 accounts at 145 branches had been loaded on to computers and, as a result of careful planning, the switch to the new system had been reduced very much to a routine by computer systems department. To the manager and staff of a particular branch, of course, the move to computer accounting meant a major change and much re-organisation of day-to-day procedures. Members of a 100-strong team in time visited every branch in the country, spending some two to three months in each.[18] At first, only current accounts were loaded but from 1967 deposit and savings accounts were included. By the summer of 1969 some forty branches and 100,000 accounts were being transferred each month to computer accounting. In little over another twelve months, in October 1970, the job was completed and computer systems department could be closed.

A total of 2,346 branches and sub-branches, with approaching five million accounts, were now on the new automatic system, linked to computer centres in the City and Birmingham, the latter opened at the end of 1967 (the West End centre no longer handled branch accounting). Entries on these accounts were running at nearly 400m. a year. Separate computer equipment was used for cheque clearings. The City centre handled a daily average of some 650,000 cheques, rising on peak days to well over a million.

Other areas of the bank's operations had also been automated. The work of the registrar's department was ideally suited to the new processes and, starting in 1963, was now fully computerised, covering some 170 companies with $1\frac{3}{4}$m. individual shareholdings. In the executor and trustee department, computer-based routines had been introduced for the control of pension funds and large investment portfolios, as well as for branch accounting. Certain aspects of the specialised work of overseas department has also been covered: in 1968 computers took over part of foreign exchange dealing routines and, later, were extended to drafts and transfers and the accounting systems.

During the whole of this period from the 1950s there were great technical advances and improvements in the design and operation of computers. Magnetic discs took the place of miles of magnetic tape. Terminals linked branches directly to their computer centres. Processing speeds became enormously faster: in only four years 1960 to 1964 there was an increase from some 2,000 to 20,000 items an hour. Questions of speed hardly arose in later years, when the bank's computers became capable not only of handling a number of jobs simultaneously—branch accounting, work for executor and trustee and overseas departments—but also of carrying out operations which could never have been done manually.

All these changes had to be studied, evaluated and adapted to the bank's

[18] Let us take Guildford branch as an example. In August 1964, when the branch had six sub-branches, 8,500 current accounts and ninety staff, the changeover process was started, aimed at switching to computer in January 1966. The following months were spent in preparing branch records, learning new methods, altering premises. In November 1965 a team of six instructresses arrived to supervise the actual transfer. The branch current accounts were loaded on to the computer on schedule on Saturday, 22 January 1966.

requirements by Howland and his staff. It was still an industry in the early stages of growth, with few professionals at first. All those in the bank engaged in this work were drawn from men and women already in branches or head office departments, who quickly grasped the new techniques coming forward and developed the new skills needed. They knew what was required for the bank's purposes, drew up the specifications and left it to the machine companies to produce the equipment. Close contacts were established with these companies. Similar relations were, of course, necessary with the Post Office, on whose facilities the whole system ultimately rested.

One of the objectives of computer automation was to save staff and this was achieved. By the end of 1969 branches were employing some 2,000 fewer men and women than they otherwise would have done. That the bank's total staff increased by more than this in 1969 alone merely reflected the increase in its general business. In addition, overtime was reduced. A group of fifty London branches had to pay £116,000 for overtime in the two years before they switched to computer accounting; in the two years after loading overtime payments were cut to £59,000. On the other hand, for the economic use of equipment, shift-working became necessary for computer operators and supervisors. In 1965 a three-shift system from 9 a.m. to 2 a.m. was introduced but in 1967, with the increasing volume of work, this was extended to round-the-clock working.[19] Benefits, however, were not obtained without cost, which was substantial. In 1960 the bank's expenditure on computer and allied equipment was only £534. By 1965 it approached £750,000 and in 1969 reached a peak of nearly £4½m.

By the end of the 1960s computer operations in Lloyds and other British banks were among the most sophisticated to be found anywhere in the world. Many of their programming techniques were the same as those used by such advanced users as the U.S. National Aeronautics and Space Administration. This study ends at that time, since when technical change and development has proceeded apace. One aspect deserves a brief comment.

With the swift spread of the new techniques there was much speculation that computers would soon usher in an economy needing neither cash nor cheques. Credit cards, black boxes, computer terminals, and the rest would mean the end of cheque books, pound notes, and coins. It is now realised that all this was little more than science fiction and that it will be a very long time before currency and cheques become museum pieces in

[19] But not until 1967 were women employed on the night shift and then they had to be over twenty-five years old.

Britain or elsewhere. Notes and coins are still used for over 95% of all payments in Britain, and cheques for most of the rest.[20] The banks play a major part in distributing cash throughout the country and in both respects, cash and cheques, they—and their computers—are likely to remain at the centre of Britain's payments system for many years yet.

Staff questions

To ensure that the bank's branches, increasing specialised services, and head office departments were adequately staffed continued to present considerable difficulties that were lightened only intermittently during the 1960s. Yet, in spite of these, it proved possible to increase the total staff by no less than three-fifths in the ten years to the end of 1969: from 20,160 to 32,510. Well over half this increase was in women. In 1963, for the first time ever, the number of women just exceeded the number of men and by the end of the decade women represented over 52% of all the bank's employees.

The numbers were there, but not always the experience. Turnover increased, particularly in the London area. In 1964–5 the wastage rate for women was 19% but by 1969 it had accelerated to 28%. In London it was even higher, with about a third of the female staff leaving during the year. For men, too, the figures were high by historical standards: 11% (and higher in London) in 1969. Moreover, the low recruitment of the early 1930s was still having an effect, nearly forty years later: in 1969 less than 4% of the male staff (excluding messengers) was in the 50–4 age-group. The upshot was that three-fifths of the female staff and a third of the male staff now had less than five years' service. At one point, indeed, the possibility of 'pairing' branches to make the optimum use of experienced staff was considered, with the manager of one branch becoming the deputy at another.

Policy on male recruitment shifted during the 1960s and the considerable changes that had taken place since the war in the social and educational environment were at last acknowledged. In the early 1960s recruitment was somewhat easier, possibly helped by the abolition of national service in 1962. By 1963, however, doubts were growing. A salary scale tied to age worked in the 1920s and 1930s but was it appropriate in today's vastly different conditions? Should the bank recruit directly for management? The increasing use of computers throughout the bank's operations would

---

[20] Peter Hirsch and John Railton, *op. cit.* Hirsch and Railton conclude that 'Far from the cashless and chequeless society becoming a reality in the near future, there seems to be little immediate prospect of even a less-cheque and less-cash society'.

itself bring many changes in the number and types of men needed. There was talk of 'two-tier' recruitment, encouraged in 1965 by the National Board for Prices and Incomes' report on Midland Bank salaries.[21] Next year the decision was taken: with the staff association's agreement, graduates were to be recruited directly to the A and B scales. Those who in the past had opposed this move had by now either been convinced that it was necessary or had retired. In 1966 only fifteen graduates joined the bank; by 1968 this had increased to thirty-six. However, Lloyds still had no special scheme to groom and train for early management the brightest of the young men and women it was now attracting from the universities. This was introduced in the spring of 1969, together with an appropriate salary differential.

Another long-standing tradition tumbled early in the decade, in the face of the need to attract more men to the bank's service. Early in 1960 so-called 'over-age' recruitment was started, of men aged 27–35 years. The result was encouraging. By September more than 2,000 applications had been received. In 1960 over 270 over-age men joined the bank, followed by another 280 in 1961. Then there was a drop in the middle 1960s, with an increase in numbers towards the end of the decade. In 1965 a special training branch was established to give these men a three-week course in the elements of branch routines. Many of them, more mature and less fickle in their attitudes than their younger colleagues, took well to banking, and by 1969 there were some 950 late entrants in Lloyds' branches.

For women, as well, new sources had to be tapped. In 1968 two women officials went to Ireland, in the hope of recruiting some 200 or so girls to work in London. Because of the competition from other banks, sights had to be lowered and inducements increased, in the form of lodging allowances and travel warrants home. A number of Irish girls did join, however, reaching a total of about 250 in 1970.

Salary scales were raised throughout the period (allowing for occasional official restrictions on pay increases) and, again, those at the lower end gained relatively more than those higher up, although not to quite the same extent as in the 1950s. The salary of a boy aged 17 went up from £310 to £445 (43%) between 1960 and 1969, while that of a man aged 31 (on the C scale) rose from £930 to £1,250 (34%). Women's status also improved. In 1966 a special 'merit scale' was introduced and salaries of women holding board and chief general manager's appointments were raised from

<hr />

[21] '. . . we think the banks' requirements would be better served if they had a salary structure which recognised the changing character of bank employment. There should therefore be a dual salary structure. . . .' (para. 48).

four-fifths to nine-tenths of their male equivalents. In 1967 the merit scale
was replaced by A and B scales, comparable to those for the men, and two-
tier recruitment was established for women. Women up to the age of
twenty-three on the C scale received the same pay as men, after allowing
for the pension contribution paid by the latter, and this covered nearly
three-quarters of all women on the staff. Developments after 1969, in
particular the Equal Pay Act of 1970 and the requirement of 'equal pay for
equal work', lie beyond the end of this study.

Changes in salaries followed discussions with the staff association which
on one occasion, in 1961, invoked the arbitration agreement signed with
the bank in 1953. In the summer of 1960, after long negotiations, pay was
raised and differentials increased. The association claimed further
improvements, based on the bank's increased earnings and the need to
widen differentials still more and to reduce wastage. The bank would not
budge and in June 1961 the staff association resorted to arbitration. In
November the arbitration panel[22] announced its award. While it ruled
against an across-the-board increase it decided in favour of greater
differentials for senior clerks and holders of chief general manager's and
board appointments.

Throughout the 1960s, how long the banks should remain open each
day, and in particular whether they should open on Saturdays, was the
subject of much discussion by the Committee of London Clearing
Bankers, in which the representatives of Lloyds played their full part. The
customers, of course, wished the banks to stay open for as long as possible
right through the week. This had to be reconciled, however, with the
banks' need to keep staff so that their branches could stay open at all. A
five-and-a-half day week, often with irregular leaving hours, was rather
less attractive, especially to young women, than a fixed five-day week in
work elsewhere, quite apart from the question of relative pay. A five-day
week for the staff with five-and-a-half day opening for the public was
possible but would mean additional men and women would be needed—
running for Lloyds into hundreds—and thus inevitably higher bank
charges. Other solutions were considered: Monday closing, selective
closing of branches on Saturday, closing on local early closing day. None
of these, on examination, proved practicable and in September 1968 the
clearing banks announced that, from July 1969, they would close on
Saturday but that their branches would be open later on one evening a
week, excluding Friday.

---

[22] Formed by Lord Birkett, S. M. Caffyn, a member of the Industrial Court and Civil
Service Arbitration Tribunal and G. G. Palmer, formerly Honorary General Secretary of the
Association of Officers of the Ministry of Labour.

This represented a change of heart. For a year before this announcement the C.L.C.B. had decided, in October 1967, that Saturday closing was not 'feasible at present'. Resentment among the banks' staff at this decision was one factor that enabled N.U.B.E., in November 1967, to call the first-ever strike in the clearing banks in South Wales, where it claimed some 90% membership. To gain recognition as a negotiating body, however, was the prime aim of this action. It lasted only two days. Lloyds had 101 branches in South Wales with a total staff of 1,150. At thirty-nine of these offices all staff stayed at work but at the rest 489 men and women came out on strike. The bank regarded it as a duty to provide customers, as a minimum, with a limited counter service and at certain branches members of the inspection staff were drafted in to help. It is a long-established practice in the bank for members of the inspection staff to move to any part of the country where emergencies erupt. N.U.B.E. could claim some success in two of the clearing banks as a result of the strike. In December the union called another two-day strike in Blackpool, Bolton, Doncaster, and Nottingham, when only sixty-five of Lloyds' staff at 306 in the bank's twenty offices in these towns answered the call. At sixteen branches service was normal.

By the early 1960s N.U.B.E. membership in Lloyds had recovered from the low point touched a few years earlier. Between 1954 and 1962 there was an increase of just over 3,000 (from 17 to 23% of the total staff) against a rise in members of the staff association of rather less than a thousand, (representing a fall from 70 to 55% of total staff). During the rest of the decade N.U.B.E. gained further ground relatively and by 1969 could claim 28% of Lloyds' staff, compared with 45% in the staff association. But those who belonged to neither body also grew in numbers: from 22% of the staff in 1962 to 27% in 1969.

Another attempt was now made to establish national negotiating machinery to settle questions of pay and conditions in the clearing banks and this, the third such endeavour, ultimately proved successful. In 1964 discussions started between the C.L.C.B., N.U.B.E., and the Central Council of Bank Staff Associations and once again, as in the 1950s, a working party was set up. This produced a draft constitution of a joint negotiating council for clerical staffs, but not until May 1968 was this ratified by all the parties involved. In 1970 comparable domestic negotiating machinery was designed for Lloyds, with the staff side composed of three representatives each of N.U.B.E. and of the staff association. After decades of rivalry and recrimination the two bodies had at last sunk their differences and come together. Unfortunately, the agreement broke down some years later, but that is outside this story.

The widening application of computers during these years, together with the start of two-tier recruitment in 1966, called for a fresh look at the training systems that had been set up after the war. Hitherto, all young men and women had started on the same mark, with equal status and opportunity. In the future, of those joining the bank each year there would be a relatively small number of potential managers and officials, with the rest destined for clerical and technical jobs in branches, departments, and computer centres. Training had to be adapted to the new policies. In 1968 'programmed learning' was introduced into branches. This had been developed in the U.S.A. and consisted of specially-written courses on various aspects of branch routines which young men and women could study on their own for an hour a day. Then, they could set out on a carefully planned programme over the years ahead: from a preliminary course at the training centre at Hindhead covering the elements of branch banking through later courses on lending and security work, and junior management duties, to a senior course at the staff college and, for a chosen few, to a course at the Administrative Staff College at Henley or one of the business schools.

To encourage the interest of the staff in improving branch and departmental routines and promoting general efficiency a suggestion scheme was started in December 1968, with a small committee of officials to determine awards. This had been tried before. In 1920 the staff were invited to make suggestions and in the next four years they submitted some 300 ideas, few of which, it seems, amounted to very much. The new scheme was more successful, possibly because there was a system of awards. In 1969, the first year, members of the staff made 4,701 suggestions, of which 138 earned awards worth £4,860. In subsequent years thousands of ideas were sent in each year, a number of which were adopted and won their authors an award.

A merger stopped

For some fifty years, from soon after the end of the first world war until the announcement of the merger of the Westminster and National Provincial Banks in January 1968, the structure of English joint stock banking remained largely unaltered. There were various relatively minor changes, approved by the authorities after the Colwyn Advisory Committee ceased to function in 1932. Martins absorbed British Mutual Bank in 1951, National Provincial acquired District Bank in 1962, Lloyds bought Lewis's Bank from Martins in 1967. But these, and other, mergers during the half century hardly affected the backbone of the system, the big five clearing banks. Any amalgamation among these very large banks, it was supposed, would not be countenanced. This appeared to be the implication of the Colwyn Report of 1918 and, as we saw in Chapter 2, was explicitly agreed among themselves by the authorities five years later. And, so far as is known, no attempts at such amalgamations were made.

So matters stood until May 1967, when the National Board for Prices and Incomes, in its wide-ranging report on *Bank Charges*, revealed that the 'Bank of England and the Treasury have made it plain to us that they would not obstruct some further amalgamations if the banks were willing to contemplate such a development' (para. 154). Did this mean that the Bank and the Treasury had now changed their minds after all these years and that a merger among the Big Five themselves would now be permitted? Some of them, at least, thought not. In June Lloyds' chairman, Harald Peake, saw the Governor, Sir Leslie O'Brien, when his understanding was that the Colwyn Report's and the authorities' principles of 1923 still stood.[23] However, the Bank of England apparently had not intended to give this impression and, as the Monopolies Commission commented, 'there was still some confusion over what the official attitude was'.[24] As the commission pointed out, this impression could not have been conveyed to National Provincial and Westminster Banks.

For some years Lloyds had been keen on a merger with Martins Bank which, with its head office still in Liverpool, would have filled out Lloyds' branch network in a part of the country where it still had relatively few offices. For one reason or another, Martins turned down these offers of marriage. In 1962 and 1964 Peake had made approaches, and again in October 1967 he wrote to Sir Cuthbert Clegg, chairman of Martins, that it had long been his ambition 'to see our two great banks brought together', and suggested a mutual exploration of the possibilities of amalgamating. In December, Martins, finally acknowledging that a merger with another bank might be advantageous, in effect put itself up to the highest bidder, with offers to be made by 25 January 1968. In the event, of the six banks which were initially interested, only Barclays and Lloyds put in bids.

[23] Barclays and Martins also believed that no merger among the Big Five would be allowed: The Monopolies Commission, *Barclays Bank Ltd. Lloyds Bank Ltd. and Martins Bank Ltd.*, a report on the proposed merger, July 1968, para. 48.

[24] Later, in a speech at the Lord Mayor's dinner on 17 October 1968, O'Brien defended the attitude of the authorities, 'which for this purpose means principally me'. He did not 'think it expedient for me actively to promote particular unions. Even if I had done so it would have made little or no difference to the end result but would have caused a great deal of heart-burning in between.' However, this still leaves unanswered the question of whether 'particular unions' did or did not exclude those between the Big Five. Some banks thought such mergers were excluded but, as events were to show, they were mistaken. That was the root of the confusion.

The next day, Friday, 26 January, Lombard Street and the City generally were astonished by the announcement of an intention to merge by National Provincial and Westminster Banks, with the approval of the authorities. These had now evidently abandoned what most people had taken to be a cardinal principle of policy. The news, Lloyds' chief general manager Michael Wilson has admitted, came as 'a tremendous shock'. The accepted order had been shattered. As things were now going to stand, there would be four big banks and Lloyds would be the smallest. There was concern, too, elsewhere.

On Monday, 29 January Peake was visited by Sir Archibald Forbes, chairman of Midland Bank and an old acquaintance. Forbes suggested that some association, not necessarily a full merger, between Lloyds and Midland might be approved by the authorities but the idea was not very warmly received and his proposal went no further. Two days later Peake himself took the initiative and called on John Thomson, chairman of Barclays, to discuss the changed position. By now Peake and Thomson knew that no other banks except Lloyds and Barclays had put in offers for Martins. Instead of competing against one another, why should they not together acquire Martins and form one giant bank? Thus was born the proposal for the merger of Lloyds, Barclays and Martins Banks. What happened is well known and can soon be told.

Just a week later, on 8 February, came the announcement that the three banks wished to merge and that approval had been sought from the authorities. This was not forthcoming. The same day the Board of Trade referred the proposal to the Monopolies Commission for investigation and report. In little over five months the idea was dead. On 9 July the president of the Board of Trade (Anthony Crosland) announced that the commission had recommended against the merger of the three banks or of Barclays and Lloyds alone by a majority of six to four. As this was not a two-thirds majority the decision now rested with the government. This was not long delayed. On 25 July Crosland told the House of Commons that the government accepted the conclusion of the Monopolies Commission's majority that the three-fold merger would be against the public interest and therefore should not proceed. Martins, however, could join any other bank, and now accepted the higher bid Barclays had put in. Lloyds was on its own.

The merger proposal was not a decision reached after careful study of the position of English banking[25] and assessment of Lloyds' likely role in probable future developments. Even so, that the detailed arguments for

[25] Nor, for that matter, was the proposed merger between Westminster and National

merging had to be formulated after the proposal was made public did not by itself weaken the case. In the wholly new situation created by the Westminster–National Provincial tie-up it seemed that Lloyds might be left behind in the competition unless it too joined in a larger grouping. The general feeling at the time was in favour of large enterprises, the bigger the better. Government itself had strongly encouraged bigger units through the Industrial Reorganisation Corporation.

All this did not, however, prepare the board and general management for their considerable surprise on hearing of what was planned—the staff in general, inevitably, first learnt of it through the press and radio. The board accepted the proposal, although if a vote had been taken it might have been turned down.[26] Among the general management there was some concern and anxiety. Whatever might appear to be the future long-term benefits to Lloyds of merging with Barclays and Martins, immediately a great deal was likely to be different, established methods upset, old loyalties broken. Among the rest of the staff there was no great enthusiasm. Nevertheless, Michael Wilson believed new and exciting possibilities for the bank had opened up, and the case for trying to realise them through the merger proposed had to be convincing enough for the Monopolies Commission.

A small team under F. J. Thomas, a joint general manager, was set up to prepare the bank's case, working in collaboration with a similar (and much larger) team at Barclays. There is no need here to rehearse again all the arguments assembled, the views of other interested parties and the conclusions of the majority of the Monopolies Commission, from some of whose views four members dissented. Very briefly, the three banks claimed that there was a need for larger units in banking to match those in industry; that savings would be gained by closing branches and from economies in administration and in computer work; that the co-ordination and development of the three banks' overseas interests would provide a wider coverage to meet British traders' varied and world-wide needs; that international banking and competition overseas required large units.[27] The majority of the Monopolies Commission accepted little of all this:

Provincial Banks. According to *The Times*, 27 January 1968, merger talks had been going on for only ten days before the announcement on 26 January.

[26] But some bankers abroad put their approval on record. Cables of good wishes for the success of the merger were received from George Champion, chairman of the board, Chase Manhattan Bank, G. Arnold Hart, chairman of Bank of Montreal, and J. Brusselmans, on behalf of the chairman and board of Kredietbank.

[27] These were, not surprisingly, much the same kind of arguments that Westminster and National Provincial Banks had advanced when announcing their planned merger. This, however, was not referred to the Monopolies Commission.

benefits to the public would be likely to be few, competition would be reduced, there was not much to suggest large industrial customers needed equally large banks, the international arguments were unconvincing. The four minority members dissented from some of these views and saw no serious risk to the public interest from the proposed merger.

This was the case put to the Monopolies Commission in written evidence and hearings. However, it was not very long before, behind the public confidence, there were private doubts.

A merged bank might well be able to close branches, make economies, streamline its use of computers, offer stiffer competition at home and abroad. But what kind of bank would it be? After the initial excitement and when the cold facts came to be studied and talks with Barclays proceeded, some on the Lloyds side began to have reservations about the project, arising mainly from the differences in structure between Lloyds and Barclays. Lloyds then had fifteen regional boards and fourteen regional offices each under a general manager, while branch managers enjoyed considerable discretionary powers. Barclays, partly because of historical influences and the way it had developed over the years, was organised very differently. Under a board with full-time chairman, deputy chairman and vice-chairmen there were over 100 executive local directors, with wide-ranging powers, at thirty-four local head offices, and branch managers had less discretionary authority than their Lloyds' opposite numbers. Whatever the merits of the two structures, it looked very likely that, once the process of merging started, Barclays would do their utmost to preserve as much as possible of their own particular system and organisation. At one point Barclays suggested that the merged bank might have fifty regional or local offices; later, a district organisation was proposed of some forty areas, of which over three-quarters would have the boundaries of Barclays' existing local head offices. If these ideas came to be accepted, it was difficult to see that much of Lloyds' quite different system would survive.

This was not the only problem. A number of working parties were set up of representatives of Lloyds, Barclays and, sometimes, Martins to consider the detailed questions of merging. These got quickly to work and found that, besides the differences in structure, there were other respects in which the three banks were not alike. For example, Barclays had no equivalent of Lloyds' legal department; Barclays relied mainly on outside architects for its premises work, while Lloyds did not; there were many differences in administrative procedures. But for most of these and other differences an accommodation of views and practices seemed possible without much friction. A high-level committee was also planned to look at the constitution of the board of the merged bank, its various committees and methods of determining policy. Wisely, however, little was done in advance of the decision of the Monopolies Commission. The merged bank, it was decided in principle, would have the not very original name of Barclay Lloyds Bank.[28] Thomson of Barclays would be the first chairman and Michael Wilson of Lloyds the first chief executive officer.

On 9 July Anthony Crosland announced that he had received the Monopolies Commission's report and this was published on 15 July. Two days later the three banks made public their own views of the report, taking exception to many of the commission's comments and criticising, in particular, those on the likely savings from a merger, the need for size in overseas business and interest-rate agreements. Stung by the accusation that cartel agreements had had a 'soporific effect' in inhibiting competition, the three banks listed eighteen examples of innovations they had introduced in recent years. On 18 July the chairmen of the three banks, together with their chief executives and the Governor, visited the Chancellor, Roy Jenkins, and Crosland at the Treasury. A week later Crosland made his announcement in the House of Commons and the curtain came down. The same day, 25 July, Lord Runciman, Lloyds' deputy chairman, confirmed to Clegg, Martins' chairman, that Lloyds' original offer still stood—equivalent to 30/- (£1·50) for each of Martins 5/- (25p) shares—and that there was no intention of increasing it. Martins thus accepted Barclays' offer, equivalent to 35/6 (£1·77) for its shares.

Lloyds was now the smallest of the big four London clearing banks, instead of the third largest of the big five. All the anxieties, long hours, discussions, plans, endless drafts had come to nothing. Peake, giving the news to shareholders, said he was 'disappointed at the Government's decision', which hardly suggests a broken heart. Wilson, on whom an enormous burden had been thrust during these months, at first keenly regretted the verdict but, when the dust had settled, he was thankful it went the way it did. Wilson was concerned about morale in the bank. Spirits, in fact, were not noticeably lower. For a fair number of the staff, most of the young women, for example, whether they worked in future for Lloyds Bank or for Barclay Lloyds Bank was not, perhaps, of great consequence. For the rest, the common reaction was one of relief. Possibly they, too, sensed that it was likely that the realities of the vast bank

---

[28] Martins Bank, the very junior partner in size, was likely to be forgotten, at least publicly. One of the sketches for a sign to hang outside the branches of Barclay Lloyds Bank showed only Lloyds' black horse and Barclays' eagle with the title of the bank, set within a triangle symbolising the merger of the three banks.

proposed would have been rather different from the hopeful plans sketched out, and that Lloyds was already an enterprise large enough for administrative efficiency. That profitability was not necessarily commensurate with size indeed soon became evident, when the bank's results for 1969 were made public, the first on the now fully-disclosed basis. As a return on resources, the ratio for Lloyds' profits was the highest of the big four.[29]

[29] In September 1969 the clearing and Scottish banks announced that in future their accounts would be prepared in accordance with the provisions of the Companies Act applicable to companies in general and that they would no longer take advantage of the exemptions available to them not to disclose true profits and hidden reserves. Lloyds' board welcomed this move; they had been in favour of disclosure for some time. As a ratio of total balance-sheet resources, group profits before tax for the big four clearing banks were as follows for 1969:

	%
Lloyds	1.72
National Westminster	1.46
Midland	1.15
Barclays	1.07

Epilogue

This book has told the story of Lloyds Bank from 1918 to 1969. A very brief glance at subsequent developments provides a fitting conclusion, for it was during these years that Lloyds Bank went on to find a new role for itself as the domestic base of a major international banking group.

The Monopolies Commission's report in the summer of 1968 and the acceptance by the government of the majority's verdict, however much this may have been welcomed in the bank, either overtly or covertly, meant that one particular road to future development was blocked. In the new situation, fresh thinking on Lloyds' position and a review of its likely prospects became urgently necessary. In a very few months this was given its direction and impetus when, in February 1969, Eric O. Faulkner succeeded Harald Peake as chairman. Faulkner, an executive director since 1950 and chairman since 1963 of Glyn Mills and Co., had spent thirty-two years in banking and had also a wide knowledge of industry. He made an outstanding contribution to Lloyds Bank during his eight years as chairman. His great dynamic abilities and immense professionalism raised significantly the status of the bank at home and abroad. Moreover and most important, by rationalising certain of Lloyds' interests and developing new ones, Faulkner helped to bring together various individual elements into the great world-wide institution of the Lloyds Bank Group. In all he accomplished he enjoyed a close and easy relationship with Sir Michael Wilson. The bank indeed owes Wilson a vast debt for all he did in the vital years after the merger failure to adapt activities to the new opportunities opened up and to plan the many changes that became necessary.

All this was against a background of continuing and wide-ranging change and innovation. In the first year of Faulkner's chairmanship came the disclosure of their true profits and reserves by the London clearing and Scottish banks. In 1971 the whole system of the Bank of England's control of the banks was radically changed with the introduction of 'competition and credit control', with its eligible liabilities, its specified reserve assets and minimum reserve asset ratio in place of liquidity ratio and the end of the deposit-rate cartel; and next year saw the abandonment of Bank Rate in favour of minimum lending rate. Term lending, wholesale banking, leasing, Euro-currency transactions, insurance broking, certificates of deposit were developed by the banks, in addition to their traditional deposit business. Competition was greater, and not only from domestic institutions. Although the number of the London clearing banks was now smaller, more and more foreign banks flocked to the City, attracted by London's position as a leading world financial centre. In this respect, the Euro-currency market was of major significance. The London banks were responsible for its birth in the late 1950s and have played a dominant role in its subsequent enormous development. One of the first to seize the initiative was Sir George Bolton. From 1957 to 1970 Bolton was chairman of Bank of London and South America, later to join with Lloyds Bank Europe to form Lloyds Bank International, and for many years BOLSA was the largest single dealer in London in Euro-dollars.

Lloyds Bank was well to the fore in all these new ventures. In 1970 Lloyds Associated Banking Company (LABCO) was set up as a subsidiary to take term deposits and to offer term loans and, later, to issue sterling certificates of deposit. In 1971, in partnership with Midland and National Westminster Banks, Lloyds formed the Joint Credit Card Company and in 1972 the Access credit card was launched. In 1972, too, an insurance department was established. In 1973 Lloyds Leasing Limited began operations, to become one of the four largest leasing companies in Britain, providing finance for firms to acquire industrial plant and machinery. A third unit trust had been launched in 1970 and the trust division—as the executor and trustee department was re-named in 1974—went on to start an overseas fund based in Jersey in 1974 and a fourth unit trust in 1976. Meanwhile, the computer was all the time revolutionising old facilities and making new ones possible.

This widening range of facilities extended the bank's operations and sharpened its competitive edge in the more aggressive market conditions of the 1970s. However, it was in organising the Lloyds Bank Group on a firm basis, with Lloyds Bank as the dominant domestic element, that Eric Faulkner's initiatives were most significant. By the end of 1978 the group's consolidated balance sheet stood at £14.8b., of which not quite half was attributable to Lloyds Bank and the rest to its various subsidiaries. Of these, Lloyds Bank International had offices and subsidiaries in over forty countries. In the U.S.A., Lloyds acquired a footing in California in 1974 with the purchase of First Western Bank and Trust Company, since renamed Lloyds Bank California. Across the Pacific, The National Bank of New Zealand had become a subsidiary in 1966.

All these, though their ownership rested with Lloyds Bank, remained independently managed and with their own traditions and ways of doing business. But they were now consciously brought together to form an integrated Lloyds Bank Group. A new ethos was born and flourished. New administrative procedures were designed, a group headquarters was established in Lombard Street and, eventually, a separate board was set up to control the group's domestic business in Lloyds Bank and its subsidiaries in Britain, leaving the main board free to devote itself to strategy for the group's institutions and interests across the continents. Until 1864 Lloyds had only one office in Birmingham, where in 1765 the partnership of Taylors and Lloyds had been formed. Today, branches of the Lloyds group of banks are to be found throughout the world, from Singapore to Los Angeles, from Edinburgh to Auckland. For Lloyds Bank, the words with which Professor Richard Sayers in 1957 concluded his history are more than ever true:

The principles on which the business is based differ little from those of Sampson Lloyd and John Taylor in 1765, or from those of Howard Lloyd and others a century later, but the size and shape of the business make it almost incredible that it has sprung from that single Birmingham office of a century ago.

Index

Abell, G. F., 36, 58, 61, 75, 87
Access credit card, 202
accounts, numbers of 8; (1918–23), 32; (1923–9), 46; (1929–33), 64; (1930–8), 79; (1939–45), 102–3; (1946–51), 148; (1952–9), 164; (1959–69), 178
advance control, 36, 96, 146, 160, 172, 175–6
advances, 6–7; (1918–22), 30–1; (1923–9), 44–5; (1929–33), 63–4, 67; (1933–8), 74, 76–8; (1939–45), 96–7, 103–5; (1944), 111; (1945–51), 145, (1954–9), 160–2; (1959–69), 174–8; in India, 129
advertising, 74, 156, 181
Aiyer, H. S., 131
Alliance Bank of Simla, 123
amalgamation see merger; problems of 25–7
Amory, Derick Heathcoat, 142
Anderson, Sir John, 117
Andrews, L. F., 135, 136
arbitration panel (1961), 192
architecture, 13–15, 47, 133
arms, 15
Armstrong & Co, 27
Austin Friars Trust, 59, 60, 61
Australia, 29
Australia & N.Z. Bank, 183
automatic sorting, 186
Avory, Mr. Justice, 61

balance sheet, 45
Baldwin, J. H. L., 20
Balfour, Lord, of Burleigh, 75, 118, 140–1, 157
Balfour Committee (1924–9), 64, 79
Banca d'America e d'Italia, 59
Banca Italo-Britannica, 57, 58
bank notes, 21
Bank of British West Africa (B.B.W.A.), 28–9, 120–2
Bank of England, 66, 93, 155, 201
Bank of Liverpool and Martins, 21
Bank of London and South America

(BOLSA), 28, 183, 202
Bank Officers Guild (B.O.G.), 43, 86–7, 110
Bank Rate, 32, 63, 95, 144, 145, 159, 160, 175, 201
Banker, The, 56
Bankers Industrial Development Co., 67
Banking Companies Act (1949), India, 125
Banking Companies (Control) Act (1948), Pakistan, 126
Barchard, E. H., 41
Barclays Bank, 183, 184, 195, 196, 198
Barclays D.C.O. (later Barclays Bank International), 183, 184
Barnett, Charles Edward, 75
Barnetts, Hoares, Hanbury and Lloyds, 15, 52, 75
Beane, F. A. (later Sir Francis) 36, 56, 61, 67, 68, 75, 87, 120, 123
Beardmore & Co., 66
Beaverbrook, Lord, 104
Bell, Henry, 22, 23, 36, 173
Beng Chong, 127
Beng Huat & Co., 127
Birkett, Lord, 192
black horse, origin of, 15
Blackett, Sir Basil, 123
Blair-Giannini group, 59
Blanch, R. J., 153
Bledisloe, Lord, 20, 142
blitz, effects of, 100–1
Bolton, Sir George, 183, 202
Boothroyd, Basil, 49
Bosanquet, Salt & Co., 52
Bowmaker, 163
branch accounts, analysis of (1951), 149
branch extensions committee, 33
branch network, 13; (1918–23), 33; (1923–9), 47; (1931–6), 69–70; (1940–5), 106; (1946–51), 149; (1951–9), 165; (1959–69), 178–80
branch profitability, committee on (1931), 69
Brand, R. H. (later Lord Brand), 31, 89, 157
British Bankers' Association, 35